This book addresses one of the major challenges faced by most areas of business. It should be read by women who wish to be part of the solution. It should also be read by men who wish to understand the problem.

— Guy Beringer, former Senior Partner, Allen & Overy LLP

In all my years of coaching professional women, I've not come across a resource to offer them that helps them overcome the obstacles outlined by Dr Suzanne Doyle: lack of knowledge about politics and lack of confidence about playing the game. Finally a book for women by women that shows how to play the game of politics in an ethical and feminine way. Increasing your power image, lobbying before the important decision-making meetings are held, networking and profiling are all political skills. These skills ensured that the women Suzanne interviewed got their ideas heard, funded, resourced, implemented and ultimately got them promoted in their male-dominated industry. Kudos for Beyond the Boys' Club for reframing politics from a four-letter word to advocacy, collaboration, and teamwork!

— Michelle Brailsford, President,
European Professional Women's Network – London

We invest in our education, health, home and wardrobe, but so often not in our career development. Beyond the Boys' Club reminds us of the importance of this investment and provides us with a variety of tools and tips from the pioneers that have shown the potential Return on Investment. After reading this book, you should have no reason not to push at the barriers to your own progression and achieve your full potential.

— Fleur Bothwick, Director of Diversity and Inclusiveness, EMEIA,
Ernst & Young LLP

In her book Beyond the Boys' Club Dr Suzanne Doyle-Morris outlines with humour and imagination many top tips and strategies for high achieving professional women to enhance their career potential by overcoming the many unconscious gender biases in a male-dominated workplace. She writes with real passion and this is an essential read for women wishing to emulate the success of those she has interviewed for this book.

— Dr Jenny Brookman, Chair,
Cambridge Association for Women in Science and Engineering

In an economy of increasing pressure, companies with few women must be ever more innovative and proactive in retaining the talented women they do have. This is a book born out of extensive research, interviews and coaching conversations with senior professionals who have each succeeded as one of the few women in their team and who have the ambition to keep climbing that ladder. It fills an obvious gap in modern business literature – on the experiences and successes of women who work primarily with men.

— Caroline Buckingham, Equality and Diversity Manager, Microsoft UK

D0681666

A gift for any woman looking to raise her profile, develop her brand, understand organisational politics and take her career to the next level. Dr Doyle-Morris has an eye for the irreverent and uses plenty of wit to keep the topics of gender equality and political savvy accessible, practical and fun. Absolutely crammed with ideas and rich in the kind of stories that feel both familiar and inspirational at the same time.

— Lesley Everett, Personal Branding Expert and author of 'Drop Dead Brilliant'

This is an important book that gives professional women well-researched, practical and tested advice based on interviews with twenty-one women in senior positions in a range of professional areas. All women in science, engineering and technology should read this book.

— Dr Esther Haines, Regional Officer, Institute of Physics

I loved this book - it's a 'must have' book for all women looking to raise their profile, understand organisational politics and really progress in their careers.

— Claire Palmer, former President, UK International Coach Federation (ICF)

This inspiring and exciting book is precisely what is needed to help women who want to make an impact and have a successful career, and to help organisations understand how to change their behaviour and culture.

— Professor Jeremy Sanders FRS, Deputy Vice-Chancellor and Head of the School of Physical Sciences, University of Cambridge

Reading this book should be top of your to-do list as a professional woman keen to build a career. Suzanne Doyle-Morris has captured the essence of how to play the game, and learning to win. She imparts the wisdom and insightful advice that are testament to her experience as a professional executive coach helping career professionals succeed.

— Lamia Walker, Director, London Business School

Suzanne brings together her clever mind with her human warmth to create a book that will inspire and inform any woman who wants to put more into life and take more from it. Ladies, if we all took even a small amount of her wisdom and put it into action the world would be a brighter, happier place and businesses would be stronger and more lucrative. I won't just be recommending this book to my female clients - I will be sending them a copy.

— Lisa Wynn, Master Certified Coach (ICF) Managing Partner, Corporate Potential Ltd

SUZANNE DOYLE-MORRIS, PhD

BEYOND THE BOYS' CLUB

STRATEGIES FOR
**ACHIEVING CAREER SUCCESS
AS A WOMAN**
WORKING IN A MALE DOMINATED FIELD

WIT AND WISDOM PRESS

Beyond the Boys' Club
First edition May 2009
Copyright © Suzanne Doyle-Morris, PhD
Published by Wit and Wisdom Press

Typeset in Times New Roman and TrajanPro
Layout design by eldamar.co.uk
Cover design Julia Lloyd Designs
ISBN 978-0-9562688-0-8

Printed and bound by Lightning Source

For more information visit:
www.doylemorris.com
www.beyondtheboysclub.com

ACKNOWLEDGEMENTS

In the writing of this book I would like to thank all the countless people who generously gave their time and energy towards its creation. I could not have done so without their contributions and am very grateful for the support they provided.

I would like to thank my fantastic editor, Fiona Cowan, and the woman who led me to her, Jo Parfitt. I would also like to thank Judith Morgan for encouraging me to write from the start and Sue Blake for her encouragement and guidance on the tail end of the process. Gratitude also goes to my assistant, Susan Moore, who helped me weave the various stories into a manageable form and Kate Atkin and Lorraine Harte for their suggestions.

I am very grateful for the contributions of Janet Davies, Laura Hinton, Ana Pacheco, Angela Mohtashemi, Joanna Hewitt, Mary Hensher, Harriet Crawford, Eileen Brown, Maggie Berry, Matilda Venter, Lis Astall, Rebecca George, Jackie Gittins, Athene Donald, Dame Veronica Sutherland, Nicky Clayton, Fiona Edington, Sharon Rynne-Coleman, Dana Brotman, Margret Fine-Davis, Zoë Ingle, Philippa Snare, Jane Lewis, Amy Cox, Sharon Webb, Carol Collins and Andy Lopata. I would also like to thank my clients: truly inspirational women from whom I learn a huge amount and with whom I relish working.

Finally, but most importantly, I would like to thank my husband, Geoff, who has been the greatest source of ongoing support and mentoring to me, as well as my parents, Lyn and Bob, who modelled consummate integrity and networking skills to me from an early age!

TABLE OF CONTENTS

INTRODUCTION

What does it mean to go *Beyond the Boys' Club?* What does it mean to not just survive, but thrive as a woman working in a male-dominated environment? What does it take to observe and learn from the boys' club, but not let those interactions define you? How can you engage with the boys' club but still be true to yourself as a woman?

Ever since I was a little girl, I have been fascinated by the stories of successful and high-achieving women. My influences were wide ranging and no doubt influenced by being an American growing up in the early 1980s. I loved reading about dynamic girl detective Nancy Drew and the outspoken and clever Jo, of the novel *Little Women.* Looking for role models in my youth was an experience that in retrospect revealed the wide variety of examples available. I loved hearing about the truly inspirational Sally Ride, the first female American astronaut and, at the other end of the spectrum, I was a big fan of *Charlie's Angels* too – three beautiful, 'take-no-prisoners' action heroines who always outsmarted the villainous evil-doers. Why, by the time I was four, I was even vaguely aware that the UK had a female Prime Minister!

So while my earliest role models ranged from the sublime to the ridiculous and back again, it started a passion for finding out as much as I could about successful women that continues today. What makes them tick? What are they doing right? What were their journeys to the top like? And as importantly — what can we learn from them?

In addition, I am passionate about working with professional women — especially women who choose to work in male-dominated fields. How do they thrive in situations where they may be the only woman round the board table, in the lab, on the trading floor, or in the judiciary? What makes the difference for them? How do they thrive in environments where they weren't always welcome and among working practices that weren't designed to be female-friendly?

How do they learn all they can from their male colleagues and eventually move *Beyond the Boys' Club*?

Historically, there have been many challenges to women working in such settings. These fields are set up around a traditional model that assumes there's a full time carer at home to service domestic responsibilities, freeing up the employee to devote most of *his* waking hours to *his* career.

Women who work in these fields compete with male colleagues who *do* have wives and girlfriends, and in some cases mothers, to take care of their day-to-day needs. The men of the office or laboratory can devote all the time they desire to work, whereas their female colleagues are generally still expected to run households in addition to maintaining and progressing their careers. In such fields even the language is masculine: 'cold facts' and 'hard science' compared to the more feminine and less valued: 'soft skills' and 'women's intuition'.

In addition to the one-to-one work I do with executive-coaching clients, I facilitate workshops on succeeding as a woman in male-dominated fields. Occasionally, people come to these workshops unsure of what to expect. There can be a misconception that the day will focus on the challenges and drawbacks of taking on such a career, and that it will deteriorate into a forum for complaint.

Without dismissing any of what are true experiences for those individuals, I like to keep the atmosphere proactive, humorous and much to the surprise of many initially dubious clients, even fun. We concentrate on what we can each do to effect change in our careers and lives, rather than looking for someone to blame for a lack of progress.

This book does not seek to diminish the difficulties faced by many women, who work in these fields and who have struggled against a male status quo. I am the first to recognise that there are systemic problems around gender bias in many companies, and even industries as a whole. However, this book focuses on the positive: women can thrive in these fields, and we can all learn from those who do and their successes. In fact, the strategies shared by the successful women in this book can benefit the careers of *all* ambitious women, as indeed most fields become more male-dominated the higher up the professional ladder *any woman* climbs.

These are lessons I myself have had to learn. While my initial interest in this group of women came from an academic standpoint, I too have chosen a road not frequently taken by others. As an entrepreneur, professional speaker and émigrée, these are lessons I am still learning. I've made my fair share of mistakes, which I will share with you — but, like the successful women I have interviewed, I've noticed patterns where women have been successful. It is important to remember, the ultimate reward is not to be 'as good' as a man, but to do the work on the interesting challenges and projects that we actually love – the work that makes getting out of bed in the morning a joy.

SENIOR WOMEN – THEIR STORIES – YOUR BENEFIT

This long-held passion started in my dim and distant past over 15 years ago at university, where I studied Psychology and Women's Studies, and I've worked with developing the careers of women either through my PhD research at the University of Cambridge or in one-to-one sessions through my coaching practice ever since. And I love spending time with such inspirational women! But when I set up my consultancy, Doyle Morris Coaching and Development, which helps companies retain and develop their talented women, I realised how much learning there was to pass on – certainly from my own clients as well as from women who were at the top of their game.

To get at the heart of what makes these women tick, these women who work in science, engineering, technology and professional services, I spent 18 months conducting in-depth interviews with 21 senior women from a range of backgrounds – so that *you* could benefit from their collective knowledge and the individual strategies that have served them well.

I had discussions with some of the most senior technical women at Microsoft and senior partners in professional service firms ranging from Deloitte LLP to Accenture to PricewaterhouseCoopers. I spent time with a retired archaeologist who led digs in Iraq and a Physics Professor at the University of Cambridge who had just won the highly esteemed L'Oréal Women in Science prize for 2009. I also interviewed an army recruit who left the service to become a criminal barrister as well as the first female British Ambassador to Ireland.

They came from a wide range of backgrounds — but what they all had in common was that they forged outstanding careers in fields dominated by men, and they were all willing to share with you, the reader, the secrets of what had made the difference for their career.

Listening to their stories, themes emerge such as the value we give profile-raising, working with key stakeholders, risk-taking, mentoring, networking and coaching — all as a means to ever greater professional success. I am constantly inspired by my clients; women who not only learn to survive, perhaps being the only woman in their office, their team or their laboratory, but who do better than that and *thrive*.

No two women had the same career path. No two had the same answer for how they arrived in their senior positions. It was exciting how different their stories were from each other — and yet how they had all succeeded. Some had known from childhood that they wanted to become scientists; others didn't decide to become technology experts until they were adults and realised that they wanted to earn 'real' money. Some had made a straight and narrow path through higher education, some made a more circuitous route through apprenticeships and military service.

This is both reassuring and daunting at once. Reassuring, because it means you can tailor your efforts according to your strengths and where you want to stretch your comfort zone. Daunting because it means that there are no excuses for not finding ideas in the book that *would* work for you.

But they did agree on certain things, and at the end of the day, they have reached levels of success of which most professional women at first only dream. And the truth is that, while my specialism is in helping *women* succeed, there is nothing in the book, no big secrets, that can't benefit men too. I make no apologies for working primarily with women because it is their male colleagues who often act faster on the strategies we are going to discuss throughout the book and hence are rewarded with a disproportionate number of the top positions in these fields.

One thing that all of the women I interviewed had in common was that they were all hard-working and very sharp — no doubt *just like you.*

My Passion ... Your Success

I first recognised the importance of these lessons when I began to search for my own first job. This was not just any job: I was looking to move to Ireland just two weeks after finishing my first degree. I had set myself the challenge of landing a job in psychology in a country where I had no family, friends or contacts. I told everyone I was going to live and work in Europe for a few years.

As most of my coaching clients will recognise, the mere act of verbalising an intention to others with a deadline gave me the confidence and accountability to carry it through. My plans were met with reactions ranging from incredulity and concern to encouragement.

Despite my Irish surname, I had not a single friend, family member and certainly no employer to cushion my landing in Ireland. What I did have in my favour was a good reputation with professors at the university I previously attended, St Mary's College of Maryland. I had laid the groundwork, often without knowing it at the time, through a willingness to speak publicly on various women's issues, volunteer work in the local community around my University and eventually by earning an Honours degree in Psychology and Women's Studies.

One of my first and most important lessons in networking was to capitalise on the strong profile I had built, and to ask each professor I knew whether *they* knew anyone in Ireland who was a psychology professional.

Most people were encouraging, even if they questioned the wisdom in my sense of adventure and were somewhat baffled as to why I would want to move abroad. Perhaps understandably for a small American college, only one lecturer remembered an Irish academic she had met some ten years previously at a conference. However, as most networkers know, it only takes one good contact to make the difference.

I arrived in Ireland as a 22 year old, wide-eyed and optimistic but certainly 'under-resourced' and perhaps a bit out of my depth. I took a series of temporary office jobs, always vaguely aware there could be more to my 'Irish adventure' and after a few months I worked up the courage to offer my services to the research team led by my one potential contact at the Centre for Women's Studies at Trinity College, Dublin. I worked there for as long as my work visa permitted before my new boss and mentor, Dr Margret Fine-Davis — herself an American expat who had lived in Ireland for 25 years — then helped me secure my next professional contact in my destination of choice, London.

Why do I share this story? Because to me it represents many aspects of what made the women I interviewed so successful: a good reputation and profile that made others willing to help me; networking; high-profile risk-taking; and mentoring. These are some of the same characteristics that make women who are successful in male-dominated fields so inspiring – and such a relevant group of women from whom to learn.

In this book, you will read some of the best strategies for success employed by 21 successful senior women in the fields where I spend most of my time as an executive coach — namely science, engineering, technology, professional and financial services and the law. It is from their experiences that I will illustrate the lessons they taught me about what it takes to be a wildly successful woman in a man's world. I will also share my own experiences as an executive coach, speaker and entrepreneur who has faced many challenges of my own.

I'll be honest about what went right and what didn't for me, my clients and the senior women I interviewed, so that you can also learn from our ongoing journeys. Every woman in this book has given a piece of herself for our collective benefit. I hope you enjoy the trip as much as we have enjoyed sharing it with you.

Suzanne Doyle-Morris, PhD

May 2009

ONE

TO WIN THE GAME, YOU HAVE TO PLAY THE GAME

Only the untalented can afford to be humble.

— Sylvia Miles

The smartest women in male-dominated industries know that you can't win the game if you are not willing to play. They are also aware that the best way to change the game is as a key player, not as an outsider. But this is a learning curve for even the savviest of women. Becoming politically savvy and understanding what is truly going to take their career to the next level is a major theme for many women, as they begin to observe and even engage with the boys' club.

Taking control of your own career is the first and fundamental step. It is the place from which the rest of the lessons covered here will flow.

If you still believe that it is enough to keep your head down and hope for the best, this is not the book for you. Obviously it is imperative that you can 'deliver the goods' on a work front — but in my experience of coaching professional women in male-dominated fields, I have yet to meet an ambitious woman who wasn't already delivering high quality work. What most women lack is not the technical skill to take their career to the next level but the *knowledge* of how to raise their profile and the *confidence* to take that next step.

Professional women at all stages of their careers tend by nature to be reluctant to draw attention to their achievements. It seems somehow wrong to boast of your success with the kind of aplomb many men find natural — whether or not it is merited!

Let me tell you this plainly: acting humble will never bring you career advancement.

One of things I love about my executive-coaching clients is how important *delivery* is to them. They take their work seriously and spend hours giving it their all. They have spent their education and most of their career believing they would be rewarded by a meritocratic system.

And why not? It is a system that has largely worked for them in the past. Meritocracy earned them 'A's when they were at school, gave them a good degree or qualifications when they were in higher education, and probably made the difference in their first jobs.

However, they inevitably reach a point when they look around and realise that pure meritocracy does not prevail in today's workplace. Eventually, we all begin to realise that the people who get ahead are those who make others aware of their wins, and those who spend time developing relationships and their own personal profile.

In the modern workplace it is simply not enough to do a good job and hope to be noticed. We must draw attention to our achievements, the quality of our work and what we are delivering. Waiting to be noticed and rewarded for our efforts simply puts too much power in the hands of other people — and these 'other people' are not mind-readers. *No one will ever care about your career as much as you do.* They are more concerned about their own advancement. Passively hoping your efforts are being noticed is tantamount to handing over the direction of your career to someone else.

Women today certainly have plenty of achievements they could brag about to others. They are entering the professions and postgraduate programmes in unprecedented numbers. However, their striving for professional fulfilment has not been matched with a willingness to claim their own strengths as boldly as the male colleagues with whom they compete.

This reluctance to draw attention to their wins costs women the most in settings where they are surrounded by men playing the game of one-upmanship. This game is natural to many men — yet most women are still unfamiliar with the rules of play.

What of the women who decide to rise above such nonsense and opt out of the game altogether? They as individuals, and the companies that are searching for the best talent, will both miss out. Most companies have just a few women at the most senior levels — yet 80 per cent of consumer decisions are made by women, and many industries are facing a talent shortage[1].

According to Meg Munn, the former UK Deputy Minister for Women and Equality, 70 per cent of women with science, engineering or technology qualifications are not working in these fields[2]. Not having enough women at senior levels is a real problem for the UK, which is expecting a shortfall of 24 million workers by 2040, with a majority being in these' traditionally male-dominated fields[3].

Many companies are beginning to realise that keeping and promoting their women is the only way to tap into the future generation of leaders that will guide them through an uncertain and ever-changing marketplace.

The reticence for many ambitious women stems from a misguided belief in the value of keeping one's head down and just doing a good job, paired with the trust that this will lead to being noticed and promoted. Unfortunately, it doesn't work like that. Once you reach a certain level professionally, your qualifications and skills are considered a given. It is the way you draw attention to what you achieve that will set you apart.

[1] Wittenburg–Cox, A. & Maitland, A. (2008) "Why Women Mean Business", Jossey-Bass
[2] Munn, M. (2007) Speech at Opportunity Now Awards, 24 April
[3] McKinsey Quarterly: A Business Case for Women, September 2008

Drawing attention to your skills and achievements feels like a stretch, particularly in British culture. Additionally, it can seem particularly foreign in certain industries, such as the sciences, where there is a prevalent belief that it is solely the quality of your research that sets you apart. While I wish this were true, this is not the landscape of the real workplace. The ability to network effectively, and explain what you have achieved in a coherent and interesting manner to a lay audience, is what will set you apart in the long run. These skills are a must if you want to grow into any management or client-facing roles, both of which rely on communication. That is the only real way to progress your career in the long term.

- No one will ever care about your career as much as you do.

- Successful delivery in your job is taken for granted, once you reach a certain level.

- You must get comfortable with the idea of self-promotion.

THE VALUE OF QUALIFICATIONS

Working women often wonder what they can do to get further along in their careers. In my experience they are always eager to take more personal and professional development courses to give them that edge. Certainly, the evidence would suggest that additional qualifications have a bottom line benefit for working women. In fact, additional years of education are shown to have a more positive effect on women's earnings than on men's[4].

[4] Eagly, A. & Carli, L. (2007) "Women and the Labyrinth of Leadership", Harvard Business Review, September

As an accredited executive coach with a PhD, I clearly believe in the added knowledge, confidence and credibility that additional qualifications can impart to an ambitious woman. However, some of the blame for a lack of female representation in certain fields should be shared by gender-biased systemic practices within organisations, such as presenteeism, a long-hours culture, inflexible international travel, networking in the evenings, and outdated attitudes towards flexible working.

For those new to the word, *presenteeism* is experienced as a pressure — imposed by others or even by oneself — to be seen to be putting in long hours. It's based on the usually-unspoken understanding that this is one of the traits upon which your commitment to your career will be judged in the future. It often goes against the company's stated policy, and will invariably be denied if anyone is accused of practising it.

Additionally, I have long suspected that the continual pursuit of more qualifications is a red herring for women in the struggle for workplace equality. It is a way for the blame to be laid at the feet of individual women — and can be a distraction from looking at how well-qualified their male peers actually are (or are not as the case may be) and what those male peers are actually doing to get ahead.

But don't take my word for it. New research also backs up the idea that lack of career progression for working women cannot be blamed on a lack of qualifications. Fifty-seven per cent of first degree graduates in 2007/2008 were women, the same as in the previous year[5]. Additionally, there are more women entering higher education as well, with women making up 58 per cent of UK undergraduate populations in 2008[6]. Not surprisingly, the figures are reversed in science, engineering and technology subjects where women make up only 38 per cent of students, but there are signs of historic progress as women are making real inroads into fields that were previously male-dominated such as subjects allied to medicine, which is now just 16.4 per cent

[5] Higher Education Statistics Agency, 2008
[6] Equality in Higher Education Statistical Report, Equality Challenge Unit, 2008

male and veterinary science, which is 22.1 per cent male. Clearly, the fact that women are not 'trickling up' to senior positions cannot legitimately be blamed on a lack of the right qualifications for much longer.

Other evidence suggests that working women in London are better trained than their male counterparts. According to the recent Women in London's Economy[7] report: 'A higher proportion of females in London gain qualifications than males at ages 16, 19 and 23. By the time they enter the workforce, a larger proportion of women in London have higher level qualifications. Despite this, women are less likely than men to attain supervisory or managerial posts.'

Of those who do hold management responsibilities, the women are much more likely to have higher qualifications than their male colleagues. Furthermore, over half of all those entering university are women, which clearly indicates that we cannot blame women's underachievement on a supposed lack of qualifications.

Does this sound familiar to you? If you feel that confidence and a promotion always seem to be one more degree, qualification or training course away, the chances are you need to draw attention to what you are *already* achieving rather than concentrating on what you perceive yourself as lacking.

Rebecca George, a partner at the global accountancy firm Deloitte LLP, is an experienced recruiter. She recounted some of the main differences she saw between male and female candidates at interview stage. 'Often, I have found that I have two candidates with exactly the same qualifications and the woman will never say she can do all of the job, whereas the man will not only say he can do it all, but that he's the best possible choice,' she laughs. Rebecca commented that while there were a few exceptions, she found it interesting to see how the dynamic of confidence affects men and women before they even start their jobs.

---

[7] Women in London's Economy Report 2008, Mayor of London's Office

What she notices in job interviews is borne out in research from University College London in 2008[8], where researchers found men, especially those of lower actual IQ scores, routinely overstated their intelligence — while women underplayed their own. They reported: 'Men are not cleverer but they appear to be more confident, which can have beneficial effects in the interview and even the examination room.'

Unfortunately, the same research also found that very bright women often believed their IQ to be much lower than their actual score.

This is precisely why smart women must not be shy about telling others what they are achieving. Even the dimmest of men know how to play up their real or imagined mental assets! And much to their credit, as they know how valuable confidence is in today's work place.

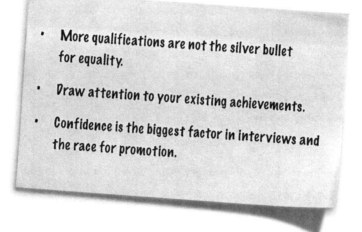

- More qualifications are not the silver bullet for equality.
- Draw attention to your existing achievements.
- Confidence is the biggest factor in interviews and the race for promotion.

THE GREAT QUOTA QUESTION

It is eye-opening, when one moves the focus away from what women supposedly lack in these industries to what they can uniquely offer.

In 2002, the Norwegian government issued a mandate that all publicly traded companies listed on the Oslo Stock Exchange have 40 per cent female

[8] Furnham, A. & Buchanan, T. (2005) "Personality, Gender and Self-Perceived Intelligence", Personality and Individual Differences, Vol. 39, pp. 543-555

representation on executive boards by July 2005 — or face punitive legislation. The government capitalised on both the business imperative and a long-held source of national pride in gender equality to enact the measure, but understandably the dictum was still not without its critics. Initially, people were sceptical of this risky mandate which was based on American research by the think tank Catalyst[9], showing that companies with more women on senior management teams enjoyed higher returns on both equity and total shareholder return than those with the fewest women.

Catalyst followed this up in 2007 and found that those Fortune 500 companies with at least three women directors experienced the most dramatic returns for sales and invested capital[10].

In Norway, progress on reaching the 'recommended targets' was steady but slow, with women reaching 17 per cent representation on boards, until the Norwegian government mandated the quotas in 2005. By 2008, women made up 36 per cent of corporate boards in the largest companies. The 77 companies that had not reached 40 per cent were issued with written warnings, and the government retains the right to dissolve any companies that do not comply. It is still too early to determine if all will reach the 40 per cent watershed, and indeed if any firms will be legally dissolved because of not reaching their quotas.

Defending the move, the Norwegian government said it was not for the sake of political correctness. Rather it just made better business sense to have executive members that were the best-qualified, across the board, so to speak — as opposed to 'being recruited on hunting and fishing trips or from within a small circle of acquaintances'. Sound familiar?

When organisations are forced to look for great female talent and potential, and nurture it through a process the Norwegians call 'pearl-diving', they are often surprised at just how much talent they actually find.

[9] Catalyst (2004) "The Bottom Line: Connecting Corporate Performance and Gender Diversity"
[10] Catalyst (2007) "The Bottom Line: Corporate Performance and Women's Representation on Boards"

The requirement has since had a positive effect on the Norwegian boards, as the women are better educated and have wider work experience than the men they are replacing[11]. Public opinion has shown both acceptance and satisfaction with the measures and no instances of women being forced onto boards and asked to play a nominal role. In most cases, the women were just not as well 'networked' or sufficiently 'high-profile' before the legislation. Since 2002, the sky above Norway has not fallen in, companies have not folded and in fact Norway is ranked year after year as one of the best countries in which to live and the most peaceful nation by the Economist Intelligence Unit[12].

Quotas are always controversial, and even some of the staunchest supporters of women's employment rights are less than happy about them. At the 2006 Women's Forum in Deauville, only 40 per cent of attendees were in favour of quotas at the start of the conference. After hearing arguments for and against, and considering the slow progress of women's advancement in the workplace, some 90 per cent saw the merit of such measures as much needed temporary intervention, at the very least, by the end of the conference[13].

Similarly, the United States federal government set guidelines in 1994 that established a five per cent goal for businesses contracting with women and minority-owned firms. This proved to be very successful in establishing ground rules and good practice, by encouraging all companies with government contracts to look for tangible ways to do business with women and minority-owned businesses.

I myself own one of the first companies to be certified under the UK version of the scheme, which encourages US-owned firms operating in the UK, such as Merrill Lynch, Microsoft, Accenture, Pfizer and Cisco, to use UK-based women-owned suppliers. The certification is certainly not a free entry into tendering processes. However, it does allow companies that want to engage with women-owned businesses to benefit from an established system of

---

[11] Toomey, C. "Quotas for Women on the Board: Do they Work?" Sunday Times, June 8, 2008
[12] Economist Intelligence Unit (2008) The Economist, Country Report Norway
[13] Wittenburg–Cox, A. & Maitland, A. (2008) "Why Women Mean Business", Jossey-Bass

outsourced due diligence. This will ensure access to the suppliers they need with the added benefit of fulfilling government targets for diversity.

It makes you wonder: how would legal requirements of this kind affect the UK? My view is that it would rock our institutions to the core — but that is not to say this controversial idea is without merit. Affirmative action is illegal in the United Kingdom but most people agree that it would be advantageous to have more women represented within companies and the supplier chain, especially when women make up a lion's share of purchasing decisions.

The majority of organisations espouse equal opportunities and lament the lack of women at the top. Still, despite much well-intentioned hand-wringing, overall, women are not gaining ground at the highest levels in any great numbers. The Norwegians illustrate what happens when companies are forced to undertake more than lip service to solve the problem — to take women's representation on the board from six per cent to 40 per cent in less than a decade. They are forced to come up with innovative measures to ensure that women do reach the top, and they have found the initial results dramatic and groundbreaking.

The general consensus of Britons is that professional women want to be treated as equals to men — and thus no special legislation is necessary. While I can initially agree, we have had supposed 'equal treatment' for decades now, and women's representation at board level still flounders at single-digit figures. I appreciate that women want to gain such positions on their own merit and be treated as equals — but I must point out that historically many men have not used merit alone when acquiring senior positions.

The 'old boy network' has ensured that the players within that system have been given favours and help from others. To my mind, it is a bit naïve and overly optimistic for women to claim they want to build their careers without any help, when most men know that building relationships for mutual benefit is the only way to build a career.

The truth is, a purely egalitarian model still does not exist. It is certainly not a career model followed by many successful men who have enjoyed deals from their university friends, promotions from their brothers-in-law, insider news from their colleagues; they understand the meaning of 'if you scratch my back, I'll scratch yours'.

I have no problem asking women to participate on a level playing field. But let us not forget just how slanted that playing field remains. Men who advance in their careers understand how vital relationships and building their professional profile are, in acquiring the most esteemed positions within senior management.

Companies who espouse equal opportunities for women should look for those whose talent has not been fully utilised, and whose potential could be nurtured. Like the Norwegians, we could ask companies to try 'pearl-diving'; to find the gems and teach them the same secrets of profile raising through intensive mentoring and career development, thereby eliminating the need for quotas.

As pointed out by Wittenburg-Cox and Maitland, in their insightful call to arms, *Why Women Mean Business*: 'They believe they are being rigorously objective in treating men and women in exactly the same way — which they do. That is the problem. They are unaware of the bias inherent in assuming everyone is the same when everything about their culture and promotion tracks is based on a traditional, linear, single income male career model. Since men and women are equal and the same in their eyes, the only difference is that women appear to bring to the table less time, less availability to travel and therefore 'less' commitment[14]'

Many firms question women's commitment to their jobs, without questioning whether the business model many have created, one of a virtual round the clock service, is in fact sustainable. While business has aimed over the past few decades to right past wrongs by treating everyone equally, they have missed the point. Not everyone can engage equally with a workplace that assumes there is a full time carer at home to service all domestic needs.

[14] Wittenburg–Cox, A. & Maitland, A. (2008) "Why Women Mean Business", Jossey-Bass, p. 51

- Companies who promote more women to board level are more successful.

- Women make most purchasing decisions.

- Building relationships is the only way to build a career.

THE MYTH OF MERITOCRACY

Once, power was considered a masculine attribute.

In fact, power has no sex.

— Katherine Graham

One of my former coaching clients — let's call her Paula — told me about an informal discussion she'd had with former laboratory colleagues, all of whom belonged to ethnic minorities or were women. Paula said the general consensus was that, while they all loved their profession, they also agreed that they considered engaging in office politics and networking to be a waste of time. They felt that they should refuse to dignify these 'lowly games' with their participation.

I can understand an initial intolerance for 'game-playing', as most of the games in these fields have never included women or ethnic minorities as key players; nor were they invited to help create the rules.

Women often say they are searching for a career that is 'politics-free'. Well, that career does not exist. What can make it easier is the realisation that *politics* is not a four-letter word; it is, in fact, the way business gets done. Politics just means understanding how 'organisational back-scratching' works. The quid pro quo aspect is never mentioned openly, yet a trade is implicit between the parties.

It may seem manipulative — but you help other people at work all the time. Is it unreasonable to expect help in return? There is nothing underhand about it. Politics is simply the work of relationships, and giving help to others so that you can call on *their* help when you need it. And let's face it, by the time you really need a helpful relationship, it is usually too late to build it from scratch. Most women will willingly go out of their way for someone else if they can help. However, most still feel squeamish about asking favours of others. The truth is that if you work with other people at any level, you can't avoid office politics — but you can remember to give out *and* cash in your credits.

The most successful women are clued-in to the importance of office politicking, despite its negative connotations. The upside of participation in healthy politics is collaboration and enhanced team work.

Another coaching client, whom I will call Lorraine, told me how she had initially been resentful of the fact that her work was not well-regarded in her laboratory. When she eventually worked up the courage to discuss this with one her line manager, he replied sheepishly that while he wanted to be an advocate for her, he did not understand the exact nature of her research into the minutiae of genetic mapping.

As surprising as this seemed to Lorraine, a lack of understanding regarding roles happens in all types of workplace. Few people feel that their line manager knows exactly what they do all day. In fact, a good manager doesn't need to know every step you take. Successful women learn that the only way to get ahead in the beginning is to tell others exactly what they are producing and why it is so vital to the business as a whole. It sounds obvious — but we often make the assumption that those around us are mind-readers. We assume they know how much recognition means to us, and that they choose to deny us their acceptance and kudos.

Lorraine came to see that briefing her boss about the detail of her work, and its potential implications for genetic research, was not bragging but simply helping him become an advocate for her. This is particularly important in the UK where anything perceived as 'bragging' is seen as an anathema to social cohesion and to be avoided at all costs.

Lis Astall, who is European Managing Director for public service in Accenture, told me that she initially believed in meritocracy alone. In the early years of her career, when she was working towards management level, she expected to be rewarded by grateful onlookers for her Herculean efforts. She quickly realised that approach was misguided.

She smiled: 'I tried to work harder than anybody else, which in hindsight was a mistake. I worked longer hours than anyone else before I realised it was not accomplishing anything I wanted — just more work. Instead I became better skilled at realising which projects were worth the hard work — and which were not.'

The steadfast belief that the best way to progress your career is by keeping your head down, delivering good work and waiting to get noticed, is not helping women progress their careers. Most men, on the other hand, seem to start out already knowing instinctively that self-promotion and relationship-building are vital. Of course, we all have to be able to deliver on our responsibilities — however, in my experience that is not a problem for the vast majority of professional women. What *is* a challenge is the idea of proudly drawing attention to their achievements and everything else they could offer other colleagues, employers and collaborators.

> • Office politics is not a dirty word.
>
> • Collect favours from other people as freely as you do them yourself.
>
> • Colleagues are not mind-readers — tell them what you are doing.

WHY WOMEN'S REPRESENTATION IS VITAL IN A RECESSION

At the time of writing this book, the current economic situation is dire. Make no mistake about that. The economic freefall is the worst seen in many decades in the UK. Formerly sound business names in a variety of sectors, ranging from Woolworths to Lehman Brothers, have fallen by the wayside, leaving thousands of talented women in their wake. Of the companies that are still operational, many are shedding staff, putting a freeze on hiring new members and cutting training budgets.

Women are the first to be downsized during a shaky economy. In the final quarter of 2008, the quarter that tolled the approach of an official recession, women in full time employment lost twice as many jobs as men. Harriet Harman, the women's minister, said: "There is a major fear about women being targeted by their employers during the downturn." Her fears look like they are being realised as the number of women in full-time work fell by 53,000, compared with a fall of 36,000 for men which meant women are losing full-time jobs at twice the rate of men, because men significantly outnumber women in the UK workplace.[15]

---

[15] Oakeshott, I. (2009) "Women Losing Jobs Twice as Fast as Men", Sunday Times, January 25

According to the International Labour Office, the global unemployment rate for women in 2009 is projected at 7.4 per cent compared to 7.0 per cent for men, with the number of unemployed women worldwide potentially rising to 22 million in 2009 as the global economic crisis deepens[16].

With initial impacts felt in male-dominated sectors such as finance, construction and manufacturing, the shockwaves are spreading into service-orientated sectors and wholesale retail trade which in most industrialised countries are dominated by women as both business owners and employees. According to the ILO's annual report 'Global Employment Trends for Women', the impacts on women can be alleviated if governments sign up to gender-equality measures, and ensure that new jobs created by economic stimulus packages guarantee fair salaries and social protection measures.

For example, whilst making redundant women who are pregnant or on maternity leave is unlawful in the UK, they are often the first to go in a recession. There is still a pervasive and untrue misconception that women don't care about their jobs as much as their male colleagues, or that there will be a male for them to fall back on during times of economic crisis.

Companies can also be keen to shed women who they perceived will cost them more in the long run due to maternity breaks and days lost due to childcare. In a recession it is difficult, not to mention time-consuming, to prove that young women are being targeted for redundancy when so many job losses are being made across the board.

However, one could argue that only greater numbers of women at the top will help us *recover* from the current credit crisis. Remember, the finance sector, where the economic crisis originated, has some of the worst under-representation of women in senior leadership roles.

As explained by *The Observer*'s business editor, Ruth Sunderland: 'Both feminist and mainstream economists have pointed out that the credit crunch is quite literally a man-made disaster, a monster created in the testosterone-

---

[16] International Labour Office, "Global Employment Trends for Women", Geneva, March 2009

drenched environment of Wall Street and the City. There is a growing body of opinion that, if there had been more female decision makers, the agony could have been avoided. The crunch has emboldened advocates of boardroom diversity, who insist we now need to get more women at the top in financial institutions as a matter of urgency, to prevent it happening again[17].'

Recent research echoes this point. Findings reported in the journal *Evolution and Human Behavior*[18] demonstrated the shortcomings of the system of homogenous men sitting in front of computer screens making financial decisions. They found men to be particularly likely to make high-risk bets when under financial pressure and surrounded by other males of similar status — which describes the modern trading floor in a nutshell.

Other biological research has confirmed this, suggesting that men are more dependent on the adrenalin of rapid-fire, high-risk situations whereas women thrive on the calming influence of endorphin-producing activities such as discussion and building relationships[19]. Imagine what the modern board room would look like, and the decisions that would flow, if both of these qualities were present in equal measure.

Having a more diverse group of board members at the top of the global financial institutions that got us into this mess in the first place would go a long way towards limiting group-think and encouraging more balanced decision-making in the future.

The current situation is enough to make even the most ambitious and resolute of career women wonder what will happen to her career. This is both a challenge and a golden opportunity, as the people who will survive the redundancies will be those who are valued most by management.

---

[17] Sunderland, R. (2009) "The Real Victims of the this Credit Crunch: Women", The Observer, January 18
[18] Emer, E., Cosmides, L. & Tooby, J. (2008) "Relative status regulates risky decision-making about resources in men: Evidence for the co-evolution of motivation and cognition", Evolution and Human Behavior, 29, pp.106 -118
[19] National Institute of Mental Health (2003) "Gender Differences in Behavioural Responses to Stress: 'Fight or Flight' vs 'Tend and Befriend'." Online version www.medicalmoment.org

And as we will see throughout this book, *value* is not measured in sheer output — but rather who is perceived to be the most useful to the organisation and its goals. Historically, this is where men have tended to shine. However, given the right tools you can use these insights to your advantage. Keeping your head down and hoping you will be noticed is a risk you simply cannot afford to take in a depressed economy.

Now is the time to think strategically about your career, rather than assume a job will be waiting for you after an extended maternity break with no contact at the office. Now is the time to explore other sectors or careers, should you be given the sudden terrifying and exhilarating freedom through a redundancy to try something new. Now is the time to rethink your image so that people can see you are ambitious and leadership material, rather than someone who merely coasts in uncertain times. Now is the time to seek a support network of people who can help you figure out where the silver lining to this otherwise dark cloud is for you and you alone.

That is where the challenge comes in. The challenge to raise your game and begin to communicate why you are of value. The challenge to make new contacts both within and outside of your organisation, so that you have more options should your job be 'downsized'. The challenge to work with a wider range of key stakeholders and demonstrate what you are doing to develop both yourself and the opportunities for your organisation.

Now, more than ever, is the time to realise that no one is going to save your job or promote your career unless you are proactive. Where you may have received training through your company, now is the time to keep investing in professional development tools, even if it means paying for it yourself.

Now is the time to work even more closely with your key stakeholders and expand your network. Now is the time to stop thinking *self-promotion is for other people.*

Now is the time to realise you must take your career into your own hands. Despite being one of the few women in your field, now is the time to stand out as the talented and ambitious individual you are, and begin to understand the dynamics of *the boys' club.*

- Women are hit hardest by recessions. But it's also a chance to embrace change.

- The market needs women to promote gender-neutral decision-making — it's less risky.

- Women in senior positions in finance could help prevent future recessions.

TWO

MAKING IT IN
A MAN'S WORLD

I have yet to hear a man ask for advice on how to

combine marriage and a career.

— Gloria Steinem

The senior women I have interviewed for this book came to their fields from a wide variety of experiences. Let me introduce them to you.

Some had MBAs, some PhDs; some didn't have traditional qualifications at all, or had come to their respective male-dominated fields much later in their working lives. They worked in finance, academia, IT, science, consultancy, the law and even the Foreign Service. They came to these fields from a wide range of backgrounds and for a variety of reasons.

There was no single path to success, no one box to tick, no attribute you had to possess, no ultimate career goal, no solitary perfect decision to make.

This in itself is reassuring. Women beat themselves up for not being ideal, for not making perfect choices at every junction, and sometimes for taking the long way round to success.

What was so inspiring was the myriad ways these women found their way to rewarding jobs they loved. What these women had in common was the success they had found in a wide range of fields that had traditionally been dominated by men.

ACADEMIC INTEREST

Women do not *fall into* male-dominated fields. They do not just find themselves working in science, engineering and technology careers, for example. To get the right background for many of these fields, a girl must choose to take maths, physics and chemistry to a high level. She must then continue to study subjects where she will be part of an ever diminishing minority of females — at an age when most young girls want to fit in with their peers, not choose subjects that deliberately set them apart.

You must have a real interest in and even passion for these fields, as there are no women who choose these subjects to take the easy route or to blend in with the crowd. They are going against the grain and must develop a strong sense of self early on; as they progress their education, they often become more formidable and determined. Both of these qualities actually make them potentially better leaders and more deserving of senior roles as they climb the ladder. Any excuses you may hear about ambitious women not entering these fields are not merited.

For example, the academics in the pure sciences whom I interviewed were more likely to have had an early love for their subject. This is to be expected, because choice of subjects at school level severely limits options for working in certain scientific fields later on. It can be a key problem for girls who are forced to decide how much they like these demanding subjects very early in their lives. If you haven't taken the right maths and science subjects after a certain age, it is difficult to acquire them to an advanced level later on.

For example, Athene Donald, a fellow of the Royal Society and a professor at the University of Cambridge, found her love of physics from an early age: 'I didn't come from a scientific family background, but even at thirteen I could see physics explained why the world was the way it was — it was a way of making sense of things. I was hooked.'

MILITARY BACKGROUNDS

Many women find their way into male-dominated fields later in their career, after a stint in other roles where they also work primarily with men. Because of their earliest career experiences, it is almost as if some women become used to male-dominated fields as the norm and are very comfortable operating within them. In fact some women, when they move to more gender-balanced workplaces, find working with other women to be their new learning curve.

Additionally, as our first experiences often have the greatest influence over us, these young women become tolerant of an all-male atmosphere and come to accept being the lone woman in a team of men as par for the course. This outlook gives them the ability to move into other male-dominated fields with greater ease later in their career.

Fiona Edington is a barrister who started her career as an officer recruit in the Women's Royal Army Corps. She left the military because of her own sense that justice could be better carried out in a courtroom. She explained her choice for the move: 'People need to be treated justly while also taking responsibility for their actions. I got a great deal from my time with the military, but increasingly I felt war was possibly being used as an economic battleground by people who were unwilling to serve themselves. Now, every day, I am affecting someone's life.'

Like Fiona, Eileen Brown, the Professional Evangelist Manager for Microsoft, arrived at one male-dominated field (IT) from a career in another (the Merchant Navy). As a thirteen-year-old, she humorously claims, she initially saw the Merchant Navy as offering free holidays to exotic locations. She then worked for Shell Tankers as the first female Navigating Officer, before moving into the role of Container Ship Planner. This is where her potential IT acumen first became evident.

She remembered: 'Every Tuesday was a scheduling day, and boats were routinely late, which made it difficult to sell space aboard since we didn't know what time they would be docking in New York or Boston or Savannah.' She recalled the hours the revisions took: 'Planners like me spent the whole day becoming frustrated at amending dates and times by hand in a logbook. I thought, *Maybe I could do this on a spreadsheet*, as Lotus 1-2-3 version 2.0 had just come out. In the end it took me five minutes to make changes that took others hours — that's when Shell decided to move me into IT!'

Jane Lewis, of Microsoft, also came from a military background. She had an early interest in gadgetry, which initially led to a career in radio telecommunications in the Royal Navy. She recalled: 'As a child, I loved to take things apart and see how they worked. I scalped my Sindy doll and took everything apart, from my bike graduating up to circuit boards — trying to see if I could put them back together, and if I could do it better. I love the fact that technology is never static, that it is always changing and getting better — it's exciting. And now my job is just an extension of that — ensuring companies are making the best use of their IT.'

'WHAT CAN I LEARN HERE?'

Many women I interviewed got into certain fields, such as IT or business management, before degrees in the field were widely available. They made their way by crossing over from other departments, or simply because they loved the emerging technology.

Philippa Snare, of Microsoft, initially wanted to be a journalist but came to IT after finding herself defending the potential of the Internet for a marketing communications degree in 1993. She remarked: 'The power of the Internet was just taking off then, and I was really excited about where it could go, but my professor was not — he said the Internet had no future, long term. I obviously took a different view and even wrote my thesis as a webpage, which was a first. I never convinced him, but it helped me find a new direction and the rest of my career has probably been driven in some part by wanting to prove him wrong!'

For others, the opportunities for advancement that came with a professional qualification were most attractive. Laura Hinton is a young mother and partner at PricewaterhouseCoopers (PwC). She is a chartered accountant, though she chose the degree not to practise as an accountant, but rather for the opportunities it could offer her.

She explained: 'Like a lot of people, I left university thinking I knew everything but then quickly realised I didn't know anything! In fact, I think I had originally told some of my friends at university, *I will do anything — but it won't be accountancy*. But I joined BDO Stoy Hayward straight from university and liked the idea that it was great training. As part of the accountancy track I knew I would get good exposure to a lot of different parts of the business, which could give me a good start in doing other things eventually.' In time Laura became the youngest female partner at BDO Stoy Hayward, at just 29.

She reflected on what her time at the firm gave her: 'I learned a huge amount there as it was really entrepreneurial and you get exposure to a wider variety of clients including start-ups and family businesses.' She learned all she could in that role before joining PwC to become a director, a risk for her as it was not a direct move into partnership. In fact, it was a step down in terms of seniority — but a risk she was willing to take in order to learn more.

Similarly, Rebecca George, a partner in Deloitte's public sector business, got into IT because of her mother's concern that she should learn 'solid skills' for career progression. She knew she would be good at selling and in 1988 felt that only two companies had great sales training teams: Mars and IBM. She matter-of-factly remarked: 'I chose IBM because I thought selling computers would be more interesting than selling chocolate.'

Matilda Venter, a South African and director within PwC, came to the company from a technical background she'd developed in her home country. Her academic background was in psychology but she quickly found that her career would be limited if she stayed in counselling: 'The circumstances in the late eighties in South Africa were very tough; I battled to get a job after finishing my studies. I always knew I wanted to be successful but felt limited by the opportunities in psychology. I saw friends doing well in IT, so I started studying part-time in information systems, analysis and design, which is where the opportunity was and gave me technical expertise. It was a conscious decision to change fields, the first one in my career.'

MEANING BEYOND MONEY

While the women I interviewed seem to join these fields for a variety of reasons, it is undeniable that most of them find deeper meaning in their work. They recognise that it fills a knowledge gap they would like to close, it impacts on the lives of others and there is a sense of satisfaction in accomplishment.

These motivators are particularly strong for women, and an Aspire study of professionals found that women rated their top five motivations for work as making a difference, being challenged, believing in their company's direction, satisfaction with their team and recognition. Fewer than half actually rated flexibility as vital and money was the least motivating factor[1] out of several options given.

Male-dominated fields are, on the whole, much better paid than the traditional *pink collar ghetto* of service sector jobs of childcare, teaching and nursing that many women favour. However, not one of the successful women I interviewed mentioned money as a primary motivator.

Another study of professionals, who work at least 60 hours per week in positions of great responsibility known as *extreme jobs*, found that financial compensation was much less motivating for women than for their male colleagues. Rather, it was the stimulating and challenging aspects of their work that encouraged them to devote long hours to the job.

While the research found women less likely to be in positions where at least 60 hours per week were required, it was not from a lack of interest in such roles but rather that the women simply couldn't afford to give that much time on top of their familial responsibilities[2].

[1] Aspire (2006) "The 2006 Aspire Survey of Executive Women" www.aspirecompanies.com
[2] Hewlett, S.A. & Buck Luce, C. (2006) "Extreme Jobs: The Dangerous Allure of the 70 Hour Workweek", Harvard Business Review, December

The gender difference then denotes not a *disinterest* in such demanding roles, but rather *the type of support* those who engage in them are likely to receive. When men engage in extreme jobs, they are more likely to be cosseted by the support of a stay-at-home partner, whereas women in extreme jobs are fairly likely still to have many of those responsibilities themselves or primary responsibility for outsourcing them. Additionally, as I find in my coaching practice, many of the most ambitious women, who might like to work in more demanding roles, are indeed also married to men who also work in extreme jobs.

The way women allocate their time between work and family is vital to them. In fact, according to the study, women were much less likely to take jobs that were time-demanding but without a great deal of responsibility or personal satisfaction. Men were more tolerant of such long-hours, low-impact roles if the compensation was great enough.

- Early exposure to working with men makes it easier to work with them later in your career.

- Think strategically about what you want to learn before picking your field.

- Anyone can work long hours if they have support at home and a job with meaning.

THE GOOD, THE BAD AND THE UGLY

There is no doubt that some of the industries of my interviewees, namely science and IT, suffer from a crisis of poor public relations and a lack of general understanding as to what these careers entail. When career development organisation CRAC surveyed 2,000 undergraduates for example, they found a perception that working in IT was 'boring'[3].

Similarly, my own PhD research found that engineering is not regarded as a high status career by students in the UK. Nor do people understand exactly what engineers do on a day-to-day basis — most likely because the variety is so huge and the term overused in non-technical parlance. People who build bridges, design cars, create infertility treatments, design city layouts and even come to fix your washing machine can all call themselves an 'engineer'. Similarly, the energy industry has had a dirty reputation — both literally and politically — and is yet another sector struggling to attract women.

Many of the women I interviewed who worked in the IT sector recognised that the field had a negative reputation as being a field for the socially inept and for technological 'geeks'. A woman I will call Caroline, the IT Director of a global logistics company and also a mother of three, recalled an experience she had on a recent holiday: 'My husband and I met another couple we really liked, and when we started discussing our careers, I joked I didn't want to tell them what I did. The very funny and gregarious husband said the same thing and it turned out we both worked in IT — but neither of us wanted to admit it because of all the negative perceptions out there. The irony of course is that if you are an engaging person in IT, you will get ahead because your energy is infectious and your extroversion is much more noticeable.'

When describing how she personally tried to combat this image, Caroline talked about a presentation she often gave about the IT industry, which begins to play with stereotypes from its title, *Geeks in Sandals*. 'When the slides begin, they start with a pair of ugly feet, wrapped in cables and wires. I then

[3] Mellors-Bourne, R. (2008) "Do Undergraduates Want a Career in IT?" Sector Intelligence Research, CRAC

talk about how female-friendly and exciting the industry can be, ending with a slide of these beautiful, manicured feet in these gorgeous strappy high-heeled sandals by a set of discreetly coiled wires. It's really fun to engage with the audience that way, and challenge their perceptions.'

Caroline found herself as trainee programmer in IT after university, simply because she noticed it was a job with a clear career path and an interesting future. She is passionate about technology and believes that to succeed, as you move up the ladder, your ability to lead others is more useful than any specific technical skills.

Despite the image crisis she believes IT suffers from, she recognises that any effective IT team must have outstanding people. Even the most impressive and innovative technology won't work without great people driving it. Even the most advanced piece of software needs people to create, implement, manage and deliver value on the product — without them you have nothing. She continued: 'Technologies don't do business, *people* do business. It takes people to make decisions on what technology they buy, which suppliers they use… it's people driven.'

BUSINESS = RELATIONSHIPS

This sentiment was echoed by many women in this field, who saw their careers as working with people first, technology and products second. It is an idea that I focus on with my clients in one-to-one sessions as well as in workshops: *Business is nothing but a series of relationships.*

If you put people first, the business will flow — if you don't, it won't. Without investing in relationships your career will flounder, especially as you progress and take responsibility for larger projects. Many of the women I spoke to agreed that people were the most important aspect of any effective use of technology. Jane Lewis, of Microsoft, agreed: 'Technology doesn't break down on its own; the problem is always that the relationship between the people responsible has broken down first.'

Philippa Snare of Microsoft suggested more women could be drawn to the field if the *impact* of the technology were highlighted rather than the technology itself. She remarked: 'If we were to ask women if they wanted to help people collaborate across countries, you would have a lot more people interested; but instead we ask if they would like to be a *Unified Communications Specialist*, which doesn't get to the core of the job and what it can achieve.'

She continued: 'If we could explain technology is about human behaviour and facilitating relationships more easily, I think that would be very attractive to women. We have to let human behaviour shape technology, not the other way around. It would be a worrying world if technology started dictating how we interact.'

Philippa is passionate about technology being shaped by human interaction rather than the other way around. She explained how all the most popular pieces of technology evolved out of anthropology and watching how people actually interact.

She elaborated on this process: 'People in a group setting discuss random situations as they experience them, asking for feedback or validation of what they are experiencing. Hence the popularity of Instant Messaging, whereby short messages can be sent and no logical sequence of conversation — no small talk — is expected. Likewise, we like recommendations for products but trust those that come from people who we think are like us.

'With this knowledge, Amazon creates predictive technology that allows the online superstore to make recommendations based on other items we have purchased, and even allows us to see what other people who have bought the same item have additionally purchased.'

These processes mimic the way we interact in real life situations recommending films, books, holiday destinations and even other people to friends. For example, the social networking site Facebook facilitates the sharing of recommendations for products, and connecting with new people through your existing friends. It is highlighting the power of these collaborative and relationship-centred technologies that could potentially draw more women to a field that has historically recruited on the strength of technology for technology's sake.

Philippa Snare of Microsoft shies away from the term *IT* itself, preferring that the entire industry would be renamed. When I ask what it should be renamed as, she can't put a finger on the exact term — but she knows that it is more about *collaboration* and *people* than virtually any other field. She says: 'I don't know what Information Technology means, but I know what I am achieving with any of my projects. I have helped develop MSN Messenger and Windows Live and Hotmail. When I get feedback from people saying they found their missing daughter through tracing her Hotmail account, or that they met their wife through Messenger, or that they are now working from home with mobile technology so they can take care of their children, I understand the impact that I am having. That's what gets me out of bed in the morning.'

There is evidence that a female aversion to IT is shifting. According to the 2007 Nielsen/Netratings survey, in the UK, the largest group of Internet users is women aged 18-34, with young women spending up to 27 per cent more time online than men of the same age[4]. Whether this will translate into a greater representation of women eventually working in the field remains to be seen.

Zoë Ingle runs Positive Energy, the UK's network for women working in the energy industry. She felt the energy industry holds great potential for women as it's now a hot topic that is current and relevant for everyone. She suggested: 'We are increasingly aware of the global energy crisis. How we supply our energy needs is something discussed in the papers every day and even within the family. It's now everyday life, it's the oil crisis, it's recycling, it's the rising cost of petrol, it's about fair trade and how our food is harvested and reaches us.'

---

[4] Nielsen/Netratings (2007) "Young women now most dominant group online"

She continued: 'Now is an amazing time to be involved since it all feels so relevant and we are developing technologies to increase efficiency and make the environment cleaner for our health and the future of our children. When I explain that, many more women can see the appeal of being on the cutting edge of that movement.'

This is one way the industry, which historically has had a 'dirty' reputation, can attract women who are engaged in avoiding an impending energy crisis.

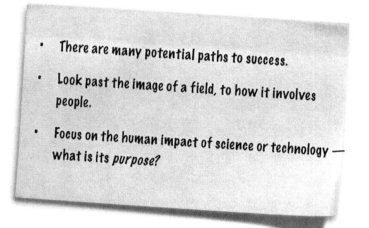

- There are many potential paths to success.
- Look past the image of a field, to how it involves people.
- Focus on the human impact of science or technology — what is its purpose?

HOW REAL IS THE GLASS CEILING?

One of the things about equality is not just that you be treated equally to a man, but that you treat yourself equally to the way you treat a man.

— Marlo Thomas

Most of the women I interviewed felt they had not experienced huge amounts of sexism. Indeed the women I coach do not come to me for help in dealing with sexism, as such. They want to understand how to manoeuvre office politics and work around the ubiquitous *boys' club* — both of which are grounded in a gendered workplace.

However, upon closer reflection, many of these women agreed it had been a tough journey at times. They certainly noticed the dearth of women in senior positions. Even when there should be ample numbers of women to 'trickle' up, the women still have a disproportionately difficult time advancing. In fact, at our current rate of progress, it will be a further 60 years before women in the UK achieve parity on company boards[5].

A few of the women I interviewed had stories about difficult men they had worked for when first starting out, and how they outmanoeuvred them to get along. However, most agreed that sexism was no longer so obvious in day-to-day interaction. Rather it is institutionalised in certain workplace practices, such as the long-hours culture, that are not female-friendly.

What was interesting is how many of the women claimed they either didn't experience overt discrimination, or merely brushed it off as a bad experience from their past but one that was no longer relevant. However, they did admit that within many traditionally female departments, such as Marketing or Human Resources, located in male-dominated companies, the most senior staff members are still mainly male.

For example, Jackie Gittins, a director in the consulting practice at PwC, has spent her entire professional life in Human Resources, an area in most companies populated primarily by women. However, that changes as you progress up the ladder within Human Resources; in many companies, the heads of HR are male.

Jackie has a Masters degree in Human Resources and is active in the Chartered Institute of Personnel and Development — but whenever she is asked to speak at a conference of Human Resources professionals, she remarked: 'The scarcity of women at the highest levels is noticeable.'

---

[5] Equality and Human Rights Commission, 2008

Caroline, the logistics company IT Director, for example, at an early point in her career, found herself working for a male boss who established credibility with his team through drinking sessions. She laughed: 'The way to establish your credibility was to drink your body weight in your chosen liquor until 4am and still make it back to the office by 7am the following day. It obviously wasn't a formal criterion, but it did influence how well you built relationships.'

When asked how she managed to establish credibility with this team, she dryly admitted: 'I learned to drink my own body weight for a while. I developed a set of male behaviours that I thought were necessary at the time. It isn't now, thank goodness, but I have it in me to be bloke-ish if I need to be.' She explained: 'If you are the only woman in a room and you make the men feel they can't talk freely, then you will be considered a threat and never be accepted as part of the team.'

Eileen Brown, the most senior technical woman at Microsoft UK, who started her career in the Merchant Navy, also initially took the route of trying to prove herself to her male colleagues by engaging in male behaviour. She remarked: 'Nobody ever told me I couldn't do the job because I was a woman — in fact, it wasn't until I arrived for my first day that I realised just what a rarity women were. It was physically the hardest work I have ever done. I drank, smoked and swore like the boys for ten years because I was desperate to be accepted — and I thought I was bullet-proof until I was thirty.'

She recalled: 'As I got older and gained credibility, I didn't need to do that any more. I was more confident in myself and getting the stripes on my arms showed my merit and changed people's perceptions of me. At the end of the day, it didn't matter what sex I was if I got the job done.'

Like other women, both Caroline and Eileen found that acting like one of the boys no longer suited who they were as individuals and therefore was unsustainable in the long run. They discovered the truth: no matter how much you may drink or swear, if you are a woman, you can be a member of the team but *you will never truly be one of the boys*. It is far better in the long run to work on what you already do well, as a woman and as an individual, than try to be something you are not in order to maintain a status quo that does not serve you anyway.

And why should you want to be *one of the guys*? As the successful professionals I interviewed have shown, women can be respected as equal players and ambitious colleagues — but to aim to be considered *an honorary male* does a disservice to the woman herself, to her male colleagues and to other women in general.

In the first instance, it does not challenge the thinking of smart men as to who should be considered for inner circle status. It encourages them to keep thinking of strong women as exceptional and not like *real women*. Additionally, it is divisive: it assumes that *normal* women generally have little to offer the modern workplace, other than a few rare individuals who are prepared to act and think like men in order to get ahead. The very nature of being included *in* the boys' club means that others — most notably women and minority groups — are *out* and continue to be excluded.

Angela Mohtashemi, a director of PwC and a mother of two, explains: 'We are aware sexism needs to be rooted out and needs to be addressed, but the issue remains. In my team, for example, we have a large number of women. For the last several years, we have looked at the pool of candidates for Director. Each year, equal numbers of women and men are proposed — and each year just the men have received promotions. We are not talking huge numbers for my group, two promotions per year, but it's still noticeable.'

This is where the role of unconscious bias must be noted. Some people assume that if ample gender-equality measures are in place, sexism can't be happening. Western countries have taken measures to root out *overt* discrimination, as well they should. However, it leaves in place the problem of *unconscious* discrimination, a much thornier issue to tackle.

There can be an assumption that if bias is unconscious, the perpetrators don't know they are doing it. If we can't prove they are doing it unconsciously, then it can't exist; if it doesn't exist, we don't have to deal with it.

Too often, equality statistics measure only the *numbers* of women in each position but not the *reasons* women are relegated to those positions — and why people think they are worthy or not worthy of promotion. This is exasperating for professional women, who find it difficult to manoeuvre amongst political structures they did not create and cannot easily infiltrate, even when those who hold the keys to those structures claim that promotions are equally available to women.

Fiona Edington, a barrister who left the military for the law, mentioned that her decision was in part influenced by the glass ceiling she saw within the military. She suggested: 'Of course there are cracks in the ceiling, and every now and then you would see a woman get to the top, but even now there are only a few brigadiers who are women and they are not technically allowed in the infantry and cavalry. Women are dying alongside men in the field — I don't see why they should be held back.'

Joanna Hewitt, a private banker at Barclays Wealth, also experienced this paradox. She felt she had never experienced overt problems simply because she was a woman — but also recognised that at senior manager level there were still very few women. When asked about how this impacted upon her, she said: 'I have to say there is one senior director I have worked with who is a role model — she's evidence that you can aspire towards the top. There is potential but it is a very difficult journey.'

- We can't wait — women are not 'trickling up' at predicted rates.

- A culture of long working hours is inherently anti-female.

- Acting 'bloke-ish' is not credible, sustainable or even desirable in the long run.

HAVING IT ALL

Mary Hensher is a partner at Deloitte, and happily married. She has no children. She says the field of professional services has the potential to be level; men and women can contribute equally because the skills required are intellectual. She remarked: 'I haven't encountered a lot of discrimination, though I don't know what it is like in other fields. There is no glass ceiling here. I think the main problem is not many women are attracted to IT as a profession.'

However, Mary continued: 'If I am completely honest, I think it would be incredibly difficult to do the job I do with children, and I admire any woman who does. It means that I can spend long hours and go away to places without having to deal with a lot of the issues working mothers have — although for me it has been a source of sadness, as it wasn't completely by choice. Can women have it all? I don't think they can. You have to always make compromises.'

In discussion with Mary, I was reminded of a talk I attended where a senior woman at a major international oil company told the audience they would have to choose between three things: children, location and profession — and they couldn't expect all three to be perfect all the time. This particular senior woman was based in Lagos, Nigeria. It was her family's choice that her husband raised their children in the United States.

Your company may not literally dictate that you move to a foreign country. However, to make the most of the opportunities available to you, you may have to make hard choices that mean that you can't have all of your ideal options all at once. Life as a professional woman is about compromises and personal choices and making the most of the decisions you take.

OTHER PEOPLE'S ASSUMPTIONS

While coming to terms with both the professional and personal choices we make can be difficult for most women, factoring in other people's judgements of those choices is unhelpful and unnecessarily divisive. Barrister Fiona Edington sometimes defends people accused of crimes against children as part of her caseload. Hers is not a background shared by most female lawyers. She finds people often make judgements about her feelings in a way they might not if she were a man.

She explained: 'A female police officer told me I probably would not want to look at the images downloaded from the defendant's computer because they were so graphic. I had to remind her that while he may indeed be found to be a paedophile, I still had a job to do that included looking at the evidence, so I could give him candid, honest and sensible advice.'

Not all the women I interviewed experienced gender bias, even when they were expecting it. Dr Harriet Crawford, a retired archaeologist, was caught out by assuming that being a woman would work against her, when seeking permission to host a major dig in Bahrain. She and another senior woman went with a junior male colleague to see the Bahraini ministry responsible.

She remembered: 'Clearly, we knew it was an Arab country that was male-dominated, so we coached our male colleague in exactly what to say the next day to the chief ministers. We walked into this enormous room with what looked like to me dozens of intimidating white-robed men. And the Minister simply said: 'Dr Crawford, we know your expertise well. Tell us how we can help you.' I immediately wracked my brain wondering, *Oh my God, what did we tell Robert to say?*'

Harriet had already worked on a number of digs in Mesopotamia and enjoyed respect from her teams of local workmen, who seemed to respect her for her academic qualifications as well as the fact that she was the *mother of sons* back in the UK.

On one dig, the Director was concerned how his team would respond to being led by a Western woman. She remembered: 'He introduced me to the workmen as *Doctora* and as the mother of sons, both of which were extremely helpful. They called me *Umm James*, which means *mother of James* — the name of my older son — and I never had any problem at all. They couldn't have been nicer, which surprised and delighted me.' While the treatment she received was undoubtedly more positive than she expected, it is disappointing some of the respect was afforded her simply because she had male children – rather than solely for her PhD and her formidable archaeological experience.

TOKENISM

For women in these fields, one thing is certain: they stand out. I spoke to many women who initially joked they had no difficulty in raising their profile; they were often, quite literally, the only woman in the room and therefore very visible. There are many ways in which women found it can be an *advantage* to be a woman in male-dominated fields; namely, that their efforts had the potential to be easily recognised and that they stood out in a crowd of men at conferences and in meetings.

For example, Laura Hinton, a partner at PwC, said: 'I sometimes think it is easier to get noticed as a woman in this field. It's a dual-edged sword: your mistakes get noticed more quickly, but so do your wins. If you are the average white male, you can blend into the background. It offers an element of safety — but it can also make it harder to distinguish yourself.'

While the advantages of being a noticeable woman can occur, the supposed benefits do not seem to be filtering up quickly enough. The rates of women reaching the upper echelons in most corporate settings substantially lags behind anything close to equity. While there are undoubted benefits for some women, tokenism is a very sharp dual-edged sword. It can help you draw attention to your wins but it also can leave you feeling like a token — either that you are there largely because you are the woman needed for the sake of appearances, or as a representative for your entire gender.

When a man in a male-dominated office makes a presentation, colleagues think, *That's obviously what John thinks*. Many women in the same male-dominated teams know when they make a presentation, there is a far greater likelihood colleagues will subconsciously think, *That's obviously what women think*.

Similarly, women who work in male-dominated fields are more likely to feel 'stereotype threat' which is 'the fear of confirming a negative stereotype about one's own group, through one's own behaviour'[6]. This can be particularly salient for those who are from a minority group, and in the case of women who work mostly with men, can seriously hinder a woman's self-belief. The anxiety around 'acting like a woman' can interfere with her performance because so much of her attention is drawn away from the task at hand onto worries about whether or not her performance is being viewed in light of stereotypes about women. Concerns about stereotype threat are real and can account for women who may become overly aggressive, or feel they need to put on a tough demeanour, so they cannot be accused of 'acting like a girl'. In effect, the female professional who is worried about stereotype threat spends so much time worrying about other people's reactions to her behaviours as a woman that she cannot concentrate on making sure those behaviours are the best for the challenge ahead regardless of gender.

Tokenism limits women's potential in the eyes of others. When they are viewed as part of a minority, their identities as women become less salient. Colleagues are more likely to lump them together in an amorphous description of how they suppose women think, feel and communicate, rather than view them as individuals.

The token is used as the standard to which all other women who might join the team are judged, for good or ill. It's a tightrope. It feels high-profile and dangerous all at once, with a crowd watching to see whether you will soar or fall.

---

[6] Steele, M.C. & Aronson, J. (1995) Stereotype threat and the intellectual test performance of African Americans, *Journal of Personality and Social Psychology*, Vol. 69, No. 5 pp. 797-811

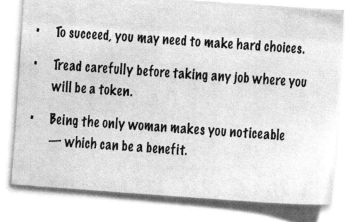

- To succeed, you may need to make hard choices.
- Tread carefully before taking any job where you will be a token.
- Being the only woman makes you noticeable — which can be a benefit.

WOMEN MEAN BUSINESS

Certain skills, such as consensus-building, the shrewd assessment of others and networking, come more easily to women and are advantages in almost any workplace. Women often rise into management positions because they use emotional intelligence strengths as well as technical prowess. A technically-skilled employee who can also read other people and communicate effectively will always be in demand. Conversely, I have seen technical wizards lose jobs simply because they can't work well with other people.

Many women who enter male-dominated fields initially pride themselves on their technical skills. As they progress, they may worry about losing these as they move into management. This is understandable: it was the technical know-how that drew them to the field in the first place. However, most people recognise that managers naturally lose some of this technical knowledge in such fast-paced industries, as they spend more of their time developing strategic skills and have to delegate much of the hands-on work they are used to doing themselves.

Furthermore, the most successful women realise this is not a *net loss* but a demonstration that they are focusing on and growing other skills — namely leadership, management and communication. In fact, as I recommend to many of my clients, if you have a choice between technical development or people management training, you should choose the people management. These skills will prepare you well for future roles in a variety of industries. In today's fast-moving global economy, they are skills that are less likely to be off-shored and are sure to remain in demand over the long term.

Research commissioned by Microsoft Windows Mobile[7] predicts that the twenty-first century will be defined by workers who are able to be 'lateral, collaborative, flexible and creative' or able to use the more feminine side of their brain. They predict a shift towards female-oriented soft skills, such as flexibility and lateral thinking.

Researchers expect the huge rise in mobile technology will see the UK workplace becoming dominated by women and female-orientated working practices, such as the rise of flexible working, which will allow women to compete on a more equal footing with their male colleagues.

- Your 'feminine' skills are invaluable to any business or organisation.

- No longer relying on your technical skills as you move up is a good sign.

- Mobile technology will help even the playing field for women.

WOMEN AS LEADERS

Rather than focus on what women lack, senior management teams would get farther by concentrating on what women offer in terms of leadership style. As Kate Ludeman writes in her research: 'Like their male counterparts, female

[7] The Future Laboratory, Windows Microsoft Mobile, October 2008

alphas are ambitious and drawn to positions of authority, but as a rule they are less likely to dominate. Better attuned to emotional climate, they are more likely ... to collaborate and find win-win solutions to conflicts. They can be just as opinionated and strong- minded, but they'll search for consensus and buy-in ... Alpha women want to lead, but they don't necessarily need to rule.'[8] Women are known more for their 'take-care' behaviours whereas men are recognised for 'take-charge' behaviours – regardless of how often these two styles are employed by a single individual.

Successful women play on their natural strengths around communication skills to help move teams forward. The value of these skills, often born out of the demands of being a good daughter, sister, friend and mother, is particularly salient for working mothers to recognise. They often return from maternity leave or a career break with a loss of confidence. More employers should wake up to the advantages they can bring in terms of project and people management.

Motherhood is an excellent training school for managers; it requires organisation, pacing, the ability to balance conflicting claims, teaching, leading, monitoring, conflict management and constant communication. These are the same skills on which good teams depend.

Research by McKinsey[9] found that companies with at least three women in senior management scored the highest on nine dimensions of organisation; most notably leadership, capability, accountability and motivation. Furthermore, having at least three women on the board increases profitability threefold[10].

Additionally, as previously discussed, those companies also enjoyed better financial performance than those firms with no women in senior management

[8] Ludeman, Kate (2009) Coaching with Women, in Passmore, J. "Diversity in Coaching", Association for Coaching, p. 238
[9] McKinsey and Company (2007) "Women Matter: Gender Diversity, a Corporate Performance Indicator"
[10] "Women Executives in the UK", Gavurin Intelligence, February 2008

positions.[11] Other studies have confirmed '...*Greater female representation in senior-management positions leads to — and is not merely a result of — better firm quality and performance*'[12].

Furthermore, according to research by the Conference Board of Canada[13], having at least one female director is correlated to better corporate governance, more board independence and greater board activity. All are great reasons to strive for a greater representation of women at the uppermost echelons of leadership.

WHAT WOMEN OFFER

Mary Hensher of Deloitte would certainly agree that women should focus on what they can bring to the table, rather than on what they perceive themselves to be lacking. To her mind, the professional services have the potential to be a level playing field.

She concluded: 'In professional services, you are selling people's brains. It's quite a leveller; you don't need brute strength, you're not making cars or widgets. Lawyers, accountants, consultants — we are all selling our brains, and therefore men and women bring equally valuable skills to the table.'

Joanna Hewitt of Barclays Wealth is single and heavily involved in philanthropy. She also felt women have much to bring to the male-dominated field of financial services. Her role involves building a trusted relationship with individuals and families, while managing their investment portfolios. She felt that private banking was well suited to what some consider more 'feminine' qualities.

She explained: 'I don't like to label attributes *male* or *female*, but I do think my approach is more empathetic to the client. I spend a longer time building relationships than some of my colleagues who would go straight to the deal.

---

[11] McKinsey Quarterly (2008), A Business Case for Women, September
[12] Deszo, Christian and Gaddis Ross, David (2007) "Girl Power: Female Representation in top management and firm performance", working paper, December
[13] The Conference Board of Canada (2002) "Women on Boards: Not Just the Right Thing ... But the Bright Thing"

In large family relationships you are dealing not just with the main asset holder, but with the wider family who in time will inherit or need assistance to manage their wealth at some point in the future — yet they have different personalities and priorities. Some will want information almost 24 hours a day; others don't want to hear from you at all. You have to be sensitive to everyone's needs. Not all people like dealing with these types of larger family relationships — but I find it fascinating.'

Joanna felt the attributes needed to be a successful private banker and trusted adviser to high net worth individuals and families, suited women well. In fact, she felt that what she brought to the table as a woman was increasingly important to an evolving client base. Her interest and knowledge around philanthropy and Family Law serve her well. Sensitivity, empathy and intuition are vital, particularly during difficult times such as divorce or after a death, when she works most closely with her clients.

She suggested: 'I think the role of private banker is a natural fit for women. You have to have an understanding about the intricacies of family relationships, as well as an interest in philanthropy and Family Law. Death and divorce are facts of life, and they are often the first time some women have held wealth of their own.'

Joanna continued: 'You must have investment and taxation skills, obviously, but the best way to work through any of the above is to have strong communication skills. These naturally play towards a woman's strengths.'

An increasingly important reason why more women are needed in banking is that the very demographics of money are changing as well. Historically, private bankers in the UK dealt primarily with aristocratic families of inherited wealth — but this is changing. She said: 'We have always had female clients, but they have tended to be the wife of a wealthy man. Now we have more female entrepreneurs and women who have been awarded large divorce settlements. Some clients will want a male private banker and some will want a female private banker. Having diversity within private banking means we can offer both.'

The increasingly diverse group of individuals with money to invest means that the old public school ties, that used to be a main breeding ground for private bankers and their male clients, are becoming irrelevant. Women are earning far more money than ever before, through private incomes and business ownership. In fact, by 2025, women are expected to own 60 per cent of all private wealth in the UK. Currently there are more female than male millionaires between the ages of 18 and 44 — and then again among those over 65 years old[14].

Women should be considered for the qualities they can bring to leadership positions, rather than be made to feel they must adjust to a male model of leadership. While it undoubtedly helps to 'speak the language' of the men, women would get further if they were truly comfortable with the attributes they brought to the table. Good leadership is gender-neutral.

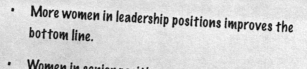

- More women in leadership positions improves the bottom line.
- Women in senior positions can better understand and service clients' demands.
- Good leadership is gender-neutral.

THE PROACTIVE CAREER

Sometimes we feel victimised by employers whom we blame for our poor treatment. Often, however, a good portion of the fault lies within ourselves. We become frustrated with our lack of career progression by concentrating on slights — whether real or imagined. Rather than wallow in the negative

[14] Carter, S. (2006) Speech at Women's Financial Advisor Group Awards, London, January

feelings of being passed over for a high-profile project or denied promotion, we need to ask ourselves how we can proactively change the situation, or at least avoid it happening again.

For example, one area around which you might feel resentful is *pay*. This is one of the clearest indicators about how we are valued in a team, and a great source of potential resentment. As we rise through the ranks, it is also one of the areas with the greatest gender disparity.

In one of my first jobs after gaining my undergraduate degree, I took a job that was so poorly-paid I had to live on my meagre savings. It was barely minimum-wage for a research job within a major university, and I resented my boss because of it. She thought my work was good and subsequently gave me a great reference — but she also knew I was *cheap labour*, a fact she informally passed on with her recommendation.

I blamed her for not paying me better but the truth of the matter is that I accepted a lot less than I was worth. I never negotiated, never made a counter-offer, never spoke up to tell her about additional aspects of the research project that I could take on. I gratefully accepted the first number she mentioned, and patiently waited for her to see how productive I was in the role and raise my salary accordingly out of her own sense of goodwill.

I became very resentful at the time, but a hard lesson was realising the fault lay with *me*. Often you will resent those around you for perceived slights, when really it is up to you to demand more respect, and more recognition of your worth.

Imagine — if we each took control of our own profile, there would be less resentment all around, replaced instead by the heady feeling of being in the driving seat of your career rather than simply waiting to get noticed.

Jackie Gittins, of PwC, similarly went through this change of perspective in her thirties. She explained: 'I looked around and realised things were happening around me, and that it was up to me to do a bit more to secure the future I wanted. So, instead of wondering why no one had asked for my opinion or thought to offer me a role within an interesting project, I had to ask myself if I had told people what I had accomplished or how I could add value.'

This feeling came to a head when Jackie was asked to apply for a promotion to a new high-profile role. 'I was surprised they asked me and I originally turned them down. It took them a week to persuade me. In many companies there is no culture of praise, so the first time I knew I was doing a good job was when I was offered this role — but my self-confidence hadn't caught up,' she remembers. Her decision to take the role had more far-reaching implications.

She declared: 'I also had to realise that I was becoming a role model to others in my team, and turning down the job would impact they way they looked at their own possibilities. People would say it was also important for them to see me moving on as it meant they could progress too. I'm lucky they persuaded me. In retrospect, it seems likely they could have just taken my *no* at face value and offered it to someone else.'

- Look for clues in your 'poor treatment' for how you can bring about beneficial change.

- This is a time to ensure your achievements are being recognised.

- Your success can help bring other people along too. You're not being selfish.

SELF-DOUBT

While I was writing this book, I had lunch with a girlfriend, whom I'll call Jocelyn, who relayed a story I thought summed up perfectly the way many women look at themselves, and why it is so important that we take credit for our own achievements.

Jocelyn spent a weekend clearing out old paperwork and looking through the various files she had accumulated during a long career. She came across an academic paper written in her specialist area within education, and read it with real respect for and growing envy of the author who had written such an accomplished piece. She wished she could write as well, and was in awe of the researcher who had penned it. When she got to the end, she found the date scrawled at the bottom in her own hand and realised that she had indeed written it herself many years before!

It was such a paradigm shift — because once she realised she had written it, she immediately questioned its quality and even *discounted* it. The irony, of course, is that it had been a brilliant paper when written by some anonymous competitor … but when it was her own work, it was nothing special.

We do this to ourselves all the time. I occasionally look at my old PhD thesis, which was a quantitative survey of more than 800 people. I look at all the Analysis of Variance (ANOVA), Regression Analysis and other tests of statistical significance contained in 80,000 words and think: *I wrote that?* I literally wouldn't believe it if I did not have my name on it, or have the memories of the hours I toiled on the thesis. As funny as my friend's story is, it is also sad if we don't take time to recognise our achievements and continue to discount all that we have achieved before.

The truth is that we all fall prone to self-doubt. The trick is not to let it silence the part of you that wants to get ahead in your career, which means you must overcome self-doubt to make others aware of your work.

When I am in a session with a client, and we are addressing the way they hold themselves back from success, we often meet a 'gremlin' — that little voice who whispers self-doubt into your ears as you work, trying to keep you in your place. It is tough enough eradicating one gremlin; most us have dozens. Mine have said: *You'll never finish that project. They made a mistake in hiring you. I can't believe I just said that. You'll never be that senior. Everybody thinks that's a dumb question.* What do yours say?

Sometimes I work with people whose gremlins are made up of the voices of other people ... teachers, parents, employers, friends ... all of whom keep whispering variations on: *Who does she think she is?* These inner voices even come from actual comments we hear from others, that we have unhelpfully stored at the back of our minds.

When I was a teenager living in the outback of Australia, one of the worst things you could say about a girl was that she 'loves herself' — implying that she was a snob. Girls would immediately defend themselves with the vehement denial: 'No, I don't!' and begin to point out their own faults in an effort to fit in and make those around them feel better. When I look back at that, I don't know whether to laugh at the ridiculousness of it all, or cry that so many girls got the message that *loving oneself* was one of the worst sins you could commit as a woman!

Think of the self-doubt those kinds of comments can create. It's no wonder women are often reluctant to draw attention to their successes and show that they *do love themselves*, and that others should too! However, if those voices of self-doubt are not addressed, they can lead to a more dispiriting feeling of Impostor Syndrome.

IMPOSTOR SYNDROME

In an era of few guarantees, I have one for you. All of the successful women you have admired, and certainly all the women I interviewed for this book, had experienced self-doubt at some point in their careers. In fact, most have a sense of *impostor syndrome* in their low moments on an ongoing basis.

This term first came into use in the 1970s when two American psychologists noted that many of their high-achieving female clients couldn't take credit for their own achievements. In spite of consistent evidence to the contrary, they would credit their successes to luck, serendipity, good contacts, timing, perseverance and even the ability to *fake confidence*[15].

---

[15] Ket de Vries, M.F.R. (2005) "The Dangers of Feeling Like a Fake", Harvard Business Review, September

Impostor syndrome occurs for many women, no matter how educated or well-qualified, and is particularly prevalent for many of my clients who work in male-dominated fields. I notice it with clients for whom confidence is the first and most important issue we will address. They admit they may have achieved the degree, got the job, worked their way up the career ladder — yet still they fear that at any moment they will be found out for not really knowing what they are doing.

This feeling can be compounded for women who primarily work with men: their mere presence is an oddity, and so surely their success is also considered unusual and even perhaps suspect in the eyes of male colleagues. When women in these fields are successful, they are often not the only ones to question their achievements.

In addition to their own feelings of self-doubt, many of their competitive male colleagues will likewise assume that chance, or perhaps affirmative action, played a role in their success. This attitude may not be made explicit — but the minimisation of a successful woman's achievements can pervade the atmosphere. This ultimately undermines her confidence and increases the cyclical pattern of self-doubt, whereby she feels she is not good enough as she is, and that she could only do better if she knew more, worked harder, had more hours in the day.

Perfection is always just out of reach. Does this sound like anyone you know?

At a workshop I ran on risk-taking and overcoming indecision, one of the delegates, a woman with a PhD in a scientific field, admitted quietly to the larger group that she often felt like a fraud at times. I asked the group who else felt that way at times and every single hand was raised — much to her relief when she cried out: 'I thought I was the only one!'

If you think success can come to you only once you are perfectly sure of yourself, you will be waiting forever. Successful women have moments, even hours of self-doubt … but they still know they can make the most of any situation. They have the self-belief to overcome the doubt and any mistakes they make along the way.

Successful women were once described beautifully to me as being 'like ducks ... all calm and unruffled on the surface but paddling like hell underneath it all'. You may be paddling, but are you getting anywhere?

If you are a woman who wants to take your career to the next level, and feel that raising your game as a woman in a man's world is both exciting and daunting, then read on because this is the book for you.

It is time to stop waiting to get noticed, and to take control of where your career is going by showing people that you do indeed *love yourself* and that they would be smart to do the same.

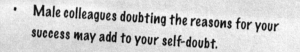

- Male colleagues doubting the reasons for your success may add to your self-doubt.

- Feeling perfection is always just out of reach is normal, but also an enemy of progress.

- Overcoming these feelings is what sets successful women apart.

THREE

PROFILE RAISING

One of the penalties for refusing to participate in politics

is that you end up being governed by your inferiors.

— Plato

There comes a time, for many women, when they realise there is more to getting ahead than simply keeping their heads down and delivering a quality product. After a certain stage, getting the work done is taken for granted and you will increasingly be judged for the larger impact you are having through your relationships, your profile and your image.

For me, that moment came when I started my own company. No matter how many qualifications I had, no matter how many letters I had after my name or how much I helped my clients, I recognised that my business would not survive if people hadn't heard of me. Trust me; if you want to take your career to the next level, *there is no point in being a well-kept secret.*

It is fascinating how many of the senior women I interviewed could also recollect a single incident that made them realise they needed to raise their game. This epiphany came in many guises — preparation for a promotion, a close call with redundancy, a move into a new team, the desire to secure larger clients or to be considered for a board appointment. What united these women was the conscious understanding that they needed to be better known in order to secure a better deal for themselves.

TIMING IS EVERYTHING

Many of the women I interviewed realised they had to play up their strengths, and start to make the most of profile-raising opportunities they would have previously ignored or not even noticed. For some it was a matter of timing. For example, returning from maternity leave was a key time to raise profile, for women who wanted to keep their career on track.

Unfortunately, there can be a tendency for colleagues to consider women on a maternity break 'out of sight, out of mind'; these women need to make a special effort to remind people of their presence and their value in the weeks, months and even years after they have returned.

Many women saw a positive performance review as the best time to start to raise their profile, as they were playing from a recently-elevated position. Matilda Venter, a director of Human Resources at PwC, is someone who can remember her own decisive moment.

'In 2006, I was at the point where I decided I wanted a promotion to Director. I watched those already in that role, what they were doing and how they behaved. I realised I needed to mirror some of those behaviours in order to be considered for the next step,' she remembered.

She quickly recognised that consistent delivery would no longer suffice as evidence that she was ready for a promotion. That was a hard realisation and a larger challenge than she had undertaken before. She explained: 'I had always been focused on delivering my responsibilities, but now I had to find time to lift my head up and look around, which was not easy. I started off by getting to know the departments I directly delivered to — not just talking to them about the details of the project I was involved in, but also asking how better I could help them serve the client. I asked them about the main challenges in their industry. I had to broaden the conversations I was having, which was new.'

Paradoxically, another good time to try and raise one's profile is on the tail end of a *poor* performance, as you need to demonstrate why you are still of value to the organisation. It may seem calculating — but making sure colleagues and clients are aware of the role you play in day-to-day projects helps ensure you will be noticed if you are ever made redundant. It's harder to hide the firing of someone if they are a well-liked figure in the office. There is no single right or wrong time to raise your profile; it is simply whenever you are ready to move your career to the next level.

Rebecca George, a partner at Deloitte, specialises in public sector work but also has corporate experience. While at her previous employer, IBM, she realised that due to a series of internal roles she had a low external profile. So, she set herself a challenge to raise her profile *outside* her organisation, partly to generate opportunities to diversify her career, and partly to be better valued *within* IBM.

Once she had set this objective, she deliberately began to say *yes* to opportunities as they arose. 'I had some lucky breaks, including being asked to join an advisory board for a local authority,' she remembers. 'I said yes, though I really didn't know much at the time about local government, and it was a fantastic experience. I did that work alongside, and in addition to, my day job — and it is important to recognise that you have to put extra effort in, over and above the requirements of your everyday job, to build your profile.

'That role, and others to do with sustainable communities and raising the profile of women in IT, resulted in the great honour of my OBE. The combination of my improved external profile, with much greater experience in the public sector, eventually led me to my current role at Deloitte.'

She adds: 'The final five years I had at IBM were the best and most successful of my time there.' She admits that it is ironic because those years followed a period of adversity, when she realised she would have few options if she wanted to leave. The reputation that she built through her *external* activities, the speaking and writing, increased her value and credibility *internally*. She pointed out: 'The interesting thing was that the higher my profile became outside IBM, the higher it got inside IBM and the more they valued me.'

In many cases, women are more likely to be better-prepared for challenges simply because they do indeed second-guess themselves and hence exercise more considered decisions. Women, by nature, are more likely to act cautiously — which arguably might seem a prudent move in light of recent market events based on short-sighted decisions, as we discussed earlier. However, when women are given the freedom to grow at their own pace, they will often turn into star performers.

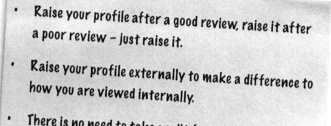

- Raise your profile after a good review, raise it after a poor review – just raise it.

- Raise your profile externally to make a difference to how you are viewed internally.

- There is no need to take credit for others' work — just make sure no one steals your thunder!

DO YOUR HOMEWORK

Understanding the public face of the organisation in which you work is often a first step in creating a strong foundation on which to build.

Mary Hensher, Head of IT at Deloitte, could have spent her career in the IT server room. However, she recognised that to advance and get the job done more effectively, she needed to become aware of all parts of the firm. 'You have to have your eyes wide open in a political sense and understand the sea you are swimming in. If you want to raise your profile, there is no excuse for not knowing what is going on,' she suggests.

For Mary, keeping on top of legislation changes that might affect the firm was a given. She felt many aspiring employees often lacked an understanding of the public face of their own company. She said. 'Organisations have a public face. I am amazed at how many people don't know what their company says on their Internet site. What exactly are you selling? What's the size of the organisation? What are your current challenges? What kind of revenue are you turning over? You really ought to know all of that.

'Moreover, are you in the right organisation and do you like your profession? You have to know pretty early on if this is the industry for you, because if it isn't, as you progress, it will show. Don't waste your time going for things you don't really want in the first place.' This is sound advice, as a lack of passion will become more noticeable as you progress, and will increasingly make colleagues resentful.

Do your homework. Google the name of your company and even some of the key players within. Don't just look at the company website; find out what customers, competitors, the Press and even bloggers are saying about your company and its services. Many companies now even have their own Facebook pages or blogs, where you can get under the skin of what image the company wants to portray. Look at the comments people post to see how well that message is being received by the wider world.

Mary agreed that working on 'advancing your career' can sound a bit calculating, and that when you start out it is best to start from a firm foundation before you look for the next promotion. She suggested: 'I think success is about doing something right. That may sound obvious, but do something that you can hang your reputation on. Make sure you are doing your job to the best of your ability, as that is your platform and the way you will initially get recognised. After you have made a name for yourself on delivering quality in that area, you can start to pick and choose more carefully your next responsibilities.'

Amy Cox, Head of Human Resources at the Internet investment firm ITG, agreed. She explained: 'I am happy to help people grow into their next role, but often people come to me looking for their next big challenge for a promotion before they have mastered what they were hired to do in the first place.' You must make sure you are delivering on the day job before you request more 'interesting' projects and greater responsibilities.

- Know your company's public profile: the good, the bad and the ugly.

- Either have real passion for your industry or be prepared to leave.

- Once you're known for delivering quality in one area, then you can choose your next one.

BUILDING RELATIONSHIPS IS PART OF THE DAY JOB

In my work with executive women, many clients are often better than their male colleagues on actual project delivery — but initially fail to realise that relationship-building is also a key aspect to their roles. If people are not made aware of how well you are handling these aspects, you will be regarded as less productive.

Hearing *both* the positive and negative feedback is often a challenge for women who want to advance their career towards the next promotion. Women often hear only the negative, which can seriously undermine your confidence — even when you are ready for the next step up.

Rebecca George, for example, has a history in managing teams. She recounted how differently men and women who had worked for her responded to feedback. She reflected: 'During a performance appraisal, you can take pains to deliver 90 per cent positive feedback to a woman, and then lightly mention she needs to work on her presentation skills. She will then go home despondent and obsess about her presentation skills, wondering which presentation you meant, where she went wrong and generally working herself up.'

She laughed: 'A man receiving the same feedback will barely remember that you even mentioned presentation skills.'

Angela Mohtashemi is a former teacher and currently a director at PwC. She is aware that performance reviews are an area where men are disproportionately given more promotions. She reflected: 'I suggested that we set aside the numbers and examine the reasons why people felt the men deserved promotion more than the women. Ask *what kinds of opportunities are they getting, what types of roles are they playing?*

'I've found that when men and women engage in the same job, they often approach it differently. Often I see men being introduced to clients earlier, being included in the network and generally being more client-facing. The women in the same role, however, tend to get involved with project management. They co-ordinate the housekeeping and write the proposals — often sitting in the office doing written work late into the night!'

Angela continued: 'Then it comes time for promotion and the inevitable question is asked: *Who got the work in and who really manages the relationship?* And it is hard to argue because it is the men! But the suggestion we even look at how the roles are divided as part of the promotion agenda meets extreme resistance — and so it doesn't get addressed.' Angela makes a great point. Focus not only on delivery but spend some of your time in relationship-building with clients and key stakeholders.

- Hear and remember the positive feedback you receive.

- If people are unaware of your achievements, they will think you are less productive.

- Consider managing relationships to be the biggest part of your job.

At Least Ten Per Cent

Rebecca George at Deloitte is an active supporter of women's networks. When she speaks, she always has a key message for her audiences of women: *Keeping your head down and doing a good job won't get you noticed on its own.*

She concluded: 'Women in these fields need to realise that men spend at least ten per cent of their time promoting their work. This doesn't necessarily sound like a great deal, but it is half a day a week — much more than most women are putting into it. They don't want to brown-nose.'

She further explained why this is so important: 'If you work in these fields, you have to understand that this is the modus operandi — and that if it is the norm for the men you are competing against, you need to get comfortable with it. The men will not credit you with diligently working at your desk, but rather interpret your reticence to self-promote as a sign you're not ambitious.'

Rebecca's previous career at IBM took off when she consciously began to take on external commitments, such as speaking and attending conferences that would raise her profile. She recalled: 'In the years before, I had been concentrating on doing my job 110 per cent — but when I realised I wanted to keep my options open, I began to think of investing in myself as well. So, whereas I would have spent 60 hours a week working solely on IBM projects, I reduced that down to 45 hours a week and spent the other 15 working on things more closely aligned to my personal agenda and *my* future.'

When talking with Rebecca, I was reminded of a coaching session I led with a group of women preparing for maternity leave, who all worked in a multinational bank. One woman lamented that she had no time to develop her relationships — she had no one she liked in her team and barely enough time to do her own job well.

One of the other participants, another pregnant woman, who was in the same position, but who looked the very picture of serenity, simply said to her: 'Then it sounds like you need to be building those relationships all the more.'

Like it or not, self-promotion is the name of the game if you are going to work in a male-dominated field. It is simply the way things are done; any unwillingness to do so will be falsely interpreted as a lack of commitment, passion for your work and overall ambition.

PROMOTING YOUR TEAM

Sometimes women in leadership positions are reluctant to push themselves forward because they perceive any wins as a 'team effort'. In their minds, any work towards individual recognition for the team leaders would denigrate and detract from the other members.

However, many of the most successful women I interviewed had come to realise that in promoting their own interests, they were also promoting the team.

Again, Angela Mohtashemi explained how she overcame this self-imposed hurdle, to rethink what promotion could mean for her. She said: 'I worked with a coach who made me realise that asking for promotion to Director did not detract from my team in any way — that it could benefit us all.

'My colleagues supported me, explaining that it would lead to better projects and more prestigious clients for all of us, if I was to put myself forward. Plus, I realised, as I progress it leaves space for my current team members to take on more responsibility and grow into more senior roles themselves. But first, I had to realise I wasn't helping any of us by holding myself back.'

Good leaders know that hardly anything gets achieved by one individual alone. Most people can see through the person who claims credit for a single large project. The fact that there are so many individual people out there, claiming credit for team efforts, should make it easier for women to claim credit for *their* part of a successful collaboration. If you give due credit to the contributors, it is easier to draw attention to your own part, whilst maintaining your integrity and credibility with those who can see through empty bragging.

Additionally, women are often hesitant to take a role where they are managing people who had previously been their peers. In fact, in my own coaching practice, women will often say they would prefer to move companies to take a promotion, rather than stay with their current company and manage their friends and former peers. They just don't want to be in charge of people they have known as equals. However, this approach is short-sighted and can potentially slow down a career. It can be faster to be promoted internally, because most professionals have greater traction within their own organisation, than having to start building a reputation elsewhere.

Jackie Gittins, a director at PwC, was put in this position by being offered a more senior role within her team. She remembered: 'I was initially shocked and I focused on the negatives, thinking about being the boss to my peers. It just felt risky, and like I would be exposed. The irony is that many of them encouraged me as it was proof you could progress your career within the team. I had to overcome my own insecurity and start to ask myself why I didn't deserve that position.'

- Spend at least half a day a week promoting your work; it's expected.

- Promoting your part of a project will also benefit your team members.

- Seek job advancement within your company before looking outside.

HANG OUT THE FLAGS

As we have discussed, if you work in a man's world, an unwillingness to draw attention to your achievements is simply not an option; it will be misinterpreted as a lack of ambition. If you are surrounded by men, you will have to play the self-promotion game like the men.

Laura Hinton, Head of the Human Resources Transformation Group at PwC, has climbed the corporate ladder all the way to Partner — but advertising her successes has never felt easy. She remarked: 'People say that women are worse at drawing attention to their good points, and that's probably true. I don't love it but I have to force myself to do it. Early on, my team won a project worth several hundred thousand pounds; I forced myself to write an email to a senior partner who I knew would be key in deciding who the next batch of partners would be.'

She visibly cringed as she recalled: 'It took me an hour to write the perfect two-line email saying that we had won a new client, and my finger just hovered over the send button for ages!' But is she regretful? 'He responded immediately, congratulating me on such a big contract after just six months in the firm, and he copied-in other key players — people who wouldn't have had any idea who I was before — but then *they* also sent me congratulations notes. It couldn't have worked out better.'

Laura was made Partner in that next round. The key was that while it wasn't easy, she got over her reticence enough to publicise her achievement to the right people.

Other women had their profile raised more publicly by winning awards for their work. Caroline, a logistics company IT Director, was a finalist in the prestigious Blackberry Women in Technology awards. It helped raise her profile in the technology media as well as her own confidence. 'I didn't win, but I was runner-up to a woman who is absolutely amazing, and that was such an honour to be considered even in the same group,' she said.

Similarly, whilst I was writing this book, Professor Athene Donald, one of the women I had interviewed, won the distinguished L'Oréal-UNESCO Prize for Women in Science. It reflected her ground-breaking work in soft matter, including approaches that could be used to help understand Alzheimer's disease as well as relating to prosthetic devices. This honour had only once before gone to a British woman.

The point of raising your profile is not to get noticed by all and sundry and feel completely out of your depth. Rather, what is important is to raise it in a way that feels like a stretch but is authentic to you. If you are deathly afraid of public speaking, try leading a small group presentation first. Ask for presentational training or invest in it yourself. If you would like to be published, start by offering to write an article for your internal employee newsletter and work your way up to contributing to industry news pieces. The key is to start where you feel comfortable and then consistently stretch yourself.

Jackie Gittins, also at PwC, stressed the importance of self-promotion in a way that is both authentic as well as comfortable for you — whilst still challenging your comfort zone. She suggested: 'For some people it might be a mass email announcing a win. I get asked to speak at a lot of conferences, which helps spread the word. I know my strengths and weaknesses; I am terrible at writing, but a good speaker, so that is where I concentrate my efforts.'

She elaborated: 'When your name is mentioned in a magazine or your name is on the speaking circuit, people aren't incredulous and looking to find fault with you. It simply reinforces the idea that you are someone who knows what you are talking about.'

When asked where a woman who is completely frozen by the idea of self-promotion should start out, Jackie suggested: 'You could update people in a team meeting, by explaining the win, what it took to achieve and what it means for both your department and the organisation as a whole.' The point is, you have to start somewhere and the options are endless.

Jackie initially found it difficult to accept that she would have to raise her profile to be noticed for her work. She remembered: 'I'm 45, but it wasn't until I was in my thirties that I noticed how much male colleagues were drawing attention to their work, the same type of work I was doing. I was put off initially, but came to realise that I had to learn to tell my story in a way that was authentic to me.' She laughed: 'I also suspect being British does not help either!'

It is interesting how the natural British reserve hinders our desire to tell people about the successes we have had. (And I say this as someone who has lived in the UK for 12 years!) The British have a natural aptitude for 'cutting the tall poppies down', which is not helpful for self-confidence and disastrous in today's workplace. It's a wonder anyone actually wants to be a tall poppy!

However, promotion and the assignment of interesting jobs only come to those who tell others about what they have achieved, rather than keeping the success to themselves. Jackie declared: 'I had to learn it from a girlfriend in New York, who was much better at drawing attention to her work.' She suggested how she had made it work for her: 'I agreed with a colleague that if either of us wins a big piece of work, the other helps brainstorm how we are going to promote it — and makes sure we do!'

There are many ways to raise your profile, in stages that keep stretching you. Speak at events: first at a team meeting, then to another department, then as an external panellist eventually offering to be a keynote speaker. Write for a company newsletter — or at least keep them apprised of your accomplishments. Copy congratulatory emails to your key stakeholders. Look for competitions or awards ceremonies in your field; enter them and also note the winners – people you can learn from who are the key players in your industry. They make great mentors!

- Set time aside to actively work on your profile: it will pay dividends.

- Raise your profile a bit at a time. You need never feel too out of your depth.

- Keep stretching your comfort zone as you go.

PUBLISH OR PERISH

> *The talk talks and the walk talks,*
>
> *but the walk talks louder than the talk.*
>
> — Fred Roach

For many women, it is the power of the written word that made the most difference to their career. Retired archaeologist Harriet Crawford took a career break to raise three children. According to her she kept her 'brain ticking over' and maintained a consistent profile by continuing to write whilst away from academic life. She took opportunities to write on related topics and present her papers at conferences when invited. Her first foray back into the world of work was in 1968, when she returned to London and took the opportunity to speak at a conference to which a former colleague had invited her.

She said: 'As an academic, it's important to publish in respected journals, rather than just your local newspaper — it demonstrates you are serious. I gave a few evening lectures for the Workers' Educational Association, which was useful in that it gave me more teaching experience. If you are considering returning to work after a break, do anything you can: talk to the Women's Institute, teach evening courses that are looking for lecturers, anything like that. It all adds to your experience and makes your CV look more convincing.'

After Harriet returned to her academic career, she could then become more selective about the types of publication in which she wrote. She remarked: 'The turnaround for an article is much quicker and you need to have them on your academic CV. It's no good saying, *I am writing a book and hope it will be finished in five years' time.*' She smiled: 'You need to be able to say, *Look, I have already published all these articles — aren't I clever?*'

Harriet explained why this was particularly important for those who have completed PhDs who want to stay in academia. She said: 'A lot of people in academia already have a PhD under their belt, but there are very few theses that are publishable as they are. I usually advise people to get a number of articles out of your PhD first and then perhaps eventually revamp the whole thing as a book, which is exactly what I did.'

Even if you are not quite ready to publish entire books, having your latest accomplishments and your name viewed in the published world will help establish your credibility. Ana Pacheco, also of PwC, saw the value of entering awards competitions and writing up case studies for internal newsletters, through watching the actions of some of her male colleagues.

She remembered: 'I used to keep my head down winning work for our team. But recently I noticed when male colleagues made large wins, they made sure they were mentioned in the internal newsletter at the very least. I am involved in winning equally big contracts, but no one except my team used to know about them. I learned not to make that mistake again.'

Sue Blake, personal publicist and media relations expert, says: 'If you consider yourself as someone who can write well, then trade press exposure would be a good starting point. Seek to engage the support of a senior member of your press office as they will have close links with the key writers on each trade press title and can make the approaches on your behalf. The internal press office will want any news related to new wins, new appointments within the company and any survey findings.'

If you play your cards right, you can raise your own profile as well as that of the company. Sue explains: 'If you have a niche role and could be considered an expert in what you do within your industry, you could write columns or articles for your trade press that capture what people are talking about, key trends or controversies - the zeitgeist in your field.

'Any articles you pen should then appear with a by-line giving you and your job title and your place of work a credit. If you do this well and often enough, it will eventually draw the attention of other media outlets such as the radio and even possibly television.'

Many women start raising their profile through the written word and find it leads to other opportunities. Sue says: 'With the support of your press office you could seek speaking engagements at your industry's conferences and perhaps run seminars or host plenary sessions. With each speaking opportunity comes further mileage for promoting yourself via the Media.'

If this all still feels a bit too much, start small: most companies have an internal newsletter and annual report in which they feature individual people and the progress they have made since starting with the firm — or, if they are new, why they were hired and what they hope to bring to the team.

The key thing is to just start somewhere, and make it a habit to stretch yourself.

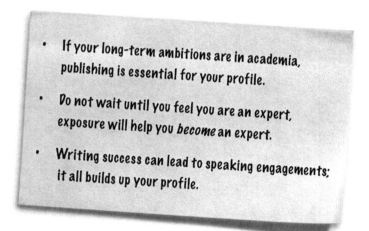

- If your long-term ambitions are in academia, publishing is essential for your profile.

- Do not wait until you feel you are an expert, exposure will help you become an expert.

- Writing success can lead to speaking engagements; it all builds up your profile.

FLUENCY IN FIGURES

In organisations, money talks. Knowing how to show the amounts you save or generate for your organisation is a fantastic way towards raising your profile. Initially, some of the women didn't always see the political value of presenting these figures in the best light, and sometimes had to learn through trial and error.

Angela Mohtashemi, of PwC, learned that presenting her budget figures in the right way determined how much spend she was given on an ongoing basis. It also established her credibility. She learned through developing a strong and much-needed relationship with the Finance Manager.

She reflected: 'The first year I was here, I didn't understand how focused they would be on the numbers and I didn't take it seriously enough. I thought if we performed well, the numbers would take care of themselves. My team consistently achieved, but the numbers were not representative of all we had accomplished. The Finance Manager began to explain to me some of the basics — like why it was better to have a larger number appear in a certain box than in another box, for example — and how important it was for your department to bill small pieces of internal work as well.'

She continued: 'Or even making simple changes as to which day you billed a client, so that the credit showed for one month and not the next. Small changes made our numbers — the same output we already had — suddenly appear much stronger. What I didn't realise was that many of my peers were getting that type of support; I just hadn't known to ask for it.'

The informal training also worked well for the Finance team, as they had received criticism that they didn't communicate their services well enough internally. This gave them valuable practice and helped make others aware of what they could do for specific departments.

Similarly, Mary Hensher at Deloitte found the need to move out of always being in the IT department, an area in which she could have become marginalised because of its distinction from the main fee-earning areas of the global firm. She knew she needed to spread her wings and build relationships in other areas. Similarly to Angela, she got the wider-ranging contacts she needed initially by presenting budgets — one of the most important things she could learn to do in an accountancy firm.

She said: 'If you spend all your time in the IT data centre, you are not going to get to talk to the people who are your customers. You have to put a real effort into being recognisable. I don't walk around with a screwdriver or a spanner because there are others who can do that, others who are fundamental to the organisation — but you shouldn't have the Head of IT doing that.'

Learning to present your best numbers is especially important for women who are not in direct profit and loss roles. Most board memberships are given to executives with direct profit and loss experience in operational roles. This is problematic for many women who may want to progress to board level positions but work in marketing, HR or even finance which are less likely to have many directors visible and reporting to the board.

Many women do not know that this type of experience is a virtually unspoken prerequisite to board membership. Some women may unwittingly hinder their careers by eschewing these types of responsibilities or not directly requesting this type of experience early on in their careers.

BEING A BROAD ABROAD

For some of the women I interviewed, foreign travel and overseas job postings provided some of the best chances for profile raising. These opportunities can be very exciting for ambitious women and are highly correlated to career growth. It shows a commitment to your employer as well as the ability to be highly adaptable in changing situations.

Getting these experiences in early, before having a partner or children, is a challenge many women take advantage of, as it helps allow them to 'tick the boxes' when being considered for advancement later. They know it is much harder to move a family later in your career when you have other commitments. If foreign experience is something many of your senior colleagues have, it is definitely something to consider. It is better to take on those challenges earlier, so that a lack of overseas experience cannot be held against you later on.

To this end Zoë Ingle, of Positive Energy, the network for women in oil and gas, also recommended learning a foreign language, depending on where your industry is growing and developing.

She recalled: 'I remember sitting in a meeting with four women who had very different career paths within the energy industry, and it arose that all four of them had learned Russian, a part of the world where now we spend a great deal of time negotiating. It was not their mother tongue, but they all recognised that learning the language had been one of the most important decisions they had ever taken.'

She smiled about another woman she had met within the network who said to her: 'You can't describe the authority you feel when you sit down to a meeting with all Middle Eastern men to negotiate and you can speak Arabic — they know instantly you mean business.'

This issue might seem a particular concern for women in certain industries only. However, it is worth bearing in mind in *any* field where you can see that progression is correlated to or even enhanced by at least one overseas assignment. This means it can be relevant for women in consultancy, investment banking, accountancy, and science and engineering as well. Working abroad demonstrates adaptability, tolerance and in many cases an ability to think laterally that is prized by employers, even if you don't learn another language.

For example, I will never know how much of my career has been helped by the fact that I have lived and worked in four different countries — but I suspect it has certainly made me more interesting to potential employers and clients, as well as giving me a wider range of perspectives. Plus, being an Australian-born American living in England is one way I am easily remembered — a plus for any woman looking to raise her profile.

- Learn how to present your reporting to best effect — truthfully but powerfully.

- Board memberships tend to go to people with direct profit and loss experience.

- Working abroad shows personal qualities that employers value highly.

WORKING OVERSEAS AND ROMANTIC RELATIONSHIPS

Indeed many women, including myself, meet their partners whilst on overseas roles. Expatriate communities can be tightly knit and even if you want to meet only locals, your rarity as a woman working abroad will make you noticeable to others. Plus there is the attractive confidence that comes from handling an overseas placement well, and your willingness to try new experiences can be a fascinating and seemingly glamorous blend to many would-be suitors!

Working overseas also hones your negotiation and communication skills as you will be working with people who have different priorities, assumptions and experiences from yours — all of which can add to the fun but also makes you a stronger woman, overall.

However, whilst overseas placements can be a shortcut to opportunities you would not have on home ground, they are not without their share of problems or compromises.

For example, overseas placements for both husband and wife are difficult to obtain. However, they are increasingly important if women are to keep advancing their careers in many industries. Dame Veronica Sutherland, a former ambassador, is a groundbreaker in this area. She ensured her first overseas placement as a Head of Mission had been arranged so that her husband could also work for the Foreign Office.

She explained: 'My husband and I very much wanted to do a joint posting abroad. We decided that he would apply for a position in the African Development Bank, and if he was successful I would submit my name for the relevant ambassadorship. It was an unusual career move for me, but it kept us together.

'It also caught the attention of senior people who were avid campaigners for equality in the workplace. They were extremely keen that the posting go ahead, as it showed it was possible for married women to reach senior positions. I wasn't looking for it to be so widely commented on, but it did heighten my profile — as, once you become an ambassador, even in a small

West African country, it is assumed you will go on to more prestigious postings. It helped prove that married women could handle such high-profile roles.'

Other women planned on going abroad as a means of developing their careers but chose other options instead. Mary Hensher came to the world of IT from an undergraduate degree in modern languages from the University of Cambridge. She went into the work world with the full intention of using her languages and going into the Diplomatic Service. However, before graduation, a supplementary numeracy course helped steer her future in another direction.

'In the early 80s, Arts graduates particularly were criticised for not having enough numeracy skills — a problem that has continued, I regret. I did a numeracy course that included a bit of computing — I had never touched a computer before that — but quickly realised it could be an interesting area,' she recalled.

Mary's plans for a life as a diplomat were quickly scuppered when she realised that: '...in 1983, if you were a graduate and worked for the Diplomatic Service, you would be sent to an Embassy for two thirds of your working life. I had no problem with that, but it would make life difficult for any husband who wanted to work outside of the Diplomatic Service. By that point, I had to do a complete rethink, as I had already met the man I wanted to marry and didn't want to force him to choose a life abroad. Luckily for me, it worked out, as we are just about to celebrate our twenty-fifth wedding anniversary.'

Not all of the senior women I met had used foreign travel as a way of building their careers, even if they had seen the positive influence it could have.

Athene Donald heads the Physics Department at the University of Cambridge. She recognised that she had not been able to build the international profile of many of her colleagues, simply because she did not want to travel when her children were young. She pointed out: 'It was my choice not to travel to international conferences but I think it has benefited my students as I have been able to spend more time with them. I get the best out of them, rather than trying to lead a lab when I am never around.'

This approach was somewhat unusual as the life of a university academic does often involve a great deal of travelling and speaking to international conferences, rather than focusing on the teaching.

It has obviously worked well for Athene, however, as she is both a Fellow of the Royal Society and a full professor — an esteemed position at any UK university, let alone the University of Cambridge. She is also the 2009 L'Oréal-UNESCO Woman Scientist of the Year.

What these women illustrate is that after starting from a solid foundation, the only way to progress a career is to be known for your efforts through concerted profile raising. One of the key rules when playing with the boys is to take control of the amount of personal PR you receive. Promote your team, promote your clients, but just make sure you promote *yourself*.

The limelight for women is scarce enough for women in male-dominated fields; make sure you keep yours burning so you can bask in its glow. Only then will others truly be able to see your potential to engage with the big boys *and win*.

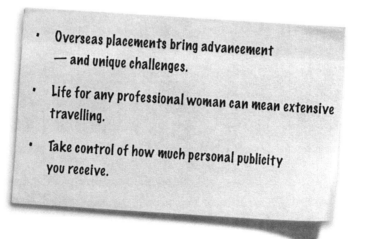

- Overseas placements bring advancement — and unique challenges.

- Life for any professional woman can mean extensive travelling.

- Take control of how much personal publicity you receive.

FOUR

CONNECTING TO THE RIGHT PEOPLE

The more independent you want to be,

the more generous you must be with yourself as a woman.

— Diane von Furstenberg

A golden rule for understanding success is: *If you don't ask, you don't get.*

If there is a vacancy or upcoming project you want, ask to be considered for it. It is important to have these larger conversations with senior people early on in your career. They are not mind-readers. They don't know what you want for your career — what projects interest you, where you want to take your role, which other departments look interesting — unless you tell them.

Waiting to get noticed for all your hard work will leave you waiting for a long time. If you are ambitious and want to be promoted, you need to tell people.

The women I interviewed all spoke about how the need to develop strong working relationships had only increased as they progressed their careers. Their networks became more vital and wider, moving outside their companies and at times even outside their industries. The need to manage relationships with a disparate group of people, even people they might not have initially liked, became a skill to master.

One of the ways that Mary Hensher at Deloitte got the key information she needed was by seeking out the right people to speak to. She suggested: 'Identify the key players — the people that other people listen to. Who are the people who have good reputations? How did they get those reputations? Talk to them if you are starting from the ground up.'

IDENTIFY KEY PLAYERS

Matilda Venter, in preparation for applying for her current Director role at PwC, knew she had to build relationships with the right stakeholders.

She said: 'After working more closely with other departments that I was delivering to, I began to seek out the partners who oversaw those projects. I sought them out and initially found excuses to talk to them. Eventually I was speaking to them about my career ambitions and asking their views and advice on how I should proceed, almost using them as mini-mentors. This was all so new for me, as I had previously focused only on delivery.'

The women I interviewed had a range of techniques for keeping interactions with senior staff positive and useful to both parties. Janet Davies, a Head of Marketing at PwC, remembered one occasion in a previous role where she helped a male colleague to refine his approach to a senior manager.

She explained: 'He was meeting with my boss for the first time and was about to go into his office carrying a large pile of papers. I warned him not to go in with so much paperwork otherwise he wouldn't be in longer than just a few minutes, even though they were due to have an hour together. He chose to ignore me, but sure enough, he was out again in five minutes. He walked over to my desk saying, *Okay, so you were right. I'm listening now. How did you know?*

'I explained that the MD was always very busy, had a very short attention span anyway, and was likely to feel overwhelmed by seeing so much paper and an hour scheduled in front of him. He knows that you will have done the due diligence but he wants you to share your proposed solution right up front. So, when he sees you with your great big stack of papers he immediately thinks, *Oh no, this guy is going to stand there droning on for ages and may not ever get to the solution. I'd better cut this short right now. I've got better things to do.*

'If you really want to get his attention,' she suggested, 'just write a couple of points on a Post-it note, hold it visibly in your hand, go the door and say, *Do you have five minutes?* With that small piece of paper, you give the impression that what you want to discuss will be quick and painless. I usually ask him how his weekend was or something, so he is more receptive to talking, and then I go in for the kill.

'I might be in there an hour but for him it seems like just a few minutes, since it all appeared very straightforward and off the cuff. Essentially, the higher up in the food chain, the easier you have to make it for them to say yes to you. It can also help to warm them up with a quick email about what you want to talk about beforehand and get to the point quickly.'

CHOOSE YOUR ADVOCATES CAREFULLY

Many women think that if they have the ear of their boss or another senior colleague, they are well protected. However, the successful women I interviewed know you should have at least four or five advocates who support your career, and who will publicly defend you during promotion time or should political trouble arise.

Angela Mohtashemi, of PwC, also felt that it was vital to establish relationships with high-profile people in order to get ahead; this was increasingly important to her as she prepared to move to the level of Partner.

She said: 'The key thing is to have several sponsors who will be supportive of you, tell you who to work with and who to avoid. My immediate leader is very supportive, receptive and fair. I trust him and know that if others are questioning my credentials, he will challenge them.'

Angela picks up a great point in recommending *several* advocates. Often a person on their own may not be willing to go out on a limb for you if they feel they will not in turn be supported by another peer. Other women I interviewed recalled the mistake of relying on one advocate who retires, falls out of favour themselves, or in some cases even dies. To this end, don't put all your eggs in one proverbial basket. Additionally, don't assume that the 'favoured basket' will always have the same key players, or even that all of those key players will be men.

Many women talked about how the addition of new people, male or female, can change the dynamics of a senior team. Just as we mustn't make assumptions that every problem faced by a woman who works in a male world is sexism, nor should we assume that every man is equally accepted into the fold of the boys' club.

Angela recounted how a committee she had belonged to went through several stages of change, depending upon who was or was not invited to attend. She remarked: 'A number of men joined the team, but each with different personalities. It wasn't just that the original team was all-male; it was that they were all alpha-male types who had grown up in Financial Services and behaved like a clan without much outside challenge.

'Individually they were fine, but as a group they took on a new persona and it was equally difficult for some of the new men as it had been for me. The new chaps who challenged the status quo were sidelined and dismissed in a way that was all too familiar to me.'

- Spot who other people listen to, and who has a good reputation. How did they get it?

- The more important someone is, the easier you have to make it for them to talk to you.

- Aim for at least three sponsors who'll advise you whom to work with and whom to avoid.

THE APPROACH IS UP TO YOU

The most successful women in male-dominated fields know that, since they are not always readily accepted into the inner circle, they have to seek out opportunities to meet the key players. They cannot afford to wait to be invited.

The onus is on *them* to demonstrate why they are worthy of an invitation.

I once had a client, whom I will call Frieda, who was a marketing director for an IT firm. She wanted to develop a better relationship with a more senior director who lived in another country and whose trips to UK were always well-planned and timed. Frieda couldn't see how she would ever get him to give her time on her own, as it was not a direct reporting relationship. We decided that it was not a question of waiting for him to 'give' her time, but rather looking for opportunities where she could 'take' his time in a subtle way.

I challenged Frieda to think whether she ever had an opportunity to be with him. She thought for a long time and then remembered that, twice a year, because of the vagaries of their presenting schedules, they shared a car to the airport when he returned to the US. It didn't seem like the quality time Frieda was waiting for, especially as he normally began to read the paper as soon as they got into the car. When she recognised that it was all the time she would get initially, she prepared some questions and comments for the next journey.

Frieda reported back that she had approached him by asking if she could get his opinion on a few things. This led to them talking for most of the way to the airport — a real improvement from the days when they would both retreat to the privacy of their respective newspapers for the trip.

Laura Hinton at PwC has also used this method with her mentor on occasion. She explained: 'I sometimes grab ten minutes in the taxi when we are on the way over to a meeting. I tell him what I've been up to and ask him about his predictions for the next few months.'

Savvy women learn to take the time — in a taxi, at the airport, in a lift, by a water cooler — *where they can get it*, rather than wait for the opportunity to arise for a scheduled one-to-one. Needless to say, with some key stakeholders, the opportunities to have longer one-to-ones won't ever arise unless you get noticed in the impromptu moments first.

MAKE A MEAL OF YOUR CAREER

One way of finding these impromptu moments is to make the most of your 'downtime', such as your lunch break. Many professional women now work through their lunch, especially if they leave on time to take care of childcare responsibilities — or indeed if they want to enjoy their private time after work, whether or not they have children.

Working through lunch is one way of seeming to achieve more in a short space of time; however it is not without its drawbacks. One of the main thrusts of what I have learned from successful women in male-dominated fields is how important networking is for career progression. One of the best times to develop these vital relationships is through *having lunch with others*.

While a proper sit-down meal is ideal, a full hour lunch may not be feasible. That doesn't mean you shouldn't make the most of what little time you do have. I wholeheartedly advocate leaving your desk for lunch. Even just walking to the sandwich shop with a colleague can be very useful, because of the interaction you have during those 20 minutes before going back to your respective desks. During the good weather, take your packed lunch outside with a colleague.

Begin to frequent lunch spots that are popular with colleagues, so that you can develop relationships and again be seen by those around you. Think of a staff canteen, a local restaurant that is popular, or a sandwich shop that many of your colleagues visit. As you develop external networks, make it a practice to meet up with people *from other companies*.

This is an especially salient point to remember in a poor economy. At a time of mass redundancies, more than any other, it pays to have good quality contacts in a wide range of other organisations.

Essentially, whilst I understand the attraction of bringing your lunch from home or ordering something straight to your desk, a greater benefit will come from taking the time at least twice a week to have lunch with colleagues or with people in other departments. The irony is that taking the time to have a break and develop relationships will save you time in the long run. You will have a larger group of people to turn to for solving problems and improving your efficiency.

Nicky Clayton, Professor of Comparative Cognition at the University of Cambridge, has been an academic at universities in both the US and the UK. She regrets the slow death of the lunch hour, first in the US and increasingly in the UK.

She explained why she values time with colleagues in a relaxed atmosphere: 'I ask new colleagues or someone from a completely different department to lunch, and we can talk and find out what things we have in common, perhaps with a view to collaboration. Lunch allows for a relaxed meal without a feeling of any greater agenda — but just to see what happens.'

The irony of course is that the more you have lunch with colleagues, the less it will ever seem that you have a specific agenda to raise and hence the more you can get accomplished. If you seem always to eat a sandwich at your desk, but then start to ask colleagues to lunch every day, people will wonder what your agenda is simply because the change is so noticeable!

Much like the woman who dresses down every day, then one day wears a suit, people can be suspicious and ask whether she has an interview at a rival firm simply because it's so out of character. However, if you *get into a habit* of sharing a meal with a variety of colleagues and potential clients or people you meet at networks, what you gain in terms of camaraderie, moral support, valuable inside information and political kudos will be worth every moment spent away from your desk, every penny spent eating out, and every calorie best forgotten!

TREAT MEETINGS AS YOUR SHOP WINDOW

To many women, meetings feel like a waste of time but they are another great way to raise your profile. The truth is, meetings are a key opportunity to see and be seen — part of marketing yourself. Meetings are airtime for your opinion to be heard, and a political way to build support for others, by publicly agreeing with opinions with which you have empathy or building support for your own causes. They are also an opportunity to read the underlying agendas of those around you. When you are ready to raise your game further, offer to *chair* a meeting.

While we love to complain about how *time-wasting* and *boring* meetings can be, we may forget how they can allow us to both observe and participate in group dynamics. Well-structured short meetings can do wonders for communications and morale.

If you think you can accomplish a lot more by skipping meetings to focus on whatever the current task is at hand, you are probably right — for that single task. However, if you routinely miss meetings to keep your nose to the grindstone, you will accomplish a lot less over time and be offered fewer interesting responsibilities.

In one of my first jobs, my team was invited to monthly teleconferences where we could hear about the strategy of the overall company, the headquarters of which were based in another city.

The teleconferences lasted an hour and then there would be time for ad hoc discussion and questions around our own board table. All members of our small staff of around 15 people were invited, though it was understood that if you had a project or a deadline looming you could skip them. I almost always attended, not because the teleconferences were so riveting but because of the time afterwards to ask questions of our local management and develop rapport.

We joked a great deal; although I had other pieces of work waiting for me in my office, I also knew *this* work was equally important, if not more so.

One of my colleagues, whom I'll call Jennifer, was a very diligent woman who was a technical whiz in putting together our presentations. Jennifer almost never attended these meetings. She always claimed she was too busy, and she probably was ... but she didn't understand the *unspoken* value of attending. As my relationship with various senior staff members developed, they would tell me about potential pieces of work, with a view to letting me have first refusal on participation.

As colleagues, Jennifer and I never quite saw eye to eye and she was difficult to win over, even though I was very happy to credit her with most aspects of our presentations. While we technically had the same title, we went about our work in very different ways. I completed my work, perhaps devoting fewer hours to any one given report, but instead I used the extra time to build relationships with those around us. She didn't see this as a value in itself, and hence it was left to me to develop relationships with our clients and colleagues — a situation from which I benefited hugely.

Eventually, people with whom I enjoyed working would request me rather than Jennifer to work on new and interesting projects. By helping to crank the machine, but not to *grease the wheels*, she missed out on opportunities that she might just as easily have shared.

Similarly, a former client, whom I will call Erin, was in the marketing department of a major FTSE 100 telecommunications company. She came to our initial coaching session feeling marginalised, since she had never been asked to deputise and lead a meeting in the absence of her boss, even though several of her colleagues had.

Rather than focus on the slights she felt from others, she let her boss know she would like the opportunity. This surprised him, as he had interpreted her quietness in meetings as a lack of interest. With some coaching around how to make her presence felt by others in meetings, she soon was offered her first chance to chair. Erin now regularly deputises for her manager in UK meetings as well as abroad.

Once you feel more comfortable presenting to your peers, ask to be invited to a meeting where you can present to senior management. Offer to talk about an aspect of a current project you are spearheading, or on an upcoming activity that needs support. You can get a lot more out of the average meeting if you *shift your focus* from just what is being superficially discussed to what can actually be accomplished for your career and the careers of those you support.

- Don't just work through lunch — invest it in networking.

- Use meetings to understand individual players and group dynamics.

- The benefits may not be immediately obvious; the payback is longer term.

SPEAK UP

As you begin to attend meetings, it is vital to contribute vocally to the discussion. Too often women are so pleased to be invited to the meeting, that they forget to speak up — or, more commonly, put huge pressure on themselves to make the *perfect comment*.

However, I have worked with plenty of clients who, in waiting for the most insightful, innovative and original comment to come to them, have let the entire meeting unfold and finish before they have opened their mouth. They then kick themselves and would love a second chance. Of course, no one thanks the person who brings up a new issue or point of view as people are wrapping up and pushing out their chairs to leave. The fact is, the reward is in *contributing*, not waiting until you have the perfect comment.

Meetings are wonderful opportunities to publicly agree with an idea you like, or to flesh out one that has been mentioned previously. It's also a great time to ask questions that will help clarify the decision-making process. If *you* have questions, it usually means you are not the only one.

I once worked with a client, Louisa, who was a senior product designer in a software company. Louisa wanted to raise her credibility among the management team, and talked about how much of an outsider she felt in their meetings.

During one session she described how the senior management team was interviewing a new software security company. Everyone around the table seemed satisfied with their proposal, yet she was still confused on many of the implications regarding their offering but felt it best not to speak up and show her ignorance.

In our session, we looked at her assumptions around the likelihood that *all the men* at the table understood something she did not. I challenged her to ask one question at the follow-up meeting with the potential provider, when they were due to make their decision. She took up the gauntlet.

During the meeting, she raised one of the issues she had understood the least — the ongoing costs of updating the bespoke security package. She had previously assumed all the men understood the financial implications of the contract. Instead, she discovered that the provider indeed included far more substantial ongoing support costs than her company could sustain. It completely changed the tenor of the meeting, saved the company from a financial decision they would not have been able to honour, and did wonders to boost Louisa's reputation around the very table she had feared. In truth, the question she feared asking *was* her perfect comment.

How many times have you been thinking something in a meeting that you didn't want to say because it seemed either so obvious or contradictory — only to hear someone else make the point, and agreement be issued all around? There is no glory in then crying out, *I was just about to say that!* or, *John must have read my mind because I was thinking the same thing!*

I often challenge clients who are new to higher-profile meetings to say at least one thing during any meeting. It doesn't have to be the ultimate pearl of wisdom, but it shows that you are thinking and reminds them why you are at the table.

SHARING BEST PRACTICE

> *The true measure of a man is how he treats someone*
>
> *who can do him absolutely no good.*
>
> — Ann Landers

One way to start showcasing your talents to a more senior audience is to prepare bi-weekly reports relaying the achievements of your team. Ask to present it as a *taster* to other departments. It demonstrates what your division does and how it can engage with others. You could ask to showcase a recent project as part of *best practice* to help guide others, and even seek their input on how you could do things even better.

A manager with whom I worked, let's call her Jody, wanted to build the confidence and profile of her team. Her division was undervalued and underutilised by other departments. As part of the coaching, Jody began having bi-weekly meetings where members of her team could discuss a learning point for them. They would discuss how the technology product for which they were responsible had a direct impact on the business as a whole, and how other individuals could refer her team's service to existing clients.

The individuals of her team took turns to shine and the profile of her division, as well as her personal profile, dramatically increased within the company.

The last time I saw her, Jody had been tipped as a potential deputy to shadow the overall Director, with a view to taking over from him in a few years' time. He had been impressed by the way she turned around the profile of her team and the individual members within it.

- In meetings, speak up. Don't wait to make the perfect comment.

- Use meetings to round out perceptions of your work persona with opinions and ideas.

- Share what has worked for your team as a series of 'best practice' presentations.

WORK WITH THE BOARD

As you stretch from leading meetings, look for opportunities to present to the board as the next step up in your career. It is a real step up for most working women, and a steep learning curve for most professionals. It will challenge your ever-developing interpersonal and political skills.

Caroline, the IT Director of a worldwide logistics company, discussed how managing an increasingly diverse group of stakeholders became her largest challenge when she was asked on to the board. She had felt naïve when first stepping into a board position.

She recalled: 'I thought I'd been doing the right things — delivering projects on time and to budget — until I got there, and realised very quickly that the buck completely stopped with me. It was a real wake-up call.'

When asked what had changed, she replied: 'You need to have a sense of emotional maturity for the board relationships, the politics and even the internal warfare sometimes. You have to develop solid and productive relationships with each and every board member in order to *survive and drive* as I call it!'

Surviving and driving means being tough enough to handle criticism, adapting if need be, and not allowing it to divert you from your goal. For women new to this type of role, adapting to a group with already-established relationships is a key challenge; the established members are testing and watching you, and are likely to close ranks when challenged by an outsider.

Caroline described the variety of people within any board and how she learned to work with such a diverse group: 'There are going to be people who love or hate my passionate approach. But I have to be able to get on with all of them effectively, which requires a great deal of self-knowledge as to what type of approach to use with each person. There are some on the board who have a loud and a commanding presence, whilst others will quietly watch. You have to know how to approach each the right way and at the right time. With the big and brash people you have to find time where you can be big and brash together, but I try to meet the quieter types one-to-one to get them on side.'

Often women who progress to senior boards and committees do not realise that *decisions are not usually taken at the meetings themselves*. Rather, they are shored up in a series of one-to-ones and small group talks that the key players engage in beforehand.

To a new person, unfamiliar with the practice, this can seem very underhand and unfair. The new person has spent their time before the meeting finding the research to back up their argument, and views the meeting as a place to engage in active debate. They are often left confused when the meeting seems to be more of a rubber-stamp exercise and people are less concerned about actually debating the merits of an idea – and even annoyed when the new person does not want to go along with what has been informally decided beforehand.

What the new person doesn't know is that the decision will have been shaped and informally agreed before the meeting ever took place, through quieter discussions and one-to-ones designed to seem informal but which consolidate support for whatever proposal the key stakeholder wants to pass in the more formal board meeting. It's vital you learn the tricks to play the game.

LIKE PUPPIES, IDEAS NEED SOCIALISING

When I raised the idea with Caroline in her interview that not all decisions were made in the board room, she agreed wholeheartedly and laughed: 'You're right — the decisions are not made in the boardroom, they're made in the pre-work beforehand. If you don't shore up support beforehand, it can get very ugly and emotional within the boardroom — so making some of these decisions beforehand is critical.'

She had learned how vital this was by watching a particularly gregarious male colleague several years before. She said: 'Every time he had to present to the board, he spent the preceding days visiting every single board member, asking them for coffee, how their day was going, if they had time for a beer later.' She continued: 'He went to every stakeholder, and nine times out of ten his proposals were accepted because he had gained the support of the individual board members before he ever walked into the boardroom.'

Caroline had clearly been impressed by her colleague's foresight as she now admitted that it was the approach *she* took to get things done. 'Now I think through my proposal, what the likely objections will be, and how to answer them. I practise on my daughter as she is the most argumentative person I know. If it makes sense to her, then my explanation is clear and coherent,' she said with a knowing smile.

She continued: 'Then I take it to work and get my Managing Director on side in terms of the general principles and direction I'd like to take. And once I have that, then I work my way around seeing each of the board members to make sure they are in agreement and I have addressed their concerns as well. I call it *socialising* the idea.'

Socialising the idea had obviously worked well for Caroline, who at the time of our interview was being considered for a more senior role. Had it ever backfired for her? She answered: 'I once accepted a challenge from my Managing Director to take an idea I had not previously socialised to the board. Needless to say, it didn't go down well and I could kick myself for doing it. I won't be making that mistake again.'

TURN SATISFIED CLIENTS INTO YOUR BIGGEST ADVOCATES

You want to please your internal and external clients – but how can they please you? Many people don't understand how much more compelling it is to your manager to hear praise about your performance directly from a client, rather than solely from you or your colleagues.

Matilda Venter explained the value of satisfied customers in helping to raise your profile: 'I had a lot of great feedback from clients, which was helpfully fed back to the partners. But eventually I learned to help that process along, because sometimes it happened and other times it didn't. I learned to take the compliment graciously. But the stretch was to ask them to *let my managers know* how pleased they were.'

Mary Hensher also built her reputation on pleasing her internal customers, employees at the professional services firm, and letting that message spread further afield. She explained: 'Clients can see what you are doing and like the results, which in my team has ranged from giving our colleagues the ability to use VoIP (Voice over Internet Protocol) or a pre-registered PDA device. External clients then hear about what you are doing and begin talking, which raises your profile. You don't have to be an extrovert to get noticed.'

This approach worked well for Mary: she had been interviewed several times on television about areas aligned to her expertise, such as how to handle spam email within corporate settings. Now she is regularly asked to help the internal PR team to speak on a variety of topics, ranging from how Deloitte handles large IT projects to whether they block employee access to the social media site, Facebook.

Joanna Hewitt is a director of Private Banking at Barclays Wealth. She finds one way to keep up with her clients is by reading about them in the Press. Since many of her clients are from wealthy families, are well known business people or entrepreneurs, they have lives that are often covered in the wider Media.

She explained: 'I have to keep up with the papers, not just to stay abreast of the economic environment as you might expect from a banker, but also to be aware of what is going on in the 'high net worth world' — and be aware of what clients, or potential clients, are doing financially but also personally, and philanthropically. It can literally come down to reading everything from the *Financial Times* to glossy magazines.' This background knowledge gives her the inside edge when dealing with her clients' issues — but also makes them aware of the extra-personal service they receive; something they then mention to others.

We have seen how vital it is to connect to the right information and the right people at the right time. You must choose your advocates carefully and think bigger when assessing who actually is a key stakeholder. We've all heard of employees poached by their former clients, who loved their work so much they brought them in-house. Even if you don't want to move, it pays to get them to help build your reputation.

Don't make the mistake a few of the women recalled, of thinking it is enough to keep your manager happy, when actually a far wider range of people will affect how far you progress. It is your clients, colleagues, your direct reports as well as those people with whom your boss interacts. As a twist from what your mother probably told you, *smile at everyone*. Be prepared to help and call in help from a wide range of people, many of whom you haven't even met yet. They can all help you through the inevitable challenges and risks you face as you get better at working with *the boys' club*.

- The impact of your work is far wider than you might think.

- Once you're comfortable leading meetings, seek to present to the board.

- As well as impressing the board, aim to please internal and external customers.

FIVE

TAKING RISKS

Whenever I'm caught between two evils,

I take the one I haven't tried yet.

— Mae West

Another characteristic of successful women is their willingness to take risks, even if it feels scary at the time. Risk-taking is part of any professional woman's life and will take many guises, both in and out of the job.

The women I interviewed refused to be 'stuck' in a job or situation that did not work for them, or in a role they did not love. They all realised that 'stuckness' is simply *inertia*; the only cure is to take a step forward.

Certainly any professional woman's career ebbs and flows. While there may have been times when they took their feet off the accelerator, perhaps for the first few years after the birth of a baby, risk-taking and love of challenge characterised their career progression as a whole.

It is because of this willingness to take risks that I identified with many of the women I interviewed. I too believe that taking calculated risks is the best way to avoid feeling stale — and it can bring substantial rewards, both professionally and psychologically.

TAKE THE PLUNGE

The first, and one of the riskiest, decisions I ever took was to move to Europe just two weeks after finishing my first degree. I had never even visited the Continent and would be arriving homeless, jobless, friendless and looking to start a new adventure.

I had lived abroad before, being born and spending my adolescence with my family in Alice Springs, Australia — an unlikely starting place, as many Australians tell me. I had spent my university years in a small liberal arts college in my home state of Maryland in the United States, which I loved.

As a Women's Studies and Psychology student, I read a variety of female authors, from Mary Wollstonecraft to Betty Friedan. One thing many female writers in history often had in common was that they had sacrificed their own ambitions to be good wives and raise children — or were women who had never been able to access opportunities for education or professional work themselves.

While I wanted to experience family life in the future, I wanted to live for myself first, before the responsibilities of a partner, children, and a career that paid too well to leave were upon me. It was a great time for me to go. I had no boyfriend, no tempting job offers and my parents had moved from my childhood hometown thus removing a tempting safety net. Plus, I had the optimism of youth. I didn't know how long the little savings I had would last, or how I would earn my living, or even how well I would adjust to being on my own in a new continent. All I did know was that I didn't want to live with regrets for taking the safe option.

Moving abroad without a safety net sounds wildly spontaneous — however I planned well in advance, and worked whilst at university to save money. It was only when I landed in Dublin, as dawn broke in a rainy and beer-soaked Temple Bar, the nightlife area of the city, and I began looking for a hostel for my first night, that the enormity of what I had done hit me. My original plan had been to spend up to two years living and working in Europe, before heading off for a year or two back in Australia. However, as most women know, even the best laid plans don't always unfold the way we expect. Two years after my arrival in Europe, I had acquired a boyfriend (now my husband) and he encouraged me to apply to the University of Cambridge for my PhD. My acceptance was both a surprise and too good an opportunity to turn down. While there certainly have been challenges, I am still here and very happy twelve years later.

Coming to the UK with good intentions and a suitcase in each hand was a huge risk, and one that certainly had its fair share of challenges — but I wouldn't have made it this far any other way.

Occasionally, some of my executive coaching clients talk about being trapped by *golden handcuffs*: a well-paid job they dislike or that no longer challenges them. However, in my experience coaching professional woman, it is not just the money and perks, but primarily the fear of the unknown, which keeps people trapped. What many successful women in male-dominated fields know is that if a new job, opportunity or responsibility *does not feel scary*, it probably isn't a big enough leap.

If you are ambitiously moving up a career ladder, you need to keep climbing each step, even if you can't see all of the rungs ahead of you. Sometimes biting off more than you initially think you can chew offers the best opportunities for growth and to avoid career, not to mention mental, stagnation.

The learning curve may be steep — but think back to how out of your depth you felt when you took the job you are in right now. We often forget how big a past challenge was when confronted with another newer challenge. We minimise the last step we took, precisely because we have already successfully achieved it, and so we no longer remember how much of a challenge it initially was. We forget how large our previous learning curves were, simply because what we see behind us seems downhill in retrospect!

- If it doesn't feel scary, it's not a big enough step!
- Remember how out of your depth you felt when you started your current job.
- You will always regret that which you *didn't* attempt.

OPPORTUNITIES IN DISGUISE

Many of the women I interviewed made a name for themselves by taking on a challenge they weren't even looking for. Eileen Brown of Microsoft was one such woman who found herself thrust into a new role after having a bit of banter with her senior Director.

She told me: 'He asked why we had so few technical women in Microsoft and I flippantly replied it was because our recruitment website was so rubbish. I meant if half-jokingly, but then he looked at me and grinned and said, *Okay, fix it*. I realised he was far too important for me to ignore this challenge, and in an area I really cared about, so we set about changing the tone of the website.'

She remembered: 'The website featured lots of statements: how only the best and the brightest belong at Microsoft. And I just knew that wasn't how even the cleverest women actually talk. I suspected women were not even applying since they didn't identify with the macho language we were using. We made it much more female-friendly, talking about collaboration and what you can learn at the job, and as a result we've had a far greater number of female applicants. And that flippant challenge came from a director — who is now my mentor.'

The challenge of attracting more women to Microsoft was a task that was more far-reaching than Eileen had anticipated, but one that developed her connections as well as giving her a sense of fulfilment. The language of the recruitment campaign changed from *dynamism, aggression* and *competition* to *enthusiasm, learning* and *innovation*.

Overall it was a far more attractive message for prospective women, and it was met with an increase in applications from women. Eileen recalled: 'When I actually looked into it, I had to speak to women across EMEA (Europe, Middle East and Asia) as to what they perceived the barriers to be, and found while there were similarities, there were big differences in legislation and attitudes towards marriage, children and working women — so it became a much larger task. It couldn't be solved by saying that Microsoft has an open policy about working from home because you would find entire offices where this just wasn't the case.'

Out of that role, Eileen became involved with the Diversity team for Microsoft UK, which additionally made her the main point of contact for people interested in this workplace challenge. She said: 'I was increasingly asked to talk about our research, so I would do a talk every time I travelled. I eventually got media training, which really helped, and the audiences became larger and larger, and ironically others now consider me a role model.

'It's funny because I've had the most unstructured of careers, but I think that makes me approachable. That's what you need in a good role model: someone who makes you realise you can do it too, despite not ticking every box.'

Other women also accepted challenges that were not initially what they were looking for, but were perhaps born out of a difficult situation. Lis Astall recalled when she first started to realise she needed to take on more challenging risks.

She remembered: 'I started out picking safe things and eventually became more adventurous. You can raise your level so substantially if you pick something high-risk, which is very tempting.' She continued: 'I once was given a project where a contract had gone pear-shaped. The sponsor felt he had no credibility with the client any longer and offered me the role of New Account Leader for the remainder of the contract. The client also put a new CEO on the contract, to give the project a completely new start. Between the two of us we got on so well, we turned it around from being the biggest money drain in the firm to one of the most successful.'

Lis is the consummate professional and doesn't give the impression of being a wild risk-taker, but rather one who takes *calculated* risks. She confirmed: 'Big risks have worked well for me — but in my twenty-odd year career, I concentrated on twenty smaller and safer projects and have probably taken just three high-profile risks that felt right at the time.' It is a pattern that has obviously worked well for her as she is now one of the most senior women at Accenture.

Just remember, it is far better to take on a challenging task and stick to it. I once had a colleague who said she wholeheartedly embraced risks; the problem was that she *did not follow through* any one challenge.

She had moved overseas to find work in Venezuela as she was a native Spanish speaker. But she found it difficult to make a go of it, and after just a few weeks she quickly decided to move back to the UK. She is known for talking about her *life-changing adventures* — which everyone takes with a dose of salt. While moving back was the right decision for her at the time, it did make those around her more sceptical with every 'big adventure' she took on after that.

In the workplace, a pattern of "talking-up" challenges that you don't quite meet will eventually undermine your credibility.

- Pick a few key risks over your entire career, and see them through.

- Opportunities often come from unlikely sources.

- Think twice before turning down a challenge from a senior member of staff.

TRACKING YOUR PROGRESS

Rebecca George is a partner at Deloitte. After 13 years with her previous employers at IBM, she was asked to take a pan-European role working with a senior executive with whom she didn't get on — partly her own fault and partly his.

She had been a star performer for 11 years, and not getting along with an important executive was a salutary lesson; one she has never repeated. In the end, she moved to another area in IBM. She licked her wounds but more importantly became aware of her own *professional mortality* — and what she had to do about it.

She recalled: 'It was a close call but made me realise that if I was ever going to leave IBM it would have to be on my own terms. It forced me to realise how limited my options were. I talked with peers who pointed out the harsh truth: though I was a star performer at IBM, I had no track record, connections or reputation outside of the organisation.'

Rebecca moved to a job where she managed relationships between IBM and the government. It was a completely new area for her — and one she immediately loved. It was also a watershed, as she realised she needed to make a name for herself so she could always keep her options open.

She confirmed: 'I realised I had this challenge ahead of me. I wanted to raise my profile but I was working in a new area. I knew I needed an objective measure: I decided to use Google mentions. So I Googled myself — and disappointingly found not a single mention of my name, which was very humbling to say the least. I checked a few times a year and worked to improve my score!'

Rebecca realised that one good way to get Google mentions is to write, publish and speak at conferences. At the same time she needed to build a reputation and start to add value in the public sector. A mentor pointed out that while she couldn't yet talk on the public sector in general, she did know a lot about other areas.

She said: 'I had spent all this time working on initiatives, inside and outside IBM, to increase the number of women working in IT. So that is what I concentrated on, leading groups, speaking and writing articles, and it grew from there. As I worked in the public sector longer, I began to expand my areas of specialism and could talk on other public sector topics like workforce planning, recruitment, cost management and shared services. I started by talking about women in IT, but I was able to build my profile and my knowledge base *at the same time.*'

While she didn't plan it that way, Rebecca's approach was ingenious. Her sobering experience, realising how little influence she had outside the organisation, made her realise that she didn't have time to wait to become an expert in her field before putting herself out there — that the two could coincide and grow simultaneously. As her reputation for writing and speaking grew, so too did her original measure: references and photos of herself on Google.

It is important not to shift *your own* goalposts. Give yourself credit for what you have already achieved – women have a habit of minimising them after the fact. Tick off your list of achievements faster than you add to your list of things to do.

Additionally, beware of goalposts that mysteriously move when you're not looking. Sometimes, managers keep team members back by continually adding to their objectives or changing the criteria for success, so they never achieve that feeling of mastery and have the confidence to go for a promotion. To avoid any chance of this, use your performance review to agree exactly how your success will be measured. Like Rebecca, be as quantitative as you can so that the goalposts will stick and you have the chance to progress.

A CHANGE OF VIEWPOINT

This type of side-stepping away from one's area of strict expertise to build knowledge in another area, also worked well for me.

While I was completing my PhD I spent a summer as the teacher of a Psychology course at a Cambridge college. Whilst there, I was asked for help by a friend who was producing a documentary about the weird and wonderful world of history re-enactors; groups of largely men who re-enact battle scenes from history. I was an odd choice, certainly — but my friend knew of my special interest in women's issues and asked me to be the 'resident gender expert'. I was to comment on psychological motivations for people who spent their weekends trudging across the country, re-enacting Roman battles or World War Two skirmishes in full costume, and speculate on why there were so few women involved in re-enactment.

I didn't seek it out, but said yes to an opportunity that was not strictly within my area of expertise. I was intrigued. And then I found there was no research on this area. So, I read as much as I could on related topics such as masculine identity, making me the default expert for the purposes of this documentary. Hence I could add '*Featured Expert on History Channel documentary*' to my CV by the time I was 27.

It was not something I was looking for, but rather an opportunity that found me, and one on which I look back and smile from the absurdity of it all.

DIVING OFF THE HIGH BOARD

> *Self-confidence is the result of taking risks.*
>
> *Once you have successfully taken risks ...*
>
> *Your belief that you can accomplish something risky is based in truth.*
>
> —— Rhonda Britten

One thing all of the women I interviewed had in common was that their careers were constant exercises in stretching their comfort zone.

Whether it was moving abroad without a position to go to, leaving a safe and secure job for a completely new industry, or getting comfortable with drawing attention to their work, all of the women knew they had to exist in the ebb and flow of challenge to stay at the top of their game. The same approach has worked for me in building my own career.

Straight after completing my first degree in the US, I settled in a Dublin flat with three other women I had never met before. I immediately sought temporary office work. Finding a temporary job was difficult to say the least. I had never waitressed and my computing skills were abysmal. I finally signed on with an agency and they agreed to place me as a receptionist.

The problem was, they wouldn't send me on work placements. They said they didn't know how well I would handle the work. When I pointed out the Catch-22 situation I was in — that they would not know what I could handle until I was sent on a job, they baulked. I had no work, my savings were dwindling and I was waiting for them to hand me work.

Eventually, I decided to prove how serious I was by showing up one morning at nine o'clock and taking up residence in their front offices. They quickly assured me they would call when a placement was found — and I assured them that as I had no work, I would just wait in their front reception office until something came through.

Lo and behold, just an hour later, a week-long position came up! By the time I finished with that agency several months later, they expressed disappointment I was leaving as I was always on time and stayed on at roles they knew wouldn't have been particularly inspiring. To them, that was surprising; to me, it was my integrity and pay packet on the line.

Three months into my Irish adventure, I left the agency to take another risk — working for the Centre for Women's Studies at Trinity College Dublin. It was a prestigious but poorly-paid risk. The role meant I used my savings in order to support myself, but I knew it was a risk worth taking. In fact, I had persuaded them to take me on *knowing* there was little budget. At the time they were unsure how my time would be filled but, through my enthusiasm, I convinced them I would make myself useful, which I did.

I knew that, long term, working on an interesting project for such a prestigious university for even a few months was a good move. It was the choice between degree-relevant work with women I admired, or more pay for answering phones at the temp agency; I chose the less remunerative option.

During those months I lived in a hostel, surviving on a diet of the free eggs and bread that came with the bed-and-breakfast rate I was paying. But at my job, I built credibility with the Director, who'd had no position or funding to offer me when I approached her initially. I was tenacious, or annoying, depending on whom you ask! She eventually found a place for me working as a research assistant on a project that looked at the relationship between women's mental health and their work experience.

It was a new and fascinating area for me, and one that no doubt helped shape my coaching specialism now. But, as in the case with the women I interviewed, it was my own personal stretch at the time.

Jackie Gittins, a director at PwC, also knows to stretch herself whilst using her key strengths. A mentor to eight people at any given time, and a consummate networker, she knows her network is one of her key strengths. She recalled when she was asked to lead an IT project — a real departure for the woman whose knowledge had always been primarily managerial rather than technical.

She explained: 'It was a surprise to be asked to lead the project, and anyone who really knew me thought it was funny since I knew nothing about IT. But I had to rely on what I did know: people. It stretched me out of my comfort zone, so I had to bring in the strengths of those people around me. So, while I was not a natural pairing for IT, I knew if I surrounded myself with the right people and enough resources, I could do anything ... which is what I did.'

She continued: 'If you are a sole trader, you aren't going to get anywhere if you don't trust people. And if you don't allow for other people's innovation and creativity, things will always be the same. So as I progressed and became busier, I still always made time to have conversations with those around me. I ask what I need to know about them, how to get the best from them and how we can work together. I always ask rather than tell, because if they feel in control, I'm already halfway there.'

Several of the women I interviewed rose to leadership roles where they were asked to manage teams of men — men who were quite unused to taking directions from a woman. This is often a big exercise in stretching the comfort zone for any professional woman in a male-dominated field.

Dame Veronica Sutherland, the former Ambassador to Ireland, had been Head of the Security Department in the Foreign Office at a relatively young age. She remembered: 'It was quite tough, supervising men who were older than me, retired policemen. They didn't know what had hit them. It wasn't easy and I made mistakes but I left that role with a certain amount of satisfaction.'

Becoming actively involved in committee work can feel like a stretch for many people — but it can raise your professional profile if you are active and make your opinions heard.

Professor Athene Donald stretched herself by accepting an invitation to participate in a cross-disciplinary committee on food immediately after the birth of a child. It was a great opportunity to learn more about the field as well as influence funding opportunities.

She remembered: 'It was a great opportunity but the timing was difficult. We had to work out how to cope with the fact that I was still nursing the baby. It was a steep learning curve, as was the subsequent Foresight Panel on Food and Drink on which I served. The latter was particularly fascinating, as there were people like the Chair of the Farmer's Union, Head of the Consumer Association, a few other academics and industrialists. I learned a huge amount in what was a very cutting-edge and topical area at the time.'

She reflected: 'Even if I am scared stiff of the challenge, I have never backed down from joining a committee if I felt there was something I could learn or contribute — but not if I felt I was being asked just to be the token woman.'

BEYOND THE BOYS' CLUB

BIG PAY-OFFS, MANAGEABLE CHALLENGES

Several of the women I interviewed had made a name for themselves by taking smaller roles where they could take bigger risks, ultimately effecting more dramatic changes for the better.

Former ambassador Dame Veronica Sutherland demonstrated this by taking lower-profile jobs where she could learn and make a difference rather than initially aiming for high-profile postings, to Washington DC or Brussels for example. She left the Foreign Office in 1999, having served in Copenhagen, Delhi, Paris, West Africa and eventually Dublin, which was her final and most senior placement having gained experience as a Head of Mission in West Africa.

The opportunities she took did give her the chance to try new things and make bigger changes in low-profile areas. She said: 'In London and other major overseas posts the work can be very competitive so I preferred to take on less fashionable roles. When I went to Delhi in the 1970s, I chose to help run the aid programme. On the whole, people don't choose that route to advance their career, and maybe that's why people never saw me as a threat.'

Similarly, she took on the role of Head of the Security Department for the Foreign Office at a time when it needed modernising — but it certainly wasn't considered a glamorous role. She declared: 'Nobody joins the Foreign Office because they want to worry about Embassy security.'

Upon reflection, she realised that these 'less fashionable' roles allowed her greater autonomy and a chance to make a bigger impact — two things that were attractive to her. Being low profile suited her personality and she was able to thrive because of it. She remarked: 'Given my personality, I figured I could make more of an impact as a bigger fish in a smaller pond. I don't like making headlines; I don't like any sort of Press interest. I'm not brash by any means. It's just not me.'

The irony is that as a result of consistently doing a good job in many diverse roles, and making the right connections for others as well as herself, she did indeed win a highly coveted role as Ambassador to Ireland — a very high-profile position for any British ambassador. The key was in being true to her values: doing a good job in areas where she could make a *real difference*, regardless of how strategic the choices appeared at the right time.

- Join committees as a way to raise profile; just make sure you speak up.

- Take lesser-paid but more interesting roles to work with people you admire.

- Accept low-paid but interesting roles early; it is hard to give up a high salary later.

ACHIEVEMENTS NOT MIRACLES

A final note for this chapter: I will always advocate taking on a challenge, and encourage all of my clients to do so to advance their careers. However, there is a point at which you need to decide whether you have been asked to perform a miracle.

A former client, whom I will call Arlene, spent her career moving from one fire-fighting role to another, creating systems on her own where an entire team is actually needed. Arlene was well known among her past employers for the long hours and weekends she consistently puts in.

She came to me because of exhaustion and a sense of disappointment that her managers didn't recognise or seem to appreciate her superhuman efforts. I pointed out that the pay-off for her employers was that they got someone who was willing to put in over 60 hours a week in a job that pays for 40. Therefore, what was motivating her managers to be the ones to change?

Arlene was a *miracle-maker* — always doing more with less, meeting or beating impossible deadlines and budgets, saving the company money — but at a serious cost to herself. The problem is that every time she delivered another miracle, she set the bar higher for herself.

Miracle-making is an endeavour to be accomplished a few times in one's career. But it is unsustainable in the long run. Attempting to do so will only lead to disappointment over time, as there is no way to surpass what you have achieved previously or even to keep pace with yourself.

Even Lis Astall, for example, one of the most senior women at Accenture, remarked that she herself took on only three high-profile and very risky projects in her long career, and these were tempered by a career of steady progress. There was a realisation that risks come in various degrees: if you take large risks every step of the way, you will not manage in the long run and could develop a reputation as a *failed* miracle-maker.

The key is in managing expectations: go the extra mile but always be ready to say if you think the goal is unrealistic without additional resources. For example, respond to an unreasonable deadline with: *I would love to take on this project and turn it around by August — but realistically, it will take until October with my current headcount.*

Pushing back when something is unreasonable won't be a career-breaker. Routinely failing to meet expectations, that you have previously set too high, can be.

Taking risks comes with the territory as a woman who must work with and around *the boys' club*, in the often fast-paced and testosterone-laden male-dominated environments. The true skill to hone is in knowing which risks are worth taking and which are not.

It may not seem obvious at the time — but a track record of *inaction* or a consistent *lack of taking risks* amounts to making a decision to stay where you are, if not actually move backwards. When you consistently stretch your comfort zone and track your progress, you will see that actions that felt like huge risks at the time are actually manageable.

This will affect both your career and self-esteem in ways you can't even yet imagine. Taking a few risks will also give you the confidence to learn vital new skills as well as take advantage of skills you don't even know you already have.

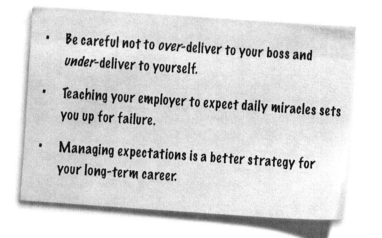

- Be careful not to over-deliver to your boss and under-deliver to yourself.

- Teaching your employer to expect daily miracles sets you up for failure.

- Managing expectations is a better strategy for your long-term career.

SIX

IF YOU HAVE SOMETHING TO SAY...

> *Because of their age-long training in human relations*
> *— for that is what feminine intuition really is —*
> *women have a special contribution to make to any group enterprise.*
>
> —— Margaret Mead

Women who work in male-dominated fields are among the best skilled employees a company can have.

Because they don't take their presence in these industries for granted they ensure they have the right qualifications, the finest degree, the most diligent work ethic. As we have seen, they are now outpacing boys in the number of A levels they take and the quality of the degrees they are awarded.

Make no mistake: women in male-dominated fields are some of the best-qualified and most dedicated workers in the world.

The bar to entry in these well-paid and highly-regarded professions is high. The internal cultures of these industries put a high premium on long work hours and informal structures that are alienating to most women. Therefore women cannot take their presence for granted.

So, they concentrate on getting the right academic skills — but their lack of progression to the top begs the question: *What exactly are the skills that help set them apart as they progress their careers?*

The most successful women know that there are skills, such as speaking in public, that they can learn and hone over a lifetime; and others, such as intuition and the *charm offensive* that they already have, but could probably use more frequently.

SPEAK NOW OR FOREVER HOLD YOUR PEACE

> *People call me a feminist whenever I express sentiments*
> *that differentiate me from a doormat or a prostitute.*
>
> — Rebecca West

One risk that pays off for the most successful women in male-dominated fields is mastering a skill that very few people love to do: public speaking.

While stereotypes abound about 'the chatty woman', the truth is that it is mostly men who present at conferences, who chair meetings and who lead presentations. Nowhere is this more true than in fields that already suffer from a dearth of women. Speaking in public is one of the most common fears, and certainly one that can be debilitating to a burgeoning career.

It can sound daunting initially but you don't have to start with speaking to an audience of thousands. In fact, most women begin to add public speaking to their careers by leading meetings and giving presentations.

As you move up, do get into the habit of chairing meetings — but *don't* offer to take the minutes, make the tea or other stereotypically female duties! If you don't yet meet with senior clients, ask to attend such meetings with a view to making a short presentation on your specialism, a new initiative or the work of the team.

Beginning to speak publicly is yet another way to demonstrate that you are serious about developing and progressing your career.

Sometimes my clients initially feel they haven't been able to raise their professional profile because a big, juicy project that is of great interest to them hasn't landed in their laps. The key to getting high-profile opportunities is to *go and seek them* — and not judge too early in the game what these opportunities might look like.

It is vital to remember: the opportunity to speak has many unexpected guises. You could be asked to deputise for your boss at an important conference because of an illness; facilitate an important meeting; or make a presentation to new clients or even senior management.

Practise first within your own team. You won't get comfortable with presenting unless you try it first with people with whom you are already comfortable. On the other hand, sometimes it is easier to speak in front of strangers. To get started, go with whichever option feels the most appealing. The key thing is to increase the frequency of how often you are speaking at all.

While it is considered one of the most common fears, the women I interviewed didn't let their fear of speaking to an audience stop them from advancing their careers. For some it is a matter of talking to the Press, such as Mary Hensher of Deloitte. For others, such as Lis Astall of Accenture, it is giving evidence to Parliament. Or it may mean taking on a role where regular public speaking makes up a good part of the job, such as Dame Veronica Sutherland, the former Ambassador to Ireland.

Dame Veronica said: 'After being made Ambassador, I had to look at my fear of public speaking. I realised I sounded nervous, which is something you can't do as an ambassador. My husband would give me feedback and I did a short course. It gave me plenty of tips and after that I'd force myself to make speeches even when I didn't want to, and gradually I began to improve. The role of ambassador in Dublin is senior, and any senior ambassador has to be able to speak well. It's what you are there for.'

KEEP IT ACCESSIBLE FOR YOUR AUDIENCE

Eileen Brown, the most senior technical woman at Microsoft UK, said that her whole career changed virtually overnight because of her first presentation skills training course.

She remembers how it changed her life: 'When I first started in IT, I was asked to lead a training workshop in Windows 3.11 — helping people get used to using a mouse for the first time in the early 1990s.'

She laughed: 'My boss watched and said I was terrible, to which I retorted that I'd never had any training! She sent me on a course, which was a complete epiphany. I'd been using aggressive body language like standing over people and getting too close. After the course I adapted my style and got rave reviews. It made me realise how vital these skills were.'

She joked: 'It was like finding God! It completely changed the direction of my life. It started me on a journey that made me realise how different presenting to ten people was to an audience of a thousand — but what was vital was that I was able to synthesise and simplify technical language to a wider audience, and build rapport simultaneously.'

Philippa Snare, another senior technical woman, also had her share of presentational skills training in her roles at BT, Scoot and Microsoft. She said the main benefit was how it taught her to focus authentically on how products are used in the real world, and how she had personally benefited from the technology.

She declared: 'People are much more interested in the personal stories as to how it has impacted you, rather than dryly hearing descriptions about the products and features.'

Focusing on the real world applications keeps her speeches engaging and compelling, even to non-technical audiences.

SPEAK BEFORE YOU FEEL READY

When you are asked to take part in a high-profile event, don't demur out of shyness, modesty or even because of a heavy schedule. If you have been invited, it is a sign of others' confidence in you; turn it down, and you are unlikely to be asked again.

Saying *no* sends a message to the world that speaking is not something you do. The truth is, there are plenty of your male colleagues, and indeed other women, who will take any opportunities you turn down, increasing the chances that it will be them, and not you, who is asked in the future.

If you feel too busy, delegate what you can and then *go*. It is nothing short of an investment in your future career.

I worked with another coach, Tanya, who told me a story that illustrated this point perfectly. She had written a high-profile government report in the 1980s, conducting the research and toiling over draft after draft. A few weeks before publication another woman was hired to help Tanya disseminate the information to the Press.

When asked to give the first interview on the groundbreaking research, Tanya demurred to her new colleague, saying she did not quite feel ready to speak to the Press. Her colleague took the opportunity and eventually became the public face of the report, ensuring a prestigious reputation for herself— much to the regret of Tanya.

The lesson? Do not wait to feel 100 per cent ready before you take up opportunities; you will never get there. Start raising your profile when you feel *80 per cent* ready, otherwise your colleagues and competitors will eventually beat you to the punch.

In any case, saying *yes* to intimidating opportunities has a way of making you put in the extra effort to get yourself to feeling 100 per cent ready. If you consistently say *no*, there is no real imperative to improve your skills and raise your game.

- Start with small audiences. Use personal stories to illustrate your main points.

- Turn down at your own peril opportunities to speak; you may not be asked twice.

- If you are *too busy* for a speaking engagement, delegate work so you *can* do it!

INVESTMENT IN TRAINING

Jackie Gittins also found presentation skills training useful in her role, where she is expected to present frequently at conferences.

She remarked: 'People think I'm a natural presenter, which is funny as I used to be petrified. I had to learn to put myself in those situations, to seek them out even when I was terrified. But I learned you can start small and build up. I teamed up with a colleague of mine for the first large conference. We created an on-stage dialogue, which was unique for that type of forum but also didn't feel as scary. I now try to create those types of joint-presentation opportunities for others in my team.'

When has she found the training most useful? She replied: 'When you are speaking to a multicultural audience, where English is a second or third language. You have to carefully think through your intentions and word choice, as phrases and humour don't always translate.'

This is a great point to understand, as many professional women have to attend and speak at international conferences where tone, humour and *industry jargon* can sometimes get lost in translation.

Jackie regarded all types of interventions, ranging from coaching, as we will discuss later, to presentational skills training, as lifelong learning. She recognised that she would never arrive at perfection — but she was continually getting better and raising her game.

For example, she used feedback forms after she had spoken at conferences to help her hone her skills further. 'While those forms can feel scary, take a big gulp and read the feedback: they give you invaluable information on how you can improve and are usually much kinder than you expect!' she laughed.

TOP-UP AT TOASTMASTERS

To help gain confidence in your presentation skills and get the feedback you need, you can't do better than to join a local branch of Toastmasters International.

Toastmasters is a non-profit organisation that exists to help people develop confidence in their speaking abilities. It has clubs all over world, and even within many larger companies. In fact the professional network, Women in Banking and Finance, has its own branch within the group, as do many larger employers.

Members of any Toastmasters can practise speaking in five-minute short speeches, as well as learn to give feedback to one another on their improving skills — which is invaluable to your development as a leader.

When I started my own company, I quickly realised that I would not make a living simply from one-to-one coaching. In fact, I realised I *shouldn't* make my living simply through one-to-one work since I enjoyed working with a larger audience. However, I knew I wouldn't be a fantastic speaker overnight and that I couldn't just 'wing it' every time I got up to speak. My audiences and I deserved better than that. So, while I knew I could speak adequately, I also knew *adequate* wasn't enough to differentiate myself as an executive coach and speaker and that I needed to get better.

I joined my local branch of Toastmasters, which enabled me to practise crafting and delivering a variety of speeches to a group of strangers who would give me supportive feedback. For my first speech, I had to give a five-minute introduction to some aspect of my life. I mistakenly thought, *How hard can that be?* I chose to speak about the circuitous journey that had brought me, an Australian-born American, to Cambridge.

I was overconfident and it showed — dreadfully. I told jokes that I hadn't first road-tested for suitability. I managed to defy the laws of physics completely, by frequently drying up and running out of interesting things to say, whilst simultaneously going over my allocated time. That was an 'achievement' I did not want to repeat.

However, that experience taught me to value my audience more, and their time, and always to prepare a presentation worth listening to.

For any woman looking to enhance her speaking skills, I couldn't recommend Toastmasters highly enough. I completed the initial round of ten speeches, on topics ranging from a past French holiday to what I loved about Britain, getting better with every speech. I then upped the ante again by joining the Professional Speakers Association, which focuses on people who earn their income from speaking publicly on their area of expertise.

- Do joint presentations to help get comfortable on a platform.

- Join a panel of speakers to talk about your field.

- Invest in training: skill in presenting and confidence mean you will be asked again.

LIGHTS, CAMERA, ACTION!

Sometimes the speaking you do may not be in front of a live audience, but rather is disseminated to a much larger audience through interaction with the Media. That is a completely new set of skills and should be treated as such. If the next step for your career is to start giving sound bites or full interviews to the Media, make sure you get adequate training.

As you begin to build your confidence and credibility in speaking, you should make it known that you would be happy to speak to the Media as a company representative, if you have not done so before.

I attended a conference, hosted by the UK Resource Centre for Women in Science, Engineering and Technology (SET), on the interplay between the Media and the portrayal of women in these fields. There was what I call a *best-intentions argument*: that journalists and the Media should seek out women in these fields when looking to interview professionals, for the sake of demonstrating that women do thrive in SET. I agree that more women should be profiled for their technical skills and opinions on industry matters, as a way of modelling that women do work and succeed in these fields.

Realistically however, the truth is that journalists are time-pressed and will prefer to speak to an expert they already know or someone who has made themselves useful through the provision of quotes or sources in the past. There is not enough time for the average journalist to seek out a woman who might be able to be interviewed.

You must make it easy for them to find you. Make yourself known to them, if you work in a field where you could serve as spokesperson for your team's research, product or even lifestyle issues, such as what it is like to be a woman working in your sector and what attracted you to the field – which is how many of the women I interviewed initially got their got their foot through the door with the Media.

A Professional Approach

To this end, ask your firm about media training. Many companies are starting to realise that if they want to engage with the Media and the larger audience that brings, it is important to invest in training that will help employees stay on message in a concise and coherent way. It will reap rewards in helping an audience to engage with both employees and their products.

Media training came in handy for Laura Hinton as her career developed. It helped her learn from mistakes she had made earlier. She recalled: 'I was interviewed for an article in *Accountancy Age* called "Top Ten to Watch Under 35" while I was still at my previous job at BDO Stoy Hayward.

'The interview itself was straightforward. But as we were wrapping up, the journalist asked if I saw myself as the first female Managing Partner at the firm. I jokingly said yes — which unfortunately became the comment the journalist used to create the main thrust of the article. I wouldn't say it now, as after the article came out, I got ribbed and more than a few raised eyebrows from other more senior women, who were probably thinking, *So, you think you're going to be the first woman?* Now I would know better and not joke so much because things can be taken out of context.'

The media training had other uses in preparing Laura for interactions with those who might wish to catch her out — but who were *not* journalists. She explained: 'Most people have their own agenda which is to make themselves look good. Now and again, you come across people who think the best way to do this is to make others look bad.'

Indeed, tearing others down *doesn't* make one look better and it's not an approach that demonstrates true confidence. But it's as likely to come from someone in your own firm or a competitor's firm as it is to be a journalist. We agreed that it had more to do with the individual than with the job they held.

Laura added: 'I've had people in my *own firm* try to catch me out publicly in a question and answer session, in front of hundreds of people. Likewise, I have worked with journalists who took pains to be fair because they wanted to create a relationship, so they could come back to me for quotes later. It's down to the individual.'

What is certain is that Laura, like many of the women I interviewed, found the media training as useful for dealing with difficult colleagues or competitors as for facing journalists.

Joanna Hewitt also had public speaking and media training at several points in her career. She remembered the first time she was invited to speak on behalf of Barclays. It was a Women's Institute event where she was expecting perhaps 20 women. However, because the wife of the bank's chairman, at the time, was a member, more than 100 women attended. She recalled: 'It was stressful; I wish I hadn't known she was in the audience.' She laughed about her first foray into public speaking as being a 'baptism by fire'.

It hadn't put her off though. While she described presentation skills training, especially if it involved cameras and watching herself later, as 'traumatic and awful', it was thoroughly useful.

She explained: 'We had a three-day media training in-house. The men groaned about it saying they didn't need it — but even they saw the value in the end. I learned that you couldn't see how nervous I sometimes feel, which boosted my confidence. I also became aware of things I would never have noticed, like my tendency to wave my arms or my legs like a windmill!

'Being able to speak to a large group of people is a confidence boost when I have to enter a networking event full of grey suited bankers — mostly men! I remind myself that if I can handle television cameras and radio interviews, simple networking should not be my undoing.'

Joanna said an important knock-on benefit was how much more controlled and confident she was, when handling private clients who were stressed about a falling market and looking to her to guide them — quite a relevant skill in a depressed economy. She reflected: 'I've learned to be more measured in my responses — just as in an interview, I remember to take a step back and remain calm.'

UNEXPECTED BENEFITS

The training also enabled Joanna to see new opportunities for speaking that she might not have noticed previously; even as we spoke, she mentioned a charity she was involved in and how they needed spokespeople. She noted that she now felt more ready to take on that type of public-facing role.

It was interesting to note that Joanna's male colleagues had not initially felt the need for media training. It is almost as if men in male-dominated fields assume they are already doing a good job and that leadership responsibilities and opportunities to speak are rightfully theirs. Women are much more likely to want to continue to invest in learning, in order to earn the right to be in top management by the continual acquisition of new skills.

Rebecca George was given formal media training while working for IBM. In her senior role there, she managed the relationship between the company and the government, which was high-profile and of great interest to the Press. Her training was intensive, held over three days, with lots of television cameras. She describes the whole experience as 'completely horrible', but is grateful she went through it 'every time I speak to a journalist'.

She explained: 'It taught me to prepare for every interview. I never take cold calls from journalists, and I write down my two or three key messages, which is vital so I don't get deflected.' One unique aspect to her preparation was that, for the first six months of her dealings with the Press, every interview she conducted was overseen by someone from IBM's press department. She laughed: 'I hated it, and felt like I was being babysat, but it helped keep me on topic and away from contentious issues. It was a fabulous bit of extra support they gave me, even if I didn't see it that way at the time!'

Matilda Venter received media training early in her career. She explained: 'I was working for the software provider, SAP, in the early 2000s, when everything 'e' was hot. I positioned myself to be the spokesperson for e-learning. It was a big area for them at the time and one of the prerequisites was that you had to have media training. It was useful in that it taught me how to focus myself to three main points, which has stuck with me in everything I have done since — from pitches to presentations to interviews.'

More recently, being quoted in the Media raised Matilda's profile amongst her internal peers and colleagues. She remarked: 'This year, we began looking at PwC's response to the sustainability question, and how that drives the Human Resources agenda. I have been interviewed by *The Times*, which was noticed by my colleagues — which is interesting, as that was a benefit I didn't initially anticipate.'

Lis Astall, the European Managing Director for Public Service in Accenture, also had to embrace public speaking, a responsibility she had never enjoyed, in order to progress her career. She said: 'I hate being on TV and speaking to large audiences, both of which I have done to get to this position.' Lis was like other successful women, in that she found media training useful, not only in handling press interviews, but also in her day-to-day communications.

She explained: 'We worked with actual presenters from the BBC, who taught us how to be succinct and handle potentially tricky questions. The irony of course is that a twelve-second spot on the News is a long news item and actually time enough for a decent sound-bite — but it takes exponentially more time to present those great twelve seconds!'

GRIST TO THE COMMUNICATIONS MILL

Matilda continued talking about the day-to-day lessons she took from the training: 'Learning to be succinct and clear with my main points has been so useful when presenting to conferences. It's made the difference between desperately clutching my note cards, looking nervous at the podium and being able to speak off the cuff using my PowerPoint slides for a little guidance, which instantly makes me more credible.'

Lis clearly knows that speaking with a minimum of notes and just a few main points gives her expert status in the eyes of her audience. She understands they will rightfully question her authority status if she looks completely lost without a detailed crib sheet and seems unsure of her topic.

Despite not loving making public presentations, Lis has accepted the challenge of representing Accenture three times on the Public Accounts Committee — a panel that answers to the House of Commons. The first time was gruelling and a good lesson to her on the impact of public image.

She explained: 'The whole process is about responding to a committee of around 12 MPs — responding to any question they may have on almost any subject. You have to think on your feet and be prepared to have your words twisted if you are not accurate and be attacked if you can't recall a specific detail.' She joked: 'Your goal is to provide the right answers without getting unfavourable headlines in the papers for your firm — I call it the last legal blood sport.'

With time she became more adept at what she describes as a three-hour 'trial by fire', but has never learned to love it. The goal for her was never to *enjoy* it, but rather to show that she was up to the challenge and willing to represent the firm — both key qualities for any professional woman.

- Media training will help keep you on message.
- Develop two or three key messages you want to focus on.
- Resist speaking to journalists off the cuff, call them back ten minutes later with your notes.

ENGAGING WITH THE MEDIA

Sue Blake, a personal publicist and media relations expert, spoke with me about how to go about engaging with the Media. Sue suggested: 'If you would love to grow a speaking career yet haven't done any real public speaking, then do seek external expert help on perfecting your message, presentation and delivery.

'The best speakers are those who are well-rehearsed, yet appear natural and confident on their topic and those who seek to engage emphatically *with* their audiences, rather than talking *at* them. Working with an expert who can help you prepare is money well spent.'

She explained how employees should engage with their press office first to discover the protocols — and if you aren't sure about these, ask!

Sue warned: 'You won't start off on the best foot with them if you go off on your own to try and make a name for yourself in the Media. Having their support is essential to making you look good in front of key Press.'

She advises: 'Make sure your company's press office team know the right things about you —your role, professional credentials and credibility and successes to date. Arrange to meet the team informally over coffee if you are new to the organisation.'

Sue is pragmatic and says: 'Avoid leaving things to chance. We're all selling ourselves all of the time, even if we don't have the word *sales* in our job title.'

She knows how frequently working with the Media can leave even the most diligent woman feeling complacent. She warned: 'When in a dialogue with a journalist, *never*, no matter how tempting, allow yourself to be caught off guard. Always take a written brief of what the journalist wants to ask and arrange to conduct the interview as soon as you can and when you will have had time to get prepared and on message.

'For example, you may need to validate certain replies you'd like to give to key questions with the press office. As your media reputation grows and you might get Press calls direct, continue to inform the press office — it's just best practice and common courtesy. Additionally let them know how they can help protect you; as in crisis management or, heaven forbid, damage limitation, things can get very awkward in hindsight.'

INTUITION IS NOT A DIRTY WORD

Not all skills that career women have in their arsenal can be learned on a training course. Luckily, these are skills that we already have within us but tend to under-utilise.

Intuition is one such powerful tool but one that women in male-dominated fields tend to ignore, often at their peril. Indeed the most successful women are those who can read others and predict their behaviours. This is not surprising as it is always hugely adaptive for subordinate group members, in this case the women, to possess a far greater inherent understanding of dominant group members and their culture than vice versa.

Your intuition is as useful when deciding on the safety of a short cut home as it is in negotiating round a board table. In both instances, recognising and understanding intuition has only helped women in the long run. Historically speaking, intuitive skills for women could be credited as survival tools in a world where access to economic security and social status has depended on an ability to please men and 'read' them accurately.

However, in fields where the *hard facts* are more respected than *soft skills*, using intuition is drummed out of professional women. Hence, few will admit to using it if it is seen as antithetical to the scientific process and all that is rational.

I have had trouble with this myself.

To assess my PhD research I crunched numbers, looking for patterns in an empirical and scientifically sound research method. In the scientific process you do not say you *feel* a certain way about findings or that *your gut tells you* an experiment will work out a certain way, for fear of adding bias to the results. Therefore I learned to rely more on my head and what I could measure, than on anything my intuition told me. I struggled with learning to use my intuition when I began to train as a coach, where listening to your gut about issues raised or indeed ignored by a client is treated as valid.

Naming things that were not being said, or making observations about what I felt was going on for a client, was anathema to me and a true challenge. To name my intuition and act on it in the absence of any background information, facts, or even in spite of what someone was telling me, was a huge personal challenge. The social 'scientist' in me still works to overcome that.

Obviously, I value research and a grounding in facts. The difference is the amount of *attention* I now give to my intuition. This can be a huge issue for women in any male-dominated field who strive to be seen as serious, credible and acting on data *alone*.

To this end, I run workshops that address how to use intuition in the workplace, which is a challenge for many delegates. In the workshop, we look at whether a decision you are making comes from your head or your gut. Professional women are initially taught to make decisions only from their head. However, when I see the same women make decisions from their gut, perhaps in dismissing a difficult team member or taking a new job, I have witnessed initial uncertainty — but never regret.

What women who say they are confused usually find, is that they know the path they must take; they just *don't like the answer* their gut gave them. It's similar to the choice of dating someone who you just *know* is going to leave you hurt in the end. This is a hard truth — but recognisable if we look over our lives and what has historically happened when we have ignored our gut feelings.

Much of the resistance to using intuition in the workplace comes from the assumption that men act on hard facts and figures more than women do. However, I think this is a fallacy, dressed up by different language. Men are dismissive of *women's intuition* and of making decisions 'from the heart'. However, they will respect a colleague who says he is going with his gut or who 'just has a feeling', in a way they don't when the same phenomenon is described *in more feminine language*. We respect the male gendering of the language, which is why it even feels more comfortable to say we *going with our gut feeling* than *listening to our intuition*.

Indeed, it has been my experience that people who listen to their intuition when making a decision are rarely dissatisfied with their choices. They will round out their knowledge with hard facts and an understanding of external factors — but this knowledge does not fundamentally affect their decision; rather, it helps tailor it.

Philippa Snare of Microsoft learned to trust her gut more in the workplace. She realised the people she respected most in her company also had this approach. She noticed: 'Most men in IT tend to want to analyse data and pull out the spreadsheets before every decision. While I also look at the data before making a decision, I notice that I already *have an idea of what I want to do* before I look at analysis, and I trust my intuition.'

She continued: 'The people I most respect here are also able to do that — and at least are honest that they are going primarily with their gut.' Philippa recognises that people who say they are only looking at the numbers forget that one can find numbers to justify almost anything and give themselves credit for a lack of bias that no one can achieve.

BLENDING COMMUNICATION STYLES

Jackie Gittins also became well versed in marrying the intuitive side of her personality with the hard facts that are so valued in modern business, and especially in male-dominated professions. She explained: 'I use what I call my *box and bubble*. I have all the facts and data that come from the figures illustrating the current situation — but I also bring in my bubble, which tells the story that illustrates what the data means in *people* terms.'

She elaborated further: 'So, for example, our CEO was interviewed by the Press to explain why profits were down. In preparation, we discussed which data he should use — but I also asked him to cover the human story, as I intuitively knew that was what people wanted to hear. So instead, he talked personally about why he is still here in a bad market and what the opportunities are for our business. It gives it a richer dimension.'

Confidence in communicating things that people would have left unsaid also characterised many of the women I interviewed, and was one way they used their intuition. Jackie Gittins often articulated the atmosphere in a group setting, even if she felt there was tension and something being left unsaid.

She explained: 'I was recently with a client group and said to them: *I sense you are finding this really difficult?* It was normally a much more vibrant group — but as soon as I spoke what I was feeling, people opened up and were visibly more relaxed. They explained there had been redundancies and that it was hard to keep motivated with the threat of more hanging over their heads. We changed the whole agenda as a result, to address what was really going on for them.'

Jackie had the confidence to name a discomfort that many people would not — but sees using this type of intuitive skill as vital to her job. She explained: 'If I didn't have the confidence to trust my intuition and be able to voice my opinions, I would risk not being the best consultant for them — I would be *colluding* with them instead.'

Fiona Edington, a barrister specialising in criminal, family and military cases, also made good use of her intuition as she faced new judges, new juries and new clients nearly every day. She suggested: 'Some people think they have to fight every case a certain way. But I think there are 101 ways to skin a cat and sometimes I have to pull back a little in my approach, or other times I have to go in swinging.' Intuition guided her every day in deciding how to address each new cast of characters in the courtroom.

Strengthen your intuition by listening to it and if you are not already doing so, make some decisions that stem from your gut first rather than your head. It's like a muscle that can be exercised to make it stronger — and it's very much a case of *use it or lose it*, as our inner voices eventually quieten the longer we ignore them.

WORKS LIKE A CHARM

Often people approach being a woman working in a male-dominated field from a negative point of view. Without diminishing the challenges faced by women in these industries, most successful women are able to turn many negative aspects into positives. To this end, using what I call the *charm offensive* is a vital skill. I wholeheartedly believe that one of the best ways for any man *or* woman to advance their career is to be charming to those around them.

Charm is a mix of humour, manners, good communication, banter and even a bit of flirting. I personally 'flirt' all the time, with both men and women. For me, it is about making people feel good about themselves. It's the joke-telling, the banter, the enquiries about their life, the genuine interest in getting to know them better that grease the wheels of communication. It's also a skill women tend to be better at than men, and therefore should use to their advantage. When I went through my scowling teenage years, my mother chastised me that 'you catch more flies with honey than vinegar'. While I didn't want to hear it at the time, it is one of the best lessons I have ever applied to my interactions with others.

I first became aware of how to use charm and humour as a method of interaction, during my university years. I like and enjoy the company of men, which is something some people who know my specialism in working with women, are surprised to find. During those years, I was known for being one of the few Women's Studies students and a passionate advocate for women's rights as well, often speaking on the subject. This was a curiosity among many men I knew, as they also knew me as someone who loved to joke, wore make-up, shaved my legs, cared about my appearance and happily dated men.

I seemed enigmatic to some fellow students who could not reconcile my proud femininity and sense of humour with my strong feminist beliefs. This is a reaction that continues to this day, with grown men being surprised to find that they enjoy my company as much as they do, after they learn I am a staunch advocate for gender equality. It is as if to be feminist and charming are mutually exclusive.

This charm offensive has also allowed me to take on contentious issues such as women's rights in the workplace. Other people are more likely to engage and actually listen when they don't feel personally threatened. I listen to what they have to say, and when they seem surprised at how genuinely feminist I am, I jokingly ask if I should remove my 'normal woman mask' to reveal the bitter, angry, unshaven, bare-faced feminist beneath.

A bit of tongue-in-cheek humour never goes amiss. Men respect a woman who can give as good as she gets when it comes to banter, and this can be used to your advantage in the office, the trading floor or the lab.

Retired archaeologist Dr Harriet Crawford saw the value of humour in what could have been a difficult situation. She took part in many digs in Mesopotamia and the Gulf region during her career. Though her attempts were far from perfect, making an effort to speak in their own language earned the loyalty of her all-male teams. It also helped to temper the firmness with which she had to lead the team.

She said: 'I attempted to learn Arabic. That's what made them laugh. Knowing that it probably wasn't being spoken terribly well, they thought it was hilarious. As long as there is an iron fist inside that velvet glove, there's no problem.'

Other women also recognised that using charm worked far better than brute force. Janet Davies, a Head of Marketing at PwC, agreed with this perspective. She declared: 'I don't view a man holding a door open for me as some kind of personal affront; it's just good manners. And naturally I would open a door for another woman; I wouldn't slam it in her face. It's simple common courtesy. People, male *or* female, will like you if you are generally easy to get on with and not looking for problems and confrontation.'

When asked how she achieved this, she elaborated: 'Having a joke with both men and women, being gracious in defeat or when winning. I helped one of our external writers renegotiate his contract with us recently, and he wrote and thanked me for 'being kind and having integrity' — he said he wasn't used to being treated with integrity, kindness or charm by many of his clients.'

This does not mean that Janet is a soft touch. She is a tough negotiator who has used her status as a woman working in a male-dominated field with humour and to her advantage.

TRAILBLAZING

Often when women are negotiating for better conditions, such as flexible working or for a four-day week, they are the first in their team to attempt to do so. Most men simply don't ever have to ask for those types of concessions, or don't feel that they can ask even when they would like to. Rather than think that your status as the first is a *handicap*, look at the *opportunity* it brings. There is no precedent — so, in many cases, you can influence the outcome rather than accepting 'standard practice', since there is none.

Janet did this when she had to negotiate for the continued use of her company car whilst on maternity leave in 1989. Her boss avoided making a decision on the issue of whether she could keep the car whilst away, until she was literally a few weeks away from giving birth. She realised no one had ever had to ask for this because none of her colleagues — all men in a manufacturing organisation — had ever been on maternity leave.

'Our HR Director told my boss he was concerned it would set some kind of precedent that he hadn't quite figured out the future implications of. But when I heard that was the objection, I was able to work around it. I pointed out he wouldn't have made a male colleague give back the car if he had been on sick leave and as I was, at that time, one of only two women who even qualified for a company car it was hardly going to be a recurring problem.

'I made a joke about my heavily pregnant form only containing a baby not a "Pankhurst-inspired time bomb". He saw the funny side and sorted out my car issue!'

Janet explained the downside to some legislation that has sought to minimise gender discrimination in the workplace. She continued: 'Unfortunately, political correctness and equality legislation often *drives such behaviour underground*. I got him to name his objection to get it out in the open, so I could address it and get a win-win outcome for both of us. I was back within a few months and was then offered a number of high-profile opportunities that advanced my career, and the fortunes of the company, significantly over the next few years.'

While women are increasingly taking senior roles within many male-dominated fields, their presence still has the ability to surprise some. This can be a great opportunity to use humour. Dame Veronica Sutherland, the former British Ambassador to Ireland, once experienced a case of mistaken identity. In 1992 she attended a formal dinner hosted by the Irish Government for Bill and Hillary Clinton, who were visiting Dublin.

She smiled when remembering: 'The place settings were out at the tables, with guests standing behind their designated seat. As I walked over to my place, marked simply with my title: *The British Ambassador*, a large American man said to me, *Ma'am, you are in the wrong place. This seat is reserved for the British Ambassador and you're sure not him.*'

Her simple reply? 'I think you will find I am.'

THE EXTRA SENTENCE THAT MAKES THE DIFFERENCE

Eileen Brown of Microsoft owes much of her success in engaging others with charm to just 'having that *extra sentence*'. When I ask what her extra sentence is, she explains that it is what you say after being asked 'how are you?' that gives the other person a hook and something to comment on.

She suggested: 'It's not about being overbearing, but just having a good response to, *Hello, how are you?* It allows you to engage with them, and if they're not interested they can back off — but it makes you approachable.'

She gave an example of how she used the charm offensive: 'It works the same way for compliments. Women love a compliment on their bag, shoes or earrings. If I see something a woman is wearing and I like it, I will tell her. And then she reciprocates by being humble and innocently claiming, *This old thing?* Or perhaps she smiles and tells me she got it as a knock-off in the market. From that we have bonded and both feel easier in each other's company, which is the best way you can start.'

This certainly was true even as we first met. When I asked her the standard 'how are you?' she joked that she was fine *and* nervously trusting her husband to harvest all the courgettes from her garden so they didn't rot while she was travelling for work for a few days. Certainly, it was more information than I normally get back when I ask what is a standard question during introductions. However, it led us to talk about gardening for several minutes and bond over our mutual love of certain types of homemade jam. This rapport-building meant we had a great start for our interview. Using charm and humour is a good starting point for anyone wanting to develop better relationships.

Similarly, she describes how the move she made from the Merchant Navy was the result of a fortuitous conversation where she offered that extra sentence. She remembered: 'I sat in an Amsterdam airport in the winter after returning from Mexico. I had flip-flops, no socks and tanned legs. I turned to the stranger next to me to ask if it was going to be this freezing in the UK. He looked surprised I had struck up a conversation — but then asked me where I had been. I explained I had just left the Merchant Navy and was now looking for work in East Anglia, as I was about to get married. As it turns out, he remarked he knew a guy in the IT sector ... and the rest is history.'

Trusting her gut and being charming has continued to work well for Eileen, as well as for many other women who are successful in male-dominated fields.

One of the things I love about working with women in these fields is that they always want to know more, to learn more, to be more. They know that even once they have the technical qualification, the learning does not stop — nor do they want it to. For example, they discover that learning to present themselves to an audience of three or three thousand becomes vital the more senior you get. They take comfort and delight in realising you don't have to know it all on your first day or even in your first decade.

The women who are the most comfortable moving *beyond the boys' club* realise that trusting your intuition is also a skill. It is an inborn skill that women in these fields are often trained to ignore in the pursuit of the rationale, the hard facts, that which is deemed *male*. However, it is a skill that must be nurtured and developed like any other if you are truly playing the game to win.

- Learn to trust your intuition; numbers help but can be used to justify almost anything.

- Charm is one of the most effective and *fun* tools to use.

- Give a piece of yourself when you are introduced to someone for the first time.

SEVEN

IMAGE

Dress shabbily, they notice the dress.

Dress impeccably, they notice the woman.

— Coco Chanel

The clients with whom I work are ambitious professional women. Whilst we work on issues around communication, leadership and management skills, I also believe that personal presentation is vital. If you want to be taken seriously and considered for promotions, you can't rest on your laurels when it comes to your professional image.

Put yourself mentally into the job you aspire to and ask yourself: *How would I dress in this job?*

I once ran a workshop on *Image and Dressing for Success* for female scientists wanting to return to the workplace after an extended career break. This was part of a larger full-day networking event, where they met other women with whom they had only ever previously had email or telephone contact. It was a huge opportunity to enhance any positive verbal first impressions they made upon each other. The women were career returners and had come from a mix of academia and industry. The level of formality in their dress varied hugely.

What amazed me in our discussions was how many women felt that the need to project a professional image did not apply to themselves, citing it as completely irrelevant. There was a virtually unspoken assumption that, if you do your work well, projecting a well-presented image is superfluous and unnecessary.

The truth is that, even if you wear a lab coat or boiler suit for work, people will still make assumptions about you based on your clothing, hair, make-up and even your posture.

FIRST IMPRESSIONS LAST

According to research from Princeton University[1], people evaluate others on the basis of the first one tenth of a second in their initial meeting — before they have even spoken. More than half (55 per cent) of a first impression in social situations is based on appearance, including facial expression and gestures; 38 per cent on vocal qualities; and a paltry seven per cent on what we say!

It may seem unfair in an ideal world ... but this book was not written for those working in an ideal world. It was written for women who, like me, have to make a good impression in the *real* world.

This is a real world where image counts and we must readjust to the way audiences really think and behave — rather than dismiss concerns about appearance as superficial. What is the use of your brilliant presentation if no one listens?

START ON THE RIGHT WELL-HEELED FOOT

Humans are visual beings. Pretending that we don't judge one another based on some aspects of appearance, or indeed that we are above such scrutiny ourselves, is a fallacy.

For example, your own quick visual judgements affect the decisions you make about whom to approach at a networking event, or how you guess who is the most senior person in a boardroom.

Image counts. In the absence of other relevant information, you will look for visual clues about who is like yourself, how they regard themselves, how professional they seem. You then let what they say verbally about themselves

[1] Willis, J. & Todorov, A. (2006) "First Impressions: Making up Your Mind after a 100-Ms Exposure to a Face", Psychological Science, Vol. 17 (7) pp. 592-598

either support or contradict your initial impression, based on your initial visual judgement — not the other way around.

Keep in mind: it is very hard to get someone to change their opinion more favourably after they have met you and already formed a negative impression. Humans subconsciously look for validation that their first impression, whether negative or positive, was correct. It is easier to start from a position of strength by offering a positive first impression through your image. For the woman looking to raise her profile, addressing one's image is not an *option*. It is vital.

Though I am still learning, I gleaned much of what I know about image from my Aunt Sharon. She was a Chanel model before taking on the construction industry as a property developer. Sharon is as comfortable in a designer suit as she is in Wellington boots. The key is that she knows when to wear each, and how to do so with aplomb.

One of my toughest lessons on image was during a visit to her and my uncle in Dallas during a university holiday. On a whim, I applied for an internship at a drug treatment centre for teenage girls. It was perfect for my undergraduate mix of Psychology and Women's Studies. They agreed to interview me quickly because I had travelled from my home outside Washington DC and was on holiday. I had a copy of my Curriculum Vitae — and as impressive as I thought that was (!) my aunt's first question was regarding *what I would wear to the interview*.

I nonchalantly told her I was sure they would understand that I was only in Dallas on holiday, and so hadn't brought anything appropriate. I was sure they would be okay with my cut-off shorts, as they knew I was a student. Aunt Sharon gave me a withering look and whisked me away to an upscale department store, Neiman Marcus, just an hour before closing.

At this high-end store I immediately felt out of my depth and nearly had a panic attack, feeling I wasn't worthy of such an extravagant gift. In the end, she treated me to my first suit: a simple single-breasted, black silk crepe suit that was perfection itself. I got the job the very next day and my future boss even commented on how well-prepared I was considering I was a college student on holiday!

Now we don't all have our own Aunt Sharon to save us, and I have learned with time that I have to save *myself* – as do you. The women I interviewed for this book were all dressed in different styles: styles that were completely appropriate for their sectors and what was on the agenda for that particular day. They dressed to have attention focused on what they contributed to the team. Their choices didn't distract from what they were saying.

For example, Laura Hinton, a partner at PwC, wore suits to work every day. It was part of her persona and had a positive impact on the way she felt about herself. Her formality of dress works for her: she is one of the youngest women at the firm ever to make Partner. She was clear however that she did not think dressing in a suited uniform was the main key to success. Rather, it was more important to *avoid* certain types of clothing, namely anything that could distract from your words and work as a professional woman.

She remarked: 'Sometimes you see a woman in the office, and when they take their jacket off you see they are wearing a top that could be mistaken for underwear.' She continued: 'If I am noticing it and thinking twice, then other people, both men and women, are probably noticing it too. It will subtly detract from the reputation of her work.'

She continued: 'You certainly don't have to wear dark colours and suits every day — but don't wear anything that could be distracting.'

CLOTHES AS CUES

Caroline, IT Director of a logistics company, was in agreement that clothes should help others focus on your ideas rather than your physical assets. She said: 'For board meetings, my choices are fairly nondescript. I've learned by watching the way men in the office respond to women who don't make the same choices. I've seen their eyes wander, and heard comments when a woman who is wearing a low-cut blouse walks by. It's not the image I want them to have of me.'

Caroline explained her particular buying patterns: 'I don't buy high-street suits — but will go to a quirky boutique. My suits will always have a jacket and the skirts will always be below the knee. Even if I have to go to a black-tie event, my black-tie dress for work will be more conservative than the one I wear if I'm out with friends or my husband.'

This is an important point, as year-end events are a time when many people feel they can 'let their hair down' and vamp it up. Don't let a too-sexy image undo all the hard work you have put in during the rest of the year.

Dress for the job you want, not the job you have. Women often promise themselves they will take their image more seriously *after* they have got the promotion. There is a double downside to this approach.

If they get the promotion before updating their image, they are lulled into complacency thinking, *I got a promotion and — how bad can I look?*

If they *don't* get the promotion, they question: *What's the point? I'm obviously not management material.*

If you want to be promoted, dress like those at the level above you, not like your peers. People aren't that imaginative; they can't see your potential unless you show it to them. Take a clue from senior women around you, as to their level of formality. For example, cleavage and bare shoulders never go down well with senior members of either gender; at best it is inappropriate, at worst threatening.

LOOK INWARDS THROUGH THE EYES OF OTHERS

When you are unsure what your current image is saying about you, the first step is to ask for feedback. It is imperative that you know how others perceive you.

You can't make any necessary changes unless you understand what people think of you and your professional image. Ask a mentor or peer you trust. Go to someone who has the career and image you would like to emulate, whether they are in or out of your office.

Maggie Berry, Director of the networking and careers organisation womenintechnology.co.uk, used this approach when starting out in her career. She wanted information about how her image was helping or hurting her.

She said: 'I definitely didn't go to my boss, initially. I started from scratch and quietly asked a few close individuals for some very personal feedback. Start with your peers and perhaps a layer or two upwards. Ask how you are managing your image: everything from project delivery to the way you dress. You have to be open to hearing some difficult things, but it's one of the quickest ways to understand where you need work. It will also tell you what you're already doing well.'

Jackie Gittins at PwC had a boss who commented on her appearance, which helped stretch her comfort zone. She remembered: 'She told me I was attractive and tall, both of which were helpful, but that I wore a lot of beige and had a soft voice — both of which were not. She asked me to consider wearing red and to project my voice. Those were challenges but very helpful to me in the long term. I can't tell you the date I began to take on that advice. But I would say it was correlated to the upward movement in my career.'

That advice comes back to her now, as she mentors others. As a senior member of staff, she now gives feedback to young women on their image. She said: 'I have worked with a few very capable young women who I have had to personally pull to the side and point out that, while I think their outfit would look great at the weekend, in a male-orientated environment they have to think about what image they are projecting.'

She added: 'Luckily, they have always responded with surprise and gratitude. They were happy to hear it from me rather than have me ignore it and affect their reputations over the long term.' Jackie learned the lessons she shares with office juniors, based on her own experiences early on in her career. She remembered: 'As a trainee at Marks & Spencer, I came into work one morning after an all-night party, with no make-up and looking like death warmed over. My boss hauled me in and told me that it just wasn't on for an executive-track job — which was humbling but I never forgot it.'

QUALITY STREET

As you progress your career, your clothes will need to be of increasing quality. However, before you buy a single item, sort out your current wardrobe. Make three piles; one to keep, one to fix and one for the charity shop. Donate anything that is too big, too small or hasn't been worn in over a year. Dress for Success is a great charity that donates business clothing to low-income women who are entering the workforce — a great way to help another burgeoning career woman. On your way there, take all the items that need fixing to a seamstress who can do all those fiddly alterations you were meaning to get round to.

Buying cheap clothes on the premise that people shouldn't worry about such frivolities is a false economy at best, and complete denial at worst. Buying professional clothes that are good quality and well-cut is not a luxury but a necessity. This is not a licence to spend your pay packet on clothing alone, but an invitation to think about how you could be honouring yourself and the quality of work you do, through your image.

Even if you can't afford or don't want to spend your hard-earned cash on designer togs, many high-street brands, such as Hobbs, LK Bennett or Jaeger do a great range of work wear. If even these seem pricey, save up to make your investment purchases during the sales.

Buy investment pieces that will last: dark wool trouser suits, white cotton button-down shirts, comfortable heels. For example, Shoon specialises in what used to be a contradiction in terms: gorgeous comfortable shoes. To complete your wardrobe you'll need a great winter coat in a wool and cashmere mix; cashmere for the softness, wool for longevity.

If you still aren't sure where to shop, ask a woman from your industry who you think always looks well put together where *she* shops. It's the ultimate form of flattery and a great conversation starter.

- It is easier to create a good first impression than to change an initial bad one.

- Dress for the job to which you aspire — not the one you already have.

- Buy nothing new until you have sorted out your current wardrobe.

A STITCH IN AN EXPERT'S TIME SAVES NINE

The presentation of women in male-dominated fields is tricky because their minority status makes them more noticeable immediately; all the more reason to get it right at the start. Too sexy and you won't be taken seriously; too serious and you'll be seen as the office matron or devoid of personality.

None of us is perfect. I don't know one woman, including myself, who is happy with every element of her appearance. Asking for guidance from a make-up artist, a personal shopper or a friendly hairdresser is nothing to be ashamed of. Many of the savviest women get support from experts on their image. Getting professional guidance is what we do in our jobs every day. In your team, you are smart enough to give people tasks according to their strengths. It should be the same in your personal life. If shopping is not one of your strengths, or you just don't have the time or interest, there is no shame is asking for professional help. Several of the women I interviewed confirmed this.

Of all the women I interviewed, Rebecca George, a partner in the Public Sector division of Deloitte, spoke the most animatedly about image. She realised on her fortieth birthday just how vital image is.

She laughed: 'My sister-in-law asked how ambitious I was. I assured her I was indeed very ambitious, and then she asked why I looked like an *overgrown hippy*. I didn't know whether to take offence or laugh — but she followed it up by sending me to see a style consultant for my birthday gift. And what a gift it was!'

She continued: 'She was a godsend! The consultant asked about everything — my industry, what type of meetings I attended, the male-to-female ratio, even how frequently I met with Europeans versus Americans. She then looked at my hair, make-up, my shape. She went through my closet, getting rid of all the things I mistakenly thought suited me best, and then helped me to choose a new wardrobe complete with handbags and shoes. She was amazing — the best gift I could have got!'

This exercise had been an eye-opening experience for Rebecca, and one that she credits with completely transforming her look and her sense of confidence. When we met, she was in a sharp suit with a red jacket, and it fitted her personality perfectly. She now swears by personal shoppers, saying they save her time and money because she wears everything they choose, rather than make costly mistakes that just hang in the back of her wardrobe.

She enthused: 'It's wonderful. I just call ahead, tell them where I am going — whether it's a client dinner, a garden party, or even when I collected my OBE from Buckingham Palace — and I just go and pick it up. It's always something I would not have picked for myself, and yet it's always perfect. It's vital, as women have a thinner line to tread, to look serious but *not like a man*.'

Similarly, Mary Hensher realised early on the importance of projecting the right image. By the time she had reached her mid-twenties, she had being given management responsibilities. She realised she needed to be dressing up, not just for herself, but for her juniors who looked to her as an example. She took matters *into her own hands* and hired an image consultant.

Mary said: 'I hired her for myself — but then was so impressed, I asked her to come in and work with my whole department. Her best advice was to be aware that, whatever image you create with your clothing, make sure it is the image you *intend*. Don't create an image by accident. She suggested, *If you want to come into work in a mini skirt and fishnet tights, then go ahead. But do it because that is the image you intend to create, not because you are unaware of the impression you will create.'*

Essentially, if you feel at all challenged on the style front, or want to raise your image to the next level, make an appointment with a personal shopper or image consultant. There is an unhelpful assumption that women *love to shop*. But think of all the people you have to delegate to on a daily basis to enable you to accomplish all that you do. I like to look stylish but I hate shopping — there is a big difference. I think of all the things I would rather be doing with my time — taking a walk, reading a good book, coaching a client — than struggling through racks of clothes with a limited imagination and budget. What's the image you would like to project ... and what would you rather be doing with your time?

No Mixed Messages

It is interesting to note that many women wear colours or a certain style without ever realising the message they are sending.

Carol Collins, a Master of the Federation of Image Consultants, has noticed a shift away from dress-down days and casual Fridays. She cited that many senior executives said they were hard to manage. There were no guidelines other than for people to use their own *best judgement* — which is widely open to interpretation.

The downside for many women was how much flesh was now on show with exposed shoulders, low necklines, short skirts and belly-skimming tops. Carol had heard of more than one City firm cancelling their dress-down days because of the mixed messages employees were sending.

As we discussed, working with the image consultant had a huge impact on Mary Hensher, who was admittedly coming out of a 'scruffy' post-college phase. She dresses conservatively now, and does this because she wants others to focus on what she is saying, not on what she is wearing.

She explained: 'It isn't appropriate to wear low-cut blouses because even the women will be staring at you. You don't want to distract people from everything you have worked so hard for. Winning your argument might be tough enough — but with the wrong clothes, you've just defeated yourself.'

Mary is very practical about what she wears, and thinks through each day's activities before choosing her outfits. 'I don't wear high heels if I am giving a presentation where I will be standing, as I might teeter in them since they are not my usual dress. If I am going to three sit-down meetings in a row, I won't wear something that crumples easily, either. Just use common sense as to what will make the best impact on that day. People wear clothes to impress other people — that's no secret. But you can spot those who feel uncomfortable in what they are wearing,' she said.

Carol Collins, the aforementioned image consultant who works with multinational banks, would agree. She regularly works with clients who are seeking job promotion or making a career change. In short, she works with women who want to progress their careers and realise that, despite all their qualifications, they are not progressing as quickly as they would like. The effect of working on someone's image can be transformative for her clients. The decision to work with Carol may be born out of a crisis of confidence or a current career challenge — but she finds that the core beliefs a client has about image stem from childhood.

She remembered: 'I once did a simple colour analysis for a professional woman in her sixties. It seemed simple at the time — but she turned to me and said that I had changed her life. She had always lived in the shadow of her prettier sister and recalled how her mother would comment that she 'couldn't make a silk purse out of a sow's ear' when she was a teenager getting ready to go out for the evening. I wanted to *cry* at the thought of this woman having to carry that comment around, her whole life. It just reminded me it's never too late to treat yourself with respect and develop your confidence.'

IMAGE REFLECTS WORTH

Carol commented that sometimes women were so busy getting their qualifications and putting their careers in order that they had neglected the first thing that people pass judgement on: the image they present to the world. A poor image can let down an otherwise stellar work ethic.

I agreed with her that I too had clients who initially liked to think that concerns about image were for women in other industries. However, I have yet to meet a woman whose career did not benefit from putting forth her best image. I also admitted that it can seem overwhelming if addressing clothing, hair and make-up is relatively new.

Additionally, since women multi-task effectively every single day, asking for help in these most personal of areas can make a woman feel as if she's on the back foot, or that there must be something wrong if it doesn't all come naturally to her.

Most professional women know they cannot do everything perfectly *at work* and hence need to have the best professional advice to support them. Sometimes they don't automatically recognise the need to get the best help for their own images; working with an image coach can help you 'reflect your worth', as Carol says, in a competitive world.

Carol explained: 'Even if you don't feel that you are the size you would like to be or have the shape you once did, we can all offer something visually. In fact, it is probably even more important when we don't feel confident in our appearance, to make more of an effort with a great haircut or well-applied make-up. No one needs heavy make-up, and even ten extra minutes spent on yourself in the morning is well-invested.

'If you put the effort in, others will notice and you will feel better about yourself. This in turn will affect everything you do, and people around you will notice the difference, even if they can't put their finger on what about you changed.'

I was reminded of Rebecca George's shock at her sister-in-law's initial referral to a style consultant, when Carol laughed that not all of her clients had initially been enthusiastic about working with an image consultant. However, they soon overcame their original dubiousness.

She remembered: 'I once worked with an ambitious young woman who was aiming for a Junior Partner role within her firm. Her mother-in-law gifted my services to her and she was very sceptical when we met. She was in her thirties but looked like the fresh-faced eighteen-year-old girl next door, with her hair scraped back in a ponytail and a bare face. She said she had no time to devote to her image in the morning — but instead of colluding with her that there was no extra time, we took it from the other end of the day!

'Rather than feeling rushed for her shower in the morning, she made a simple switch to a relaxing bath and hair-drying in the evening. She also got up ten minutes earlier in the morning, giving herself the few extra minutes she needed to put on a bit of make-up. She called me two months later, thanking me for my help as she had just been made Partner. That was a fantastic call to receive!'

No doubt the work this junior partner had contributed to the firm also spoke volumes — but addressing her image probably helped *tip the balance* in her favour.

THE LANGUAGE OF COLOUR

Like Jackie Gittins, who used to wear a good deal of beige, Carol was also an advocate for the importance of colour. Carol joked: 'When I want to make a clear point in a meeting, I wear a red jacket — it shows I'm "on" and powerful. On the other hand, if I wanted to take a back seat to proceedings, I would wear a neutral colour.'

She recalled a particular client who was a board member of a major UK retailer: 'She arrived at the Annual General Meeting in a slick black pantsuit, but with the most wonderful red patent leather stilettos, and a black belt cinched in with a red clasp. You knew she was there to do business! She was enjoying *being a woman* and understood the impact she had on others.'

To keep your accessories as professional as the rest of you, invest in a few key pieces. A good dark leather handbag, which will hold unfolded A4 papers plus your diary, laptop and blackberry or mobile, should be a staple. The handbags I reach for on a daily basis can fit all of these plus whatever book I am currently reading, at a pinch. I'm a big fan of keeping your ensemble to just one bag, as a laptop case, a too-small handbag plus briefcase and gym kit detract from a polished look. When packing for business travel, stick to one neutral as a base colour for your accessories: either brown or black.

Your clothes will then coordinate with shoes, handbags and belts for every outfit. Buy a wheelie suitcase, ideally one small enough to fit the regulations for the overhead compartment in airplanes.

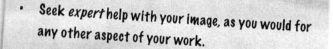

- Seek expert help with your image, as you would for any other aspect of your work.

- Your image should enhance, not distract from, your work.

- Keep your bag simple, practical and of excellent quality.

ALTERING YOUR IMAGE

If you are starting to recognise how much you might benefit from re-addressing your image, now might be the ideal time.

Sometimes women change their dress as a clear message to themselves; others are saying that they want to be regarded by other people differently than they had in the past. If you are looking for a promotion or want to be taken more seriously, dress like people in the rung above you, not like your existing colleagues.

The truth is, people can't see your potential unless you visibly show them — and that might apply to how you see *yourself* as well. I once worked with a client in New York whom I will call Tammy, an administrator in a large hospital. She was a very spiritual client and had a strong belief in God, and she wanted to move to a more fulfilling role. We often discussed her experiences in terms of the lessons she was learning spiritually.

During our time together, Tammy realised she had a history of not respecting or valuing herself. For example, she earned well but had not bought herself a new winter coat for more than ten years; this was the same length of time since she had moved from one unfulfilling role to another.

With my encouragement, Tammy found a new job. The weekend before she was due to start, gale force winds and a record-breaking winter storm hit the mid-Atlantic region. This *forced* her to buy her first 'good coat' in ten years. She bought the coat on the Sunday. As we talked, Tammy made sense of this by recognising that '…God sent the storms to force me to take on this new image and value myself well.'

It was fascinating that the worst storm in over a decade hit the same weekend she was about to start a new job where she would have to take herself and her image seriously, and the meaning she assigned to this freak occurrence. To paraphrase from L'Oréal, Tammy had to believe she was "worth it" before she would invest in her image.

DRESSING FOR GRAVITAS

Other women made changes to their image that demonstrated how comfortable they were in their own skin — a change which is instantly attractive to others. Ana Pacheco at PwC fell into this category. She *glowed* when I met her. Ana seemed very at ease with herself and, as we discussed image, she opened up about her recent transformation.

Ana had started her career wearing suits in the palette of colours that is the choice of many professional women: black, grey and navy. She did this to convey that she wanted to be taken seriously. She was in the marketing department, an internal support function and one that was not always as valued as the client-facing departments.

Being taken seriously can feel relevant for those who are young and want to portray more gravitas. I certainly cut my own long blonde hair very short in my first job, to rid myself of the image of being the 'office baby' since I was just 22, and a good ten years younger than even the next youngest member of staff.

Ana continued: 'I enter rooms with strangers all the time, and I wanted to be respected and even taken for having a client-servicing role until introductions were made. I wanted them to know that I took my job seriously and the suits helped,' she explained.

I met her in August. She had become fed up with wearing suits for the previous six years, and had started to make changes the previous January. She remarked: 'I noticed there were other women who were more senior to me who didn't necessarily wear suits like a coat of armour. I decided to experiment and began wearing dresses, which was so much more comfortable and made me feel like a woman again.'

She explained: 'It all started during the sales when I saw a wrap dress I absolutely loved but realised I would never wear to work — which was just silly. I realised that I had become too prescriptive, which was limiting me. I bought the dress and started wearing it to work … and getting compliments. Since then everything has changed. I wear make-up now, and got new glasses and treated myself to new shoes.'

Maggie Berry also went through a change in her everyday working attire. When she first started her role, she wore suits every day in an environment where it wasn't necessary on a day-to-day basis. She eventually found it stifling, and over time she made a change. She would also recommend gradual change to others looking to update their image.

'You don't need to suddenly start wearing suits every day — people will think you are interviewing for other jobs! But you can do it *gradually*. I started this job by wearing suits every day and then began to ease skirts and then dresses in. I am most comfortable now, as I really like dresses but I still wear my suits when I'm going to meet a corporate client, for example,' she explained.

REBEL IN A RED DRESS

I have often noticed that women who are more established in their careers tend to become more comfortable introducing elements of brighter, more feminine colours over time. They seem less inclined to wear the traditional suit or play by the established rule of dress.

As a woman progresses her career and her confidence increases, she is often more willing to shed her 'armour'. She may be more experimental with the rules of dress, knowing she has earned the right to do so and is unlikely to be challenged as she has already established her professional credibility.

Lis Astall told a great story about how she stretched her boundaries in this regard. Her clothes were immaculate and very expensive-looking but she teased that while she stayed within the bounds of what would be acceptable dress for her role — suits, primarily — she did test the limits now and again.

She laughed when remembering one example: 'We received a memo in the office saying that people could not wear leather trousers or skirts in the office because of the tone they set.' Lis, being one of the most senior women at Accenture in Europe, did not take kindly to the diktat. 'I had never worn leather before, but that day I went out and bought a leather skirt. Now, it's a *designer* leather skirt. It's a very conservative cut and of the softest, buttery leather imaginable, and it fits well with all my jackets — but it's still leather!' she laughs knowingly.

The same thing occurred when they issued a statement banning dangling earrings. She matter-of-factly explained: 'I went out and bought the most understated but dangling pink diamond earrings I could find. I didn't need them but I wanted them and now I wear them all the time.'

Needless to say, in neither case was she reprimanded for her breach of 'the rules'. These were simply exercises in retaining a sense of style and self-image whilst remaining within otherwise strict boundaries of the City dress code.

When I mentioned to Ana Pacheco this tendency to disobey the rules as you become more confident in your role, she wholeheartedly agreed. It is perhaps not coincidence that this change in her style came after proving herself at the company for several years.

Ana added: 'I just feel much better about my style now. I feel like more of a woman and I'm much more confident. Once I had started the change, I realised how much I liked it and it just snowballed from there.'

How had others reacted to the change? She replied: 'People are very positive. I realise now that I can wear dresses and still do a good job and people won't take me any less seriously.'

Several of the women I interviewed discussed how make-up was one factor that made the difference for them, giving them a more polished feel, even if it was just blusher, mascara and lipstick. Paying attention to these details gave them a sense of finesse and confidence that sealed the package for them.

CLOTHES HORSES FOR COURSES

Like other women I interviewed, Maggie Berry, Director of womenintechnology.co.uk, knew the importance of putting clothing choices *in context*, both for your sector and depending on your day's activities.

These women know that there is no single right look for every day — only that which is right for each role you play on any given day. She explained: 'I wear a lot of dresses — but tailor my choices according to where I am going each day. If I was going to see one of the investment bank sponsors, such as Morgan Stanley, I would wear a suit. But if I were going to see Google, then I wouldn't, because they don't wear suits and I'd feel uncomfortable and overdressed.

'One size does not fit all and you have to take that into account. I always stick to my guns on this and say, *Dress and presentation are really important.* I don't believe your work simply speaks for itself — you have to do everything else as well as delivering on your day job if you want promotion. It's about taking pride in your appearance, your work and what you deliver. They all go hand in hand.'

Science and IT are industries where there is no single set dress code; rather, it is the *type* of organisation in which a woman works that dictates what she wears. For example, most women I know, who are in IT in the financial sector or in management consultancy, wear suits or dresses. However, the standard dress is more informal within other types of IT organisations, such as start-ups or some large organisations such as Google and Yahoo. In Microsoft, for example, people dress fairly casually on a day-to-day basis. However, even if you work in an organisation like this, there are still general rules that set the successful women apart from their colleagues.

When I met Jane Lewis of Microsoft, for example, she was wearing tailored jeans and a casual shirt. However, she made a specific point of mentioning that, when she is conducting interviews or working with clients, she wears a suit. She said: 'If I am visiting a client I've never met, you sometimes see them looking behind you for the man in your team. So I am always impeccably dressed in a suit to remind them that I'm the senior engineer on the project.'

Additionally, there are discrepancies to be aware of, even if presenting to internal clients and colleagues. Jane added: 'When I am doing an internal presentation, like at the Windows 2008 launch, I dress in what could be considered the standard issue blue shirt and khaki trousers — so, more formal than normal, but still casual as is appropriate for the occasion.'

NOT ALL UNIFORMS HAVE EPAULETTES

On the other hand, Mary Hensher, also in IT but working at Deloitte, wore a suit when I interviewed her. She is a partner at a global professional services firm and works in the City of London where suiting is the standard practice. She recognised that dress code is not sector-specific, but *company*-specific. She explained: 'I work in IT — but if I had gone to a different company and was going to be in a dark bunker writing software, I would probably be wearing a black tee shirt. IT companies have a dress code too, but it is a completely different dress code. It's tee shirts and chinos — but it's still a uniform, isn't it? The uniform for the City, however, is a suit and most people know that going in.'

Nicky Clayton, a Professor of Comparative Cognition at the University of Cambridge, admittedly loves clothes, but also knew to dress appropriately for her daily activities. Before our meeting, I had seen an article in the national Press about her research, with an accompanying photograph where her hair was straight and she wore a tailored navy trouser suit. I was surprised then, when on the day of our interview she wore a short frilly skirt and high heels. Nicky looked fabulous but knew that, for professional photos that will reach a wider audience, she had to dress more conservatively. She admitted she is much more comfortable in feminine clothing, partly because she primarily spends her days in the laboratory and her free evenings in a dance studio.

Nicky remarked: 'I am only five foot tall, so I use heels to help give me height — but also because I love them. I hate the idea that women need to dress like a man to be respected. Sensible grey clothes and your hair in a bun — that's not me. And like most women, I give my best when I am confident and not feeling dowdy.'

Nicky learned how important it is to contextualise your clothing, early in her career. She remembered: 'When I went for my first Junior Research Fellowship in my twenties, I wore a little red mini skirt. Disappointingly, I didn't get the position.'

She quipped: 'My mentor tactfully pointed out that with my flowing blonde hair and cute red outfit, I may not have fitted their idea of what a Junior Research Fellow looked like. So, the next time, I wore my outfit from the Oxford Symphony Orchestra: a long black skirt and a plain white top. I got the Fellowship that time!'

Whether the panel's decision could be pinned down to her attire remains uncertain. What *is* certain is that she learned not to leave her image to chance in important situations — thereby removing any lingering doubt someone might have about her credibility and judgement.

SUMMERTIME AND THE DRESSING'S NOT EASY

I met Maggie Berry for our interview on a particularly hot June day. How did she steer clear of the minefield that is summer dressing? Maggie answered: 'Summer dresses without sleeves or flip-flops are never appropriate. If in doubt, wear more, not less. I will still wear summer dresses to the office, but I buy a matching cardigan as well. I will put a tank-top underneath a button-down shirt to give it a higher neckline. So I still buy what I want to wear but I dress it up conservatively for work.'

When asked why she took these precautions, she echoed the voices of the other women I had spoken to, saying it was her sense of professionalism. Besides mentioning the impact on others, she also felt *stronger* when appropriately dressed. She declared: 'I just feel so much more confident when I go into a new place and think, *Yes, I've got the right clothes on.* There is nothing worse than starting a meeting from a position of thinking, *I am not as smart as they are.* It undermines the very confidence you need to succeed in your meeting.'

One issue that particularly vexes me is summer shoes: open-toed or not? I do wear open-toed sandals with a slight heel for work — but it depends where I am working. If I am in the City and at a corporate client, then closed toe or sling-backs are the order of the day. However, if I am working with a more informal employer or meeting private clients then I will wear open-toed shoes.

I do think if you are going to wear open-toed shoes, in or out of the office, then a pedicure is a basic act of public kindness!

As for summer dressing in general, tailored and knee-length shorts are doable; however, stick with skirts if you are like me and don't quite have the pins to pull off the 'city shorts' look. And while you may want to wear your latest summer dress, add a cardigan or tailored short-sleeved jacket to an otherwise sleeveless or strapless dress to make it office-appropriate. This is more professional as well as practical, as most offices are over air-conditioned in any case. Your co-workers should be talking about your last report, not your tan lines — warm weather does not mean you can dress as if you are on holiday.

- There is no single right look that works for every occasion or every day.

- For important occasions, consider changing your look to suit your purpose.

- Take particular care choosing what to wear in summer.

MAKING UP IS HARD TO DO

I also believe that going completely without make-up is no longer a sensible option. This is not about vanity; it is about projecting the professional image that matches the professional job you do. Women who do wear it earn up to 30 per cent more than those who don't — an ugly truth, perhaps, but reality all the same[2].

[2] Hamermesh, D. & Biddle, J. (1994) "Beauty and the Labor Market", American Economic Association

156

This is not to say that you must wear make-up to get ahead in a male-dominated workplace; it is, rather, to be aware that when it is mainly men who are awarding promotions, you will find it valuable to play at least *this* part of their game in order to get and keep their confidence in your professional ability. Taking care about your appearance and being taken seriously for your contribution to the work are not mutually exclusive.

Hair is also part of the package and must be considered accordingly. An odd but good tip is to use newsreaders for guidance – attractive but not overdone, not too trendy to be distracting. It is part of their job to have an image that is universally appealing, and not offensive to anyone.

Curly hair should be tamed if you want to appear businesslike and in control. To that end, straighter, glossy hair is a good look for most professional women. Frizzy locks give the impression you are not in control of your hair, that your eye for detail is not great and you can't be bothered. This perception was evident even in the creation of the cover for this book. We initially looked at images of women and those images of women with curly out-of-control hair were universally given the thumbs down from my clients.

A professional image is a subtle hint that you are ready to raise the bar on your career.

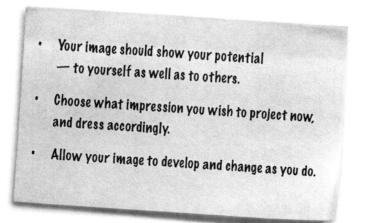

- Your image should show your potential — to yourself as well as to others.

- Choose what impression you wish to project now, and dress accordingly.

- Allow your image to develop and change as you do.

STYLE CONQUERS AGEISM

Middle age is the awkward period

when Father Time starts catching up with Mother Nature.

— Harold Coffin

Some of the women I interviewed pointed out that, while the odds might have been stacked against them as a woman, *ageism* can be a pernicious problem too — particularly in roles where creativity and fresh perspectives are highly valued.

Janet Davies, who is in her late forties, said: 'I'm still young and future-focused enough to have plenty of decent ideas in my head yet. I think there is a particularly annoying misconception that older people somehow can't add value with innovative ideas and this affects men, too.'

Unfortunately, her concern is borne out by the evidence. At the tail end of 2008, reports of ageism in the workplace had more than tripled from just a year earlier[3]. In a poor economy, older workers are often prime targets for redundancy, especially in industries that thrive on a young and fresh image, such as IT.

She continued: 'Warren Bennis and Robert Thomas refer to this interesting and valuable quality they call *neoteny* (the retention of youthful characteristics in adulthood) in their book *Geeks and Geezers: How Era, Values and Defining Moments Shape Leaders*[4] — I wish more people would read it.'

This also affected the way she presented herself. 'When I was in my twenties, I had to dress more conservatively than I would have otherwise done in order

[3] Syal, R. & Hill, A. (2008) "Claims Against Ageism at Work Triple in a Year", The Observer, December 7
[4] Bennis, W. & Thomas, R. (2007) "Geeks and Geezers: How Era, Values and Defining Moments Shape Leaders", Harvard Business School Press

to be taken seriously. No one does that now, thank goodness: we all worship at the altar of youth! Now I'm in my forties, I almost have to do the opposite to be careful not to look frumpy!' she laughed.

Other women also admitted to dressing to downplay the effect their perceived age had on others in the office. As opposed to Janet's example, Matilda Venter found dressing older useful when she first started her career. She naturally looks very young, and initially found this a disadvantage when working in South Africa where she started her career.

She remembered: 'When I was starting out at 23, I looked 18, which wasn't helpful. South Africa is very chauvinistic, and to look so young was a real challenge. So I dressed formally and never provocatively to exert a presence that seemed older.'

This was a trend she had continued, even some 20 years later. On the day of our interview, she apologised for her informal dress. This was notable as she was still one of the most formally dressed women I interviewed. She wore heels, a skirt and immaculate make-up — but was not in her standard attire of a business suit. She explained that dressing the part had been of absolute importance to her from the beginning, explaining that it showed 'pride in yourself and in your work'.

Similarly, when interviewing for my first post-PhD position in Washington DC at a market research company, I pulled out the trusty black skirt suit my Aunt Sharon had bought me to bolster my confidence and credibility. My future boss commented on how much she liked the suit, and that she and other members of the team rarely dressed so professionally. I joked that she and other members of the team were not applying for a new job. She smiled knowingly and said: 'No, you are right. You're right to make an extra effort' — just before she offered me the job.

I would love to think that the fact that I've been offered almost every job I have ever applied for is testament to my sheer brilliance! Actually, it probably has more to do with the fact that, regardless of what the situation calls for on an ongoing basis, I have always tried to put my best foot forward when it comes to the image I project.

FASHION VICTIMS FALL PREY TO CAREER BLUNDERS

Like all women, I certainly do not get it right all the time. I have had mishaps with an oddly-placed scarf or belt, flats when I should have worn heels, bare legs when I should have worn tights. Dressing down when I should have dressed up.

I even recall interviewing one senior executive for this book on a hot summer day, wearing a dress and deciding on a whim that since it was a warm day I didn't need tights. As soon as I got to her office and saw all the other professional women clad in the sheerest of silk hose, I realised my mistake. When we sat down and I crossed my legs, she gave me a quick once-over, barely perceptible to anyone else. But I noticed it as I had already been aware that I had perhaps not made the best choice. And as Maggie Berry pointed out about being comfortable, while there were other women at the office doing the same, I felt self-conscious throughout the interview, which meant I wasn't at my best. It was a reminder for me: if in doubt, *dress up*, not down. I still make blunders if I haven't made the right enquiries or scoped out the environment before attending. Despite such gaffes, which happen to all of us, I always try to look my best when doing anything public-facing. But more often than not I get the response I want: one suggesting that people take me and my potential contributions seriously.

That's all you can ask when you want to raise your game in the workplace and gain the credibility that's needed to engage with *the boys' club*.

- Dress for your age but on-trend; it reminds people that your ideas are fresh.

- If you wouldn't want your boss to see you in it, don't wear it.

- When in doubt, always dress up.

EIGHT

ESTABLISHING YOUR PRESENCE

No one can make you feel inferior without your consent.

— Eleanor Roosevelt

As a woman in a male-dominated field, it is vital to establish your professional presence. It will give you a sense of gravitas, and let people know you are key player in the game of success. Your presence comes from both your communication and your non-verbal skills. It is the way you hold yourself, the way you command attention for your ideas, and what people say about you when you are not in the room.

However, establishing a credible presence does not mean that you should establish a *male* presence. One of the main issues I hear from women in these fields is how to create a presence that inspires confidence in men, without losing yourself as a woman. The examples of the women below illustrate that you do not have to act like a man to be taken as seriously as a woman.

SAVVY SOCIALISING

As a woman in a male-dominated field, entertaining clients and building relationships through social contact are vital though not always straightforward. For example, I have yet to meet a woman who has the interest or time to take a client golfing, a long held networking tradition for men. Women who want to develop relationships during office hours, through activities traditionally associated with male-dominated fields such as drinking or at sporting events, are rare.

Equally, women don't tend to enjoy 'impromptu' after-works drinks that go on late into the night. Most women can engage in after-works drinks now and again if given enough forewarning. However, impromptu get-togethers can be difficult for women with families, or even for women who just happen to value their own social lives and time away from work.

Maggie Berry, Director of womenintechnology, agrees. She indicated that, for her members, some of the key draws for her events were the focused attention on career development and the advance marketing that allowed women to *plan* to attend.

She explained: 'One of the comments I hear is that women can't just spontaneously decide to go to the pub after work. They have different interests and responsibilities. If you know your team is going out on a Tuesday, you can plan around that. A woman can get the appropriate childcare and make transport arrangements ahead of time. Our members like to network — but like to set time aside specifically for it, rather than having to make themselves available *all* the time.'

If you avoid socialising completely, you will not be privy to political discussions, strengthening relationships or hearing about career opportunities that are almost always first discussed informally. Furthermore, you will send out the message that you are an outsider with *no interest* in becoming an insider.

That being said, most women recognise that they need to make time to socialise with clients and colleagues on work trips or dinner out — which, while it has its obvious benefits, also has potential pitfalls.

In addition to taking up what precious little time working women have, there is the danger of sending mixed messages to clients or colleagues — especially in settings where alcohol is involved. This is a potential time to shine, as people promote those with whom they feel comfortable and who will make a good impression on their clients. Tread carefully, though, because if you get it wrong, you can backtrack your career considerably.

PICK YOUR MOMENTS

Laura Hinton said that, if she enjoyed working with a client, she was happy to take them to dinner as and when she needed to. However, like other women, she was wary of asking a client to dinner early on in the relationship, in case it should be misconstrued. Laura explained: 'I don't want to have to spell it out for them by asking them to dinner and taking pains to say that it is only to talk about work. It's best if I avoid dinners and drinks and do lunches or breakfasts, which are less open to any potential misinterpretation. As the relationship progresses, however, shared meals are a good way of showing you like the other person and want to develop the relationship.'

Breakfast, lunch and coffee meetings are unlikely to be misconstrued, and have the additional advantage of being less likely times to feel obliged to order alcohol with the meal. For example, you can invent a deadline back at the office if need be. With dinner, you end the evening when you want to go home, which can be harder to negotiate your way out of if your dinner companions pressure you to stay. During the day, you can always say you have a meeting at the office, which is a more socially acceptable way of curtailing the evening than saying you just want to go home.

A word of caution: women's alcohol tolerance is much lower than men's. This is especially important to remember when you work primarily with men, who expect everyone to participate equally in rounds of drinks. If you are going to share a drink with a client or colleague, you can surreptitiously alternate your drinks with soda or fizzy water, or say you are driving home. Have a good time but just don't let one night undo all the careful hard work you have put in throughout the year!

My own husband was chief executive of a children's charity for six years, and we were expected to attend a great number of fundraising social functions and gala dinners as part of his job. On the face of it, I was merely invited as his guest, and so it could seem like a social event. However, I knew we were *always 'on'* and still at work. Accordingly, I always limited how much I drank so that I remained sober. It was amazing how much more useful I was to him by doing this. I remembered obscure conversations, and points of action that were to be taken, namely when someone mentioned making a large donation that they might otherwise have conveniently forgotten the next day!

I was of much more use to him and the charity, as well as to myself, if I just sipped my drink slowly and alternated it with water throughout the night. I learned this from an early job where I got drunk on a work trip and felt shamefaced at the breakfast buffet the next day. It was a humbling experience to see people whispering and smiling — and I didn't get drunk at a work event ever again. It may be called a 'work party', but remember it's still *work*.

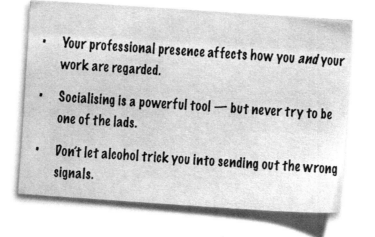

- Your professional presence affects how you and your work are regarded.

- Socialising is a powerful tool — but never try to be one of the lads.

- Don't let alcohol trick you into sending out the wrong signals.

FLIRTING AND OTHER CONTACT SPORTS

When socialising with colleagues or clients, it is easy to forget that there is a fine line between being charming and being too flirtatious. This is particularly important to remember for women who work primarily with men, as male colleagues are not always the greatest judges of the difference between friendliness and genuine romantic interest! There are ways to be fun and humorous without your intention being misconstrued.

It may seem obvious — but steer clear of telling sexual jokes. It suggests you are 'game' and can open the floodgates to being on the receiving end of many more jokes — most of which you won't want to hear. It can also give the impression that you are comfortable with sexist jokes or trying to be *one of the lads*.

Interestingly, research in the US police force, another heavily male industry suggests that the telling of gender-related jokes, long-considered a safe way of 'letting off steam' for the men involved, actually *increases* levels of stress in the workplace for both female police officers *and* their well-educated male colleagues[1]. Sexist jokes can no doubt be uncomfortable for women who want to maintain their credibility, and not draw attention to their sense of 'otherness' in a profession where being 'tough' is the standard. However, the researchers suggest that well-educated men's perceptions of gender roles might have been challenged during their education and they were therefore less likely to tell such jokes themselves as well as be more uncomfortable when they were told by others – even if they do not speak out against such joking. The bottom line is that sexist jokes are not good for *anyone*.

Also, speaking intimately about your private life is another area that can easily be misconstrued, with confusing ramifications for everyone. Talking about your love life or relationship problems with any colleague you are attracted to, or who *might be attracted to you*, is a definite no-no. It may signal to your colleague that you don't know your boundaries well or are open to advances. Additionally, other colleagues who witness what they perceive as flirtation will not rate you as credible or professional — two of the very things for which women looking to raise their profile want to be known.

I once worked with a client, whom I will call Sonia, whose colleague — a Human Resources manager no less — brought to an after-work drinks party a board game that focused on the sexual proclivities of all the participants. Sonia talked about how the colleague lost all credibility within the team. This was particularly damaging to the woman's reputation as she was the HR representative to whom others should ostensibly go in times of distress, such as if they had experienced sexual harassment at work.

[1] Kurtz, D. (2008) "Controlled Burn: The Gendering of Stress and Burnout in Modern Policing", Feminist Criminology, Vol. 3, No. 3 pp. 216-238

Another client mentioned how some of the 'bimbos' in her team frequently instant-messaged male colleagues their opinions about other colleagues. The men involved were seen as engaging in playful banter; however, the women who participated were soon thought of as gossipy and not considered to be serious management material; the ultimate double standard, I know, but reality all the same. Additionally, it contributed to an *us and them* mentality within the unit, which became divisive and ultimately hurt the team's performance.

If in doubt, consider what you would think if you saw another colleague behaving in the way you are behaving. Or, indeed, whether you would feel the need to hide what you are doing from your husband or partner. That is always a sobering thought that can help keep you out of trouble.

Laura Hinton remembered a woman she had worked with, whose flirtatious reputation damaged her credibility. She related: 'She had a reputation for being a bimbo, taking out clients and flattering them to get work. The downside for her is that I know there was a lot of work put into the contracts once she had won them — but colleagues were oblivious to this. Her *reputation* suggested that she fluttered her eyelashes without any knowledge to back it up, which wasn't true but ultimately discredited her all the same!'

While this former colleague was clearly bringing in work and delivering on these projects, her behaviour diminished any and all of her achievements. When asked how to draw the line between being charming and unhelpful flirtation, Laura remarked: 'It should be obvious: don't rub their knees or get involved in games where you sit on their lap or drink too much — know your limit. Or abstain from drinking altogether.'

PITCH IT JUST RIGHT

I am by no means advocating a 'hands-off' approach to interacting with colleagues. I firmly believe that the happiest women working in these fields are those who do authentically engage in convivial and warm relationships with their colleagues. You spend too much time at work not to enjoy the people, or to keep up a deadpan facade. You must be authentic and friendly with your colleagues. We can all smell a phoney a mile away, just as we resent someone who artificially seems to keep her distance. It is a fine line to tread, and indeed a particularly unfair one for women who work primarily with men.

However, always be aware that what you say about your private life, such as joking about woes in your love life, or what you would like in a future partner, or troubles with the nanny or getting childcare, can all be used against you in a way they are not for your male colleagues.

When your male colleague leaves early for a sick child, he is considered a concerned and admirably 'hands-on' dad; if a woman does the same, too often her commitment to the job is questioned. Be social and enjoy your colleagues by all means, just know that no matter how laid-back and easy-going you are, you will *never* be truly considered one of the boys.

It should be noted that for all the warnings against flirtation, more and more people are meeting their partners in the workplace simply because both men and women are spending a larger proportion of their time in the office. This is one area where I have to admit I haven't always followed the best advice. I did date a colleague after I came to the UK; for a while it was an uncomfortable tightrope for us both, and one that could have left me flat on my face. In fact, shortly after we began dating we both left the company. We had tried unsuccessfully to keep our relationship a secret, and we certainly didn't get a warm send-off from colleagues, with whom we had previously had good relationships. But overall, we lucked out and ten years later are happily married.

However, I recognise it was a huge risk and could just as easily have gone wrong. In truth, most office affairs do not end well — especially for the woman. As more companies are recognising this, some firms are taking the precaution of asking employees they know to be in relationships to sign waivers saying they will not hold the company legally responsible if a romantic relationship ends badly.

The key is to minimise the risk by being careful about the messages your behaviour sends out. It is tricky enough to be heard for your contributions as a woman in some of these fields; don't let anyone put a question mark against your reputation because of your *own* actions.

- Networking with clients and colleagues is a must.
- Schedule meals with clients for breakfast or lunch.
- If you tell non-pc jokes, expect to hear more — some of which you won't like.

CONTROLLING EMOTIONS

It is ironic that professional women invest so much effort, time and passion into their work — and yet are expected *not* to take things personally or become emotional if things go poorly.

This is a greater challenge for many of these professional women, than it is for women who are in jobs for which they don't care so much. It's a fine balance: we ask professionals to give their all to their jobs but then hold it against them if they bring their emotions to work.

For example, weeping at work is a particular taboo, though most of my clients admit to having cried at least once during their professional lives — more frequently in the privacy of a locked toilet during particularly difficult times. During coaching sessions, clients sometimes cry because of an issue we are looking at, and they routinely apologise. While crying is never the goal of any particular session, it is certainly not a problem. To me, it just shows me how passionate they are as individuals for both their careers and personal lives.

It does not make them do their jobs any less effectively; it merely shows they are human with a great deal of emotional and intellectual energy invested in their careers. We wouldn't question it if a mother cried when her child was failing at school. Should that mother's *career* be going through a tumultuous period, however, she is expected to put on a brave face.

When asked what advice she would give other women working in male-dominated fields, Matilda Venter agreed that managing emotions was a key issue for many women. 'Junior colleagues often struggle with stressful situations and tears are not uncommon. If you are young and still developing, there is more tolerance — but patience eventually wears thin, and you have to find ways to channel that energy outside of work and maintain a professional persona in the office.'

Managing and interpreting emotions was a theme mentioned by several of the women, who noted that men often showed their emotions through being argumentative or combative. Many male colleagues were also considered poor at reading the emotions of those around them — namely their female peers.

Angela Mohtashemi at PwC compared the attitudes, of her mostly male colleagues, to those of her colleagues in her earliest career as a primary school teacher where most of her peers were women. She recalled an incident more recently that was enlightening for her. She remembered: 'I had come in to a meeting a few minutes late, a rarity for me, because of a problem at home. There was only one chair left at the end of the table, which I slunk into.

'After the meeting, one of the senior partners came to me and chastised me for looking so miserable during the meeting, as well as sitting at the head of the table when I had the audacity to be late.' She pointed out: 'If the same thing had happened at a *teachers'* meeting, all the other teachers would have immediately asked what the matter was and if I was okay. It had not occurred to my male colleague that something other than work may be an issue. Instead he thought I couldn't be bothered to turn up on time and then was so bored that my misery showed all across my face!'

Professor Athene Donald agreed that controlling emotions is an important issue for women: 'There have been times when I felt I was being ignored simply because I am a woman, and it has been difficult to see my ideas accepted only after a man suggests them. But I have had to learn to control my emotions. It can be a vicious circle because if you think you are likely to get upset, you probably will.'

Things improved for her when she finally challenged a man who had historically been difficult with her. The final straw came when he publicly complained to the virtually all-male committee that 'women were getting the best roles on committees' with the understanding that he felt that his own career was suffering from the ills of reverse discrimination.

She continued: 'It was very upsetting, and I received some coaching so I could confront him. The coaching was helpful in that I was able to de-personalise it, and I approached him privately. We talked about communication skills and how people did not always know how they came across to others. I gave him the example of what he had said and how it had made me feel as the only woman in the room. He seemed genuinely shocked and surprised. Things have since improved between us.' No doubt Athene is pleased she controlled herself during the meeting itself, but did address it later when she was calmer.

The Tightrope of Objectivity

The balance between emotionality and objectivity is a fine one for many women who work in these fields and is made more tenuous by the *micro-inequalities* that exist within the system[2]. These micro-inequalities are subtle but can cumulatively make a woman feel unwelcome and unsure of her place within the workplace and even her industry.

It is the rolling of the eyes, the interruptions or crossing of the arms when someone speaks, the 'forgetting' to share information with all players, the only hearing of the suggestion when it is made by a male colleague. If questioned, these acts are explained as a simple mistake; a one-time event, but

[2] Sarfaty, C. (2006) "Rooting Out Subtle Office Insults", New Jersey Biz, 3 July

as they are often repeated, they can eventually send a message that certain members of a team are more valued than others. Because those who most often suffer micro-inequalities in a male-dominated field are women, it heightens their sensitivity to these slights. They then are more likely to question their own decisions or leadership potential when they feel difficulty being heard or recognised. The problem then becomes cyclical because this heightened awareness means that women can overreact to such slights, which only *reinforces* the idea that they are too sensitive and not objective.

Interestingly, Fiona Edington, a barrister specialising in criminal, family and military cases, said that some of her most difficult foes in the emotional stakes were other women. She felt they could become over-involved and emotional when trying cases or trying to protect clients.

She said: 'Women who have been successful in the Law can be aggressive, and the issues I deal with are very tough: Family Law, child abuse and murder. There can be a tendency to personalise both yourself as the hero, and the other side as the villain. You have to remain calm and remind them you are not your client — but it is your responsibility to put the best case forward. There can be a tendency for them to see you as the beast they claim your client is.'

The stakes are high for her clients, who are facing the possibility of long jail sentences and public shame. Naturally, emotions are always involved and as a professional she has had to learn to manage not only her own feelings but those of her clients as well. She often spends time calming or reassuring them before Court, to help them appear less flustered or more sympathetic or whatever is called for in each case. Like the other women I interviewed, whose dramas played out in the boardroom rather than in the courtroom, Fiona manages emotions for the sake of image.

She explained: 'The judge and jury only get a snapshot of you in time. So, you have to make sure it is a snapshot you want them to see. I had a case recently with a professional woman whose children the local authority were considering taking away from her. She had to come across as more sympathetic, less angry and less domineering. It is hard because emotions are running so high.'

While it certainly might not seem fair that women in particular have to do so much 'emotional maintenance', it is clear that managing their emotions for the sake of their image was never far from their minds.

- **Crying at work will not be tolerated for long.**
- **Keep your personal problems at home — they subtly affect the way you are perceived.**
- **Unfairly, men are considered 'passionate', women 'emotional'.**

KEEPING THE PERSONAL PRIVATE

Most people know that, when others ask, *How are you?* as part of daily salutations, they are merely being conversational. It's not an invitation to go into a litany of the problems in your life.

Concentrate on describing all that is going well, even if that just feels like one thing; for instance, that you just landed a new client, saw your child's school play, were promoted to manage a bigger team, spent time with your favourite mentee or even just got back from a good holiday. It may initially feel like putting on an act — but if you focus on what is going well, it is amazing how authentically positive you can feel on an ongoing basis.

Staying upbeat not only reminds you of your power to choose how you want to be on any given day; it also engenders a feeling of confidence in you from the other person. How often have you met a naysayer and sarcastically thought, *I can't wait to work with them!* People want to engage with those who are *positive*.

For example, Caroline, the IT Director of a global logistics company, like many of the women I interviewed, found keeping small talk positive and emotionally safe to be the best option, whatever the setting. She explained: 'If you are out with colleagues and the topic drifts to family, you can talk superficially about how well your children are doing at school, where you are going on holiday. Don't talk about childcare woes or if your children are struggling. It has to seem as if it is all under control, even if it doesn't always feel that way. It's part of your credibility.'

In an *ideal* world, women would be able to be upfront about any childcare difficulties or family challenges they have, and it would not be seen as a reflection of their level of commitment to their job. But as pointed out by Caroline, women who work in male-dominated fields live in the *real* world.

Again, small talk has a role to play in creating your image. I became aware of what happened to a former client, whom I'll call Miranda, an investment banker. Whilst on maternity leave, Miranda mentioned to several of her colleagues, in an offhand manner, that she was finding it difficult to make childcare arrangements in preparation for her return. No doubt she was merely venting with people whom she considered to be supportive friends, as I know it was her intention to return to work. However, the word soon spread around her division that Miranda was perhaps not returning, which had knock-on effects for the way she was perceived by her team. Unfairly or not, this affected Miranda's chances for promotion or interesting work upon her return to work.

As a woman, you must be careful to whom you divulge any personal problems. This is especially true for work/life balance issues, as these informal conversations can plant seeds of doubt in others' minds which may be unwittingly used against you.

COMPETITION IS THE NAME OF THE GAME

It is essential for professional women to own their successes and original ideas. You cannot afford to wait for others to compliment you or give you credit. You *teach others how to treat you*, based on how you treat yourself.

For example, women in male-dominated fields often complain of having their views silenced, or colleagues taking credit for their idea at a meeting. While this is a common complaint, several of the women had learned to take matters into their own hands.

In fact, you only have to experience the phenomenon of suggesting something and having it ignored, only for the same idea to be taken up by a male colleague with congratulations to him all around, once to learn to modify your voice.

Laura Hinton learned from experience how to moderate her communication style in the boardroom. She said: 'I attended many meetings early on, where I had something to say but couldn't get a word in edgewise. I could bang the tables as some people do — but that's not my style. That being said, I no longer wait for everyone to stop talking; I get in there when I can.' She explained: 'You have to play them at their own game because if you wait for them to ask your opinion in that environment, it will never happen.'

Verbally holding back in a meeting once things become heated, is a common practice for many women. However, as we have seen, for many of their male colleagues, becoming argumentative may be just a way of asserting themselves and *testing out* their colleagues and does not mean the men are more justified or correct in their stance. Sometimes people enjoy arguing and competition as if it's a game.

Interesting research points out that it is in these settings that men are more likely to want to compete where women are more reticent to do so[3]. In a contrived game situation, men were far more confident in their ability to win

[3] Niederle, M. & Vesterlund, L. (2005) "Do Women Shy Away From Competition? Do Men Compete Too Much?" National Bureau of Economic Research Working Paper, No. 11474, July

even when they did not know if their competitor had been a previous winner or indeed if they themselves had won a round – 75 per cent of men thought they had won, whereas just 43 per cent of women did. The men were more likely to view themselves as exceptionally competent and therefore relished visible and high-risk competitions if they thought they could possibly win, whereas the women were more reticent about competition or even about taking a contrary stand, *even when they stood a good chance of prevailing*. It is worth remembering that in some cases, your colleagues may be simply over-confident or even just spoiling for a fight.

DIRECTIVE VERSUS COLLABORATIVE LANGUAGE

It has been a long-standing double standard of the modern workplace that women resent being labelled a *control freak* while men who express the same sentiment are labelled as *passionate*. Most women use *collaborative* language. Clients sometimes ask about how they can strengthen the language they use to be more *directive*, when engaging with people who report directly to them.

One of my first bosses, a man who was well-respected by all my female colleagues, had a very collaborative way of phrasing requests, saying things such as, *It would be great if we could get statistics by the end of the week*. I always knew it was a straightforward request to indeed get the statistics by the end of the week. However, I was always perplexed at how many of my male colleagues took his statement as just blue-sky thinking and react with, *Yes, it would be great if we could get that information by then, but who knows if that is going to happen?*

The underlying assumption among the men was that they would not make the effort because it had not been a direct request.

There is evidence, however, that more collaborative and tentative styles of speaking are indeed more powerful that those using straightforward and directive speech, when conferring status and giving directions[4]. The downside

[4] Fragale, A. (2006) "The Power of Powerless Speech", Kenan-Flagler Business School, University of South Carolina, March, www.sciencedirect.com

is that many *women don't get credit* for being warm and building consensus the way their warm and collaborative male colleagues might, as it is expected that *that is what women do.*

However, research suggests that these expectations create a double bind for women in leadership positions[5]. Men who do build consensus are considered exceptional and enlightened. Similarly, they are not penalised when being directive and authoritarian; they are given respect for whichever type of leadership stance they take.

Women, on the other hand, are damned if they do and damned if they don't. They are regarded as 'soft' if they seek to build bridges and 'shrewish' is they take a more directive approach. In fact, it is undoubtedly because of the historical domination of men in leadership positions that we are unable to distinguish between what are stereotypically male behaviours from behaviours that make a good leader. Unfortunately, the connection between the two is too often now automatic, even if inaccurate.

Considering the potential backlash around women's leadership, it is not surprising that a Catalyst study of Fortune 100 female executives found that 96 per cent said it was important that they find 'a style with which male managers are comfortable'[6].

The traditionally-male workplace also makes an assumption that those who are most directive, shout loudest about their wins, take the most credit and are a commanding presence are by default best suited to leadership positions. However, if one looks at leadership as being *in the service of your team* in order collectively to accomplish larger goals, a different assumption arises.

[5] Eagly, A. & Carli, L. (2007) "Women and the Labyrinth of Leadership", Harvard Business Review, September
[6] Catalyst, 2005 "Catalyst Census of Women Corporate Officers and Top Earners of the Fortune 500

- The answer to 'how are you?' should always be something positive.

- Be prepared to interrupt, if it enables you to get the credit for your own ideas.

- Some colleagues will only respect and follow directive language.

RE-DEFINING LEADERSHIP

Perhaps if the responsibility of a leader is to model good corporate responsibility, create a sense of egalitarianism and facilitate good teamwork, then the best people are *not* those who shout the loudest about their individual accomplishments. Rather, they are those who see the value of a team and do not particularly seem too attached to the idea of gaining credit for an alpha-male style of leadership.

Women are often criticised for not having enough confidence in their voices; and most senior women do indeed become more firm in their tone and language with time ... and as they begin to wield more power.

It is not altogether surprising that women's voices don't always demonstrate a sense of unshakable confidence and self certainty. Low self-confidence is a *side effect* of not being used to having power to exercise. It is not surprising that women as a whole are considered to be less confident as they have historically not held a great deal of actual power. However, to mistake an initial insecurity for a lack of leadership potential is an error businesses make at their own peril. Women's sense of confidence and the courage of their convictions only grow when they find themselves in the relatively new position of *actually being heard*.

LIKE IN THE LIBRARY, LOWER YOUR VOICE

It is often as women grow into power that their voices cease to reflect their strength adequately.

Caroline, the logistics company IT Director, received communication training with a top actor to help her career, after being told her erratic communication style was reminiscent of a 'bumblebee in a glass jar'. She explained: 'I had to learn that *less is more*. When I am nervous, my natural tendency is to speak more, which was not helpful for my image in the boardroom.'

What did the training give her? She replied: 'Now I take the audience on a journey from where we are, to where we want to be, and how we are going to get there. He helped me work on my breathing, the structure of my comments, the way I engage with the team.

'The training sounded *pink and fluffy* to me initially, but I am smart enough to know that I'm not perfect. I have to be prepared to give anything that could help a try. Initially, because I work with so many men, most of whom would be dubious of this approach, I felt a bit inferior for seeking help. I now realise it's the people who think they know it all who are stupid not to try.' The end result for Caroline? She concluded: 'Since then, there has been virtually unanimous feedback that others have seen a step change in my delivery. The key is in keeping an open mind.'

Ana Pacheco was also conscious of her voice in meetings, and the impact it had on others. She explained: 'I naturally talk fast, and to develop my credibility I slow down. In interviews or big presentations, I make a concerted effort to slow my pace, though I do have to think about it.'

Like many of the women I interviewed, Ana knows a slower pace and a lower tone of voice give the impression of being in control — and a certain measure of gravitas.

Janet Davies also found it useful to moderate both the volume and the tone of her voice when speaking in meetings. She exclaimed: 'Try not to make your point with a quiet or squeaky voice! The way some people get ignored you might almost think some women have voices that only dogs can hear!' She suggested: 'Take it down a couple of notches in tone, and make it more measured. Make your comments succinct and maintain eye contact so they have nowhere else to look but your face.'

Regarding communication, Janet shared some useful advice on eye contact when you are the only woman in the room. She said: 'There will be one person in particular you want to make an impression on. If it's a man, keep your eyes on him — because if there are five men in the room, the other men may look to him as to whether they should listen to you. That's why it's a good idea to find out people's job titles or positions in the organisation. Do a little research beforehand if they are strangers. Sometimes you won't know who's the main decision maker. Just look for the little hints as to who is the *alpha male* — as the rest of the pack will look to see if he is approving of you before they will give your their open approval.'

'BIG UP' YOUR LANGUAGE

One way to make sure others don't try to steal your thunder, on the assumption that they will not be challenged, is to work on how you verbally establish your presence through your choice of words. As a rule, when asked what you do, don't minimise your achievements. Men are much better at 'bigging it up' and it's a lesson that women who work in a man's world must learn.

Laura Hinton's media training included videotaped analysis of her presentational style, which was invaluable to her. She remembered: 'I didn't realise how much I prefaced my comments with *I guess it might...* or *This is just my opinion, so it could be wrong but...* Those types of throwaway comments gave the impression I was uncertain or not confident of my facts, when actually I knew exactly what I was talking about.'

Most professional women I know have plenty to be proud of. I know women who are senior managers in legal, banking, science, engineering and technology firms, many with MBAs and PhDs. Yet, to hear some of them talk about themselves and their accomplishments, you'd be surprised to find they have a qualification to their name. I am not advocating bragging about things that are not true, but most women I know minimise their achievements, usually for the perceived comfort of others, in a way that men do not.

This is a mistake you can't afford to make if you want to compete with those in *the boys' club*. To this end, remove the words *small, only, kind of, just* and *little* when talking about your own achievements. No matter what you do for a living, you do not have a *little job on the side.* You have not just landed a *small project* — every new piece of business has the potential to be larger than we think.

Dismiss phrases such as *I only work part-time* when you work four days a week, and check your messages on the day you are meant to be 'off'. Chuck out weedy explanations such as *I am just doing a post-doc at the moment* when you have landed a research position in a field you love. Minimising your accomplishments in the hope others will see through your humility rarely works in the workplace and certainly not in job interviews or appraisals. Nor does it belie true confidence, which is what employers are looking for when considering hiring and promotions.

Similarly, learn how to take a compliment. Saying, *I was just lucky*, is one of the single most debilitating statements a woman can make in her career. Of course you don't have to gush, *Yes, I am wonderful, aren't I?* when given a compliment. Instead, accept it with a gracious *Thank you, I'm pleased how well it turned out,* or *Thanks, the team and I worked very hard on this project — it's great that you noticed!*

Minimising a compliment in the workplace (rare as they often are!) is the career equivalent of saying, *Oh, this old thing?* to someone who has noticed the brand new dress you love. Good social graces? Perhaps. Honest and ambitious? No.

To help you get used to taking credit for your accomplishments, display your qualifications or awards around the office to help you internalise that you do actually deserve that compliment. And learn to simply say, *Thank you.*

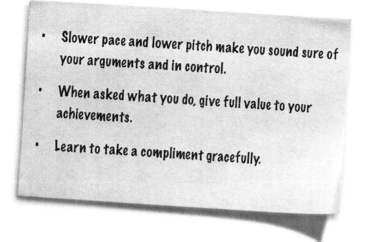

- Slower pace and lower pitch make you sound sure of your arguments and in control.

- When asked what you do, give full value to your achievements.

- Learn to take a compliment gracefully.

LEARN THE LINGUA FRANCA

> *If I had eight hours to chop down a tree,*
>
> *I'd spend six sharpening my axe.*
>
> — Abraham Lincoln

When communicating, women in these settings also learned how to speak a language that men learned and respected: the language of data and 'cold, hard facts'.

Again, Janet Davies learned to communicate with men according to their preferences. She declared: 'You usually need to go in with facts, and be concise. If you start to talk about things they don't feel are relevant, you will lose credibility quickly.'

It is interesting to note that, after a long career in both financial services and management consultancy, Janet was circumspect about blaming such things on sexism. She reasoned: 'I've learned to take responsibility for my communication style. If I don't get my point across, I don't automatically cry *sexism* because you need to find out if you really did do something wrong. Think if there is anything you can do differently next time. If not, chalk it up to experience and move on.'

When asked how she was able to do that, she explained how frequently she saw men make similar mistakes — and how often she could advise them, based on what she had learned herself.

Similarly, Mary Hensher, a partner at Deloitte, had learned to adjust her language to suit her colleagues — many of whom were accountants and not IT-savvy. Rather than force them to adapt to her 'language' of programming and computer systems, she worked around them by changing her own. She said: 'When you say you work in IT, people can glaze over. Sometimes they think you're going to be really nerdy or boring — but much of it is because they don't understand what you do. I use this to my advantage as it gives me plenty of opportunities to explain what I do, but in words they will understand. But I had to *learn* that.'

She explained: 'You need to talk *business* language; you need to speak in the language of the people whom you are talking with, and not expect them to understand yours. I don't mean in a condescending way, but in business speak.' She had to learn a new set of communication skills, and put it like this: 'I am not an accountant, but as a partner I'm now in charge of budgets. If I go to my executive with a budget, I am aware we are speaking a language they understand much better than I. So I got coaching in how to *speak accountant* and understand and draft budgets, balance sheets and Profit and Loss statements. You have to make an effort to *understand* in order to *be understood*.'

Mary honed this skill over a long career and it became increasingly important as she progressed. It is particularly important for those who might be in a minority within their office — such as an IT expert in an accountancy firm, or a woman working primarily with men.

YOUR JARGON IS A COLLEAGUE'S CONFUSION

The point of not assuming everyone speaks the same language was brought home to me as I was writing this book. I was sent a message submitted to employees at a large, non-technological organisation from their IT department, explaining a temporary lapse in email service. The note said:

*Dear all, There was a **service interruption** to the **Remote Access service** at 15:39 today which caused **user connections to be dropped**. This was due to **unexpected behaviour** of a **software update** to the **remote access appliance cluster**. Future updates will be notified and scheduled for a **vulnerability window** of 7:00am – 9:00am. Apologies for any inconvenience caused.*

When I looked closer I realised the long message, sent in technical speak to a largely un-technical audience, was sent by a man who incorrectly assumed that everyone else in receipt of his email would understand and appreciate his jargon. It is a mistake not made by those who know that the onus of communication is always on *them*. They don't rely on others adapting to the language they use.

The women who are the happiest and most successful are those who have established their own presence, not the presence of the men they see round them, or even of other women who have gone before. They are authentic to themselves while still engaging with *the boys' club*.

To be sure, women in these industries have a fine line to tread. The smartest know they need to stay upbeat and to control their emotions in a way that men are rarely expected to. These women know all too well that what is interpreted as *passion* in a man can be considered *hysterical* in a woman. They also know how and when to socialise with colleagues, and what topics to give a wide berth. Rather, they have established their own authentic voice and communication style that feels true to them and inspires confidence in those around them.

- In a male-dominated field, be ready to talk facts and be concise to be understood.

- You may require coaching if the language you need to learn feels foreign.

- Establish your own presence — don't just copy men or even other women.

NINE

BUILDING RELATIONSHIPS AND CREATING OPPORTUNITIES

It had long since come to my attention that people of accomplishment

rarely sat back and let things happen to them.

They went out and happened to things.

— Elinor Smith

When I speak to women I meet at events, and talk with my clients about how they could initially raise their profile, I am always struck by how many overlook the power of networking.

Most women recognise it is a potential boon to their careers — but some do not embrace it as readily as others. Perhaps they believe they are shy, or hold an unhelpful assumption that only *salespeople* network. It is this image that often puts women off: the idea of wearing a stiff suit, shaking hands endlessly and trying to deliver an unsolicited 'elevator speech' whilst the person you are speaking to looks over your shoulder for someone better to speak to.

At the start, while you build a community and get an idea of which networks suit you, it may feel that way. However, while that may play a part, your network is simply those people you like and trust, who may or may not be in your industry. They are a good source of information and are happy to recommend you to others who may need your services.

The most successful networkers I know say very little about themselves initially, and are much more curious about helping *others*. This is an approach that brings far better results in the long run — but is also one that comes more naturally to women who don't like *blowing their own trumpet*.

It's also an approach I learned early in life.

YOU'RE NEVER TOO YOUNG TO START

Like most women, my first lessons in life about getting on socially came from my mother. Networking was certainly no exception.

She is a woman who can talk to anyone and make them feel like the most interesting person in the room, which is a real gift. She has a Masters degree in European History, and it is not without a tinge of guilt that I say she gave up a full-time teaching career to raise my brother and me. However, the importance of being able to relate to anyone was passed on to us both, and is something I aspire to each day.

My mother was forever hosting dinner parties with a wide range of people, and leading committees for various charities. I am ashamed to say that I did not always appreciate this talent, and my feelings for the way she talked to anyone would range from boredom to annoyance to embarrassment, depending on my age and disposition that day.

However, she did instil in me the ability to talk with a wide range of people. She taught me to connect them with others, even when I had less in common with them myself, so that they could benefit from each other.

I could often come home to find dinner being served for an odd mix of a widowed neighbour, a NASA research scientist on sabbatical, our Methodist pastor, one of my mother's graduate school roommates and the adult child of one of my mother's friends from her years in the Peace Corps in Brazil. And the surprising thing? They would all be talking and laughing by the end of evening, as if they had known each other for years.

Strength in making others feel comfortable in social settings, and finding commonalities between seemingly disparate groups, is a skill many women have. However, it is an especially important attribute in a strong leader, and something women should *capitalise* on more in the workplace.

As an adult, my initial reluctance to network professionally came from a self-imposed pressure to make a 'sale' at every event I attended. I used to put enormous pressure on myself when I first started my coaching business, assuming that if no one asked me on the spot for one-to-one coaching, I had failed.

When I look back, I see how ridiculous that is. This is especially true in the realm of coaching, which is a very competitive field where most clients rely on word of mouth, or understandably want to get to know me better before delving into more personal territory.

When you first start out, go to a wide variety of networks to get a feel for what they have to offer and who attends them. For example, I used to attend lots of events all over London and East Anglia. It was only after I began to whittle them down, to the few I enjoyed the most and that I was able to become more heavily involved with, that I was able to start to reap the benefits of belonging to just a few groups.

Marketers will tell you that potential customers need to be exposed to a new product — in this case, you — *seven times* before they make a decision to buy. It is unrealistic to think you can get this type of repeated exposure with more than just a few organisations. And this applies to everyone, not just those who have a widget to sell. We are *all* selling, all the time — we are selling ourselves as a potential client, colleague, useful contact and if all goes well, even as a friend.

WHY NETWORKING MATTERS

> *Without an army, Napoleon was just a man with a hat.*
>
> — Anonymous

Maggie Berry is Director of womenintechnology.co.uk, one of the UK's leading job boards and independent networking groups for women working in IT. She is passionate about the importance of networking to improve career development.

She declared: 'I think networking is one, if not *the* most important aspect, to career development. It's not a short-term quick fix. It might be six months, a year or longer before a contact provides help for you. It could be anything from crucial business knowledge to a tip-off, or an introduction to another contact who could possibly use your product — but if you continue with it, things will happen. It's vital not to go to an event and think you're going to find the perfect person to solve all your problems in one go; it's an investment in time.'

She continued: 'It is something that you should be doing *continually* throughout your career. You may be looking for a job, you may want to meet potential clients or you may want to find possible collaborators on a project. Or perhaps you may want to know where a certain technology is moving or what web trends might be like in the future. You never know what kind of opportunities you'll hear about.'

What do women who attend womenintechnology events like about them? She replied: 'People tell me they love the mini-boost of confidence! It's easy to feel overwhelmed in your day-to-day job — but hearing a great speaker is a chance to remember all the things you already know you are doing well and where to hone your skills. It's also a great opportunity to meet other women in these fields. Most women who come to our events may be the only woman in their team. It's easy for them to forget just how many other women actually work in the sector! It is hugely reassuring to know you are not alone, and to see other women thriving in these environments.'

Many of the women I met in corporate settings were very clear about how important networking had been to their success. Janet Davies was one such woman. She has headed large teams in corporate settings as well as running successful businesses of her own — the New Life Network and Davies Development Consulting — in addition to working at PwC and American Express. As a woman with such a diverse background, she knows the value of networking.

Janet echoed Maggie's sentiments: 'Networking is everything. It's essential in today's fast moving market that people share information. It's been valuable to me as I've been offered great projects and opportunities I wouldn't have come across otherwise. I've got almost every job I've ever had through networking. And then I love to network to pay it forward.'

Interestingly, while most women considered it a vital aspect of their job, very few were instructed to develop a larger network as part of any performance review. While it's a great way to raise your profile as well as that of the company you work for, most employers did not specifically encourage women to build their network. Yet, when I work with women's internal networks, it is the opportunity to meet other women which is one of the greatest draws for participants.

Jackie Gittins describes herself as 'naturally curious' about people. Whilst networking has played a huge role in her success for the last 20 years, it is not overtly valued by most organisations. 'It's never been written into my objectives but a *huge* part of my job depends on it,' she observed.

A large network of your own clearly has benefits for your employer, as we will discuss later. However, this is one area to which you may have to devote some of your own time, as many events take place in the evening. Many employers will pay fees for you to network, through paying for your professional membership dues and event costs — but if your employer doesn't, that's no excuse not to participate. Think of it as an *investment in yourself.*

- **Your network is people you like and trust; they may not work in the same industry.**

- **Making others feel comfortable is an important skill for a strong leader.**

- **A large network of your own benefits your employer as well as yourself.**

IDENTIFY YOUR GOALS

Think carefully about what you want from a network. Are you looking for a new job, a mentor, good contacts with suppliers, industry knowledge, new clients, somewhere to hear inspiring speakers? Many women who come to my workshops simply say they want a chance to meet other women who also work in male-dominated fields.

The best networks will give you a chance to have all these benefits and more. You just need to think through these priorities when deciding which ones best serve your purpose and find the right networks accordingly.

For example, I am an accredited member of the International Coach Federation, so I can tap into best practice, an ethical code within the highly unregulated world of coaching and a system of peer-reviewed accreditation. I'm also a member of the Professional Speakers Association so I can develop my speaking business. I am also a member of various networks focused on women in the sciences, technology and the professional services, that my *clients* attend. My *personal* network is the women I meet at those organisations with whom I develop very strong relationships. That's not to say I made these relationships overnight. Networking certainly didn't start out well for me and I cringe to remember the first events I ever attended. Ignoring my intuition, I forced myself along to one Chamber of Commerce informal networking event after another. I was often the only woman and certainly the only woman looking to develop relationships with women in male-dominated fields. I received polite disinterest at best, and lightly veiled hostility at worst, when talking about my new company that focused on professional women. I always left feeling disheartened and as if I had not really connected with anyone.

It was a steep learning curve, but it taught me the value of deciding early on which networks are best for your aims. There is nothing wrong with Chamber of Commerce events — but their crowd of mostly male small-business owners was not my target market. *My* market was individual professional women in male-dominated fields and the employers who see their value and want to develop and retain them. It was only when I started attending networking sessions that focused on *these* groups that I began to make inroads … and to *enjoy* myself.

As you progress your career, your network may start out with team peers. Before long you will begin to develop good relationships with colleagues in other departments, then favourite clients, others in the industry, people in other industries. The women who get the best results from networking start within their own organisation and then attend independent networking events to grow a wider range of relationships.

- It is unrealistic to think you will make a 'sale' at your first networking event.

- Network like a gardener: consistently to reap the best fruits of your labours.

- Try a variety of networks but then focus on just a few that you really enjoy.

NETWORKING BY ANY OTHER NAME

If you focus on others first and yourself second, you will soon find you have a large network of people. The focus on the *relationships* is vital. Interestingly, it is this approach which made so many of the women I interviewed expert networkers, even when they didn't necessarily regard it as networking. Some were still in contact with colleagues they had worked with 30 years ago.

Many had an enviably long list of people who would recommend their services to others but they still didn't identify themselves as *networkers* at all. Others, mostly those in corporate settings, immediately recognised networking as simply meaning *relationship-building*. While all successful women do it, they had different comfort levels with the term *networking* itself.

Some of the women nearing retirement, for example, didn't use or recognise terms such as *networking* or *mentoring* to describe parts of their career success. That is definitely not to say they did not *engage* in networking. For example, Dame Veronica Sutherland was dismissive of the term when I asked about networking. But that did not mean she was any less aware of the power of connections.

Dame Veronica explained: 'I've been working since 1962 but I have never given any thought to networking. On the other hand, I do enjoy *talking to people*. I never consciously thought, *I must be nice to so and so, in order to get something for myself*, but I have made friends throughout my career and most often said *yes* to an invitation to go out when I have enjoyed the other person's company. I have said, *Let's have lunch to discuss a piece of work* — but that's just getting business done.'

It was apparent that her husband Alex had been a great source of support to her, and she said she could not see how unmarried ambassadors handled the responsibilities, with both social engagements and work commitments and a great deal of overlap between the two. Dame Veronica described how he would help her fulfil the strategic work of hosting dinner parties so that the right connections were made between people.

She explained: 'People laugh and call it the Gin and Tonic Circuit — but it does have a real purpose of bringing people together. You want to bring together people who will have something to talk about. Alex and I have spent many a long hour reviewing seating plans, asking, *Who can we put with him?* It's all part of diplomacy. When your boss, the Prime Minister, comes to visit, you need to make sure he or she is meeting the right people.' She laughed: 'Occasionally, you need to make sure other parties steer clear of each other!'

Her comments could be true for any savvy networker who brings people together and looks to make connections for other people, based on what she knows about their common interests.

While speaking with her, I was reminded of a favourite exhibit I saw with my husband several years ago, at the Metropolitan Museum of Art in New York City. It was a collection of Jacqueline Kennedy's dresses and the exhibit was very popular and well-attended. As glamorous as the clothes were, my favourite piece from the archive was the seating plan for a state dinner at the White House hosted by the Kennedys. The seating plan was detailed and included comments that Jacqueline and her husband, John, had passed between each other. Next to each guest's name were intimate comments they made to one another such as, *You can't sit her next to him, he's married but has a wandering eye or, Put these two together as they both work in the oil industry and love baseball.*

I am sure neither of them thought the seating plan, one of hundreds they probably created over their life together, would ever find its way into a museum for public display. What I loved was how it demonstrated the importance of diplomacy in creating connections for others, as well as the sense of true partnership, that came from this aspect of their marriage.

CULTIVATE YOUR WEAK TIES

Most professional jobs are not primarily found through the Appointments pages, by registering with an agency or by sending out CVs.

Think back to your own job experience. How many senior roles have you actually gained through a cold application? How many jobs have you had where you knew no one within the company, or no one you knew pointed out the opportunity in a place where you weren't looking? Did you *really* find it in the Appointments pages all on your own? The chances are that someone you knew, someone from your *extended network*, helped point you in the right direction.

When I looked back over my own professional life, I realised I had found only one job through a traditional Situations Vacant advertisement — and it was the worst career choice I ever made. If you are looking for your next job, this is the time to cultivate your *weak ties*. Most jobs gleaned through personal contacts come, not directly through friends or colleagues, but rather through people they know — those 'weak ties'; people who will take the recommendation about you from a mutual friend.

Networking becomes even more important as you age, as most senior jobs are filled through the method and as most people recognise that they have landed at least one job initially through networking. Additionally, many companies will reward, at the very least with kudos, people who introduce friends who become employees. They rightly figure that if they like you as a colleague, you are likely to socialise with great potential employees. In a way, you have done the first round of interviews for them.

The truth is, it is *always* easier and more authentic for a mutual friend, past colleague or satisfied client to tell others how great you are, than to hear it straight from you! Tell everyone you know that you are looking to make a change, and what types of roles or sectors you are interested in.

I once worked with a client, whom I'll call Susan, who was looking for a new role in the biotech industry. She had been using recruitment agencies and open adverts to drive her search. She was frustrated and felt she was not making good progress. Early on in the coaching, we decided to expand her search by going to those who were already interested in her success — her friends and past colleagues.

Susan sent a short email detailing her key skills and what she was looking for in a new position. Instead of sending it purely to those she knew in the industry, she sent it to neighbours, to women in her swimming class and to past colleagues. She didn't ask directly for a job, rather only that they pass it on to anyone they knew who worked in the sciences. In the end, Susan shortened the time she spent between positions, and now has a management position as a team leader in a large and well-regarded research institute.

KEEPING THE INITIATIVE

Networking may seem frightening at first, especially for those who are feeling vulnerable after a job loss or redundancy. However, it offers you the opportunity for a proactive job search, rather than just sending out applications and passively waiting for a reply. As I did with Susan, I recommend networking to all my clients who are in the midst of seeking their next role.

In fact, whilst writing the book, I led a group coaching session with women from an investment bank, all of whom were facing the very real threat of redundancy. What surprised me was how no one in the room of a dozen or so women attended external networks, where they might meet people from other sectors or companies. While most admitted they had got their current job through a personal recommendation, they did not see the impending need to grow their network outside of a potentially sinking ship. If there is ever a good time to network, it's when you think you might want or *have* to make a career move in the future — which, based on the way people change roles and even careers, is *all* of us.

Matilda Venter, at PwC, was another such woman who admitted that her network has meant she has never had to go through a normal recruitment process in the UK. Instead, she finds roles initially through friends and past colleagues. That being said, she was clear that she didn't think of herself as a *networker*. She explained: 'I wouldn't say I am one of those people with 1,000 names in a Rolodex, most of whom I don't even know. I place a great deal of importance on building close relationships with those people I know, who are then ready to let me access their networks if need be. I maintain the relationship long after we have technically stopped working together.'

To this end, sending Christmas cards or LinkedIn updates or other emails, when you are not making requests but just checking in is very helpful.

And here's a tip: if you go to the trouble of sending LinkedIn requests or Christmas messages, do personalise them. I once received a Christmas card that only had my name but with no internal signature enclosed. Because there was no return address or signature, I never even knew who had sent it — someone who probably felt I *should* be on their list, but couldn't be bothered to include a message that was personal to me and indeed had even forgotten to sign it! Needless to say, it didn't leave me with the greatest impression — but I guess it doesn't matter since I never knew who it was, which defeats their original intention in the first place!

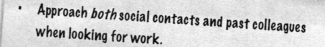

- Approach *both* social contacts and past colleagues when looking for work.

- Start networking *before* you need the network.

- Give your network updates of what you are up to — and ask what *they* are doing.

BUILD YOUR NETWORK BEFORE YOU NEED IT

Some women build networks informally without understanding their value.It may be months or even years before you actually need to turn to your network for support. A good group of supporters and mentors to whom you can turn is invaluable in any career, but especially when you are switching jobs. Keeping your old contacts is one way to ensure you have more than just your own skills to bring to your new job — a vital asset as you become more senior. Janet Davies didn't realise the value of her network until she left one of her earliest jobs, a mistake she never made again.

She remarked: 'They say it takes you five years to build a good network and when I left my first company I'd been there ten years. I didn't realise what I had *until* I left. To make matters worse, my new boss who hired me left under a cloud very soon after I arrived, which left me with no real allies and very exposed. That was a big lesson for me, and so when I later moved to American Express, I nurtured my networks and have never stopped since! You can tick all the boxes in your work, but the recognition of your achievements and your security can disappear overnight if you have all your eggs in one basket.'

Staying in touch has served Janet well in an industry — consulting — that gets smaller the higher you progress. She said: 'I was interviewing for a new contract just last year and the marketing director turned out to be a man I knew from a company I had worked with ten years ago. He knew I had done a great job there, so that helped.'

Others also had to learn a tough lesson about the value of networking early on in their career — realising how much they needed one when they were looking for work. The truth is that the best time to build a network is before you need one. Harriet Crawford, a retired archaeologist, was a woman with a similar experience. After completing her PhD in London under Professor Max Mallowan — Agatha Christie's husband and a well-respected archaeologist — she moved to Edinburgh to be with her husband and raise three children. This move took her out of the academic circuit for many years. It was only when she returned to Cambridge that she realised she wanted to find employment in her field.

Looking back, she admits she should have put more effort in staying in touch with her former colleagues and supervisors. She remembered: 'I tried to break back in after ten years away and that was difficult. My PhD supervisor had forgotten who I was by that stage and he wrote a pretty unsupportive reference, which was polite but virtually said he didn't remember much about me.' Additionally, one of her supervisors at Cambridge had died in the interim, which exacerbated her problem of rekindling old connections.

When asked what she would have done differently, she exclaimed: 'Keep in touch at all costs!' She continued: 'Knowing what I know now, I would have made a much bigger effort to keep in touch by sending them anything I wrote and would have said, *I'm planning on returning*, as well as asking their advice so I could continue the dialogue even after we had finished working together.'

LIKE THE DISNEY RIDE, IT'S A SMALL WORLD AFTER ALL

In a global economy, employees from the same industry are in an ever-diminishing pool as they become more senior, where people stay in contact and come across each other time and time again.

This is particularly vital for women in male-dominated fields, as they are much easier to remember by virtue of their minority status. It is important that people have a good impression of you. These industries may seem huge to outsiders — but are actually small and well-connected to true insiders.

Jane Lewis explained this phenomenon: 'IT can seem like a huge industry — but if you blot your copybook, it's amazing how many people will find out about it. It's just a small world. Tomorrow, for example, I am meeting with a man I met when I was first working in the public sector back in 1997. I met him again on a separate project in 2003 and now I am actually doing some work for him on site, all of which was coincidental.'

This type of small world serves as a reminder not to burn bridges or make enemies easily. Several of the women confirmed that when considering applicants or project partners, they will use this *informal grapevine* to make decisions.

Jane confirmed: 'You may see a CV on your desk and you may not recognise the name — but chances are, a colleague or client might, and can give you insider information.' As Jane explained, it is indeed a small world and your reputation will often precede you. Before making job offers, companies will use inside contacts to 'informally' find out your reputation — rather than just what is written on the formal letter of reference.

Maintaining a good reputation is vital, as it is becoming increasingly easy to find out more about people in this digital age. Amy Cox, Human Resources Director at Investment Technology Group, said: 'Keep your Facebook or other social media site entries clean and never say anything disparaging about colleagues and your boss. Anything you write online is held in cyberspace and can be found later and used against you.'

It may not seem fair but keeping your nose clean and your reputation intact is vital. The above illustrates just how a network can work for or against you. The choice is yours.

- Keep in touch with former colleagues; those contacts follow you from job to job.

- The best time to build a network is *before* you need one.

- Keep your online presence clean; be discreet about your boss and colleagues.

YOUR REPUTATION DEPENDS ON IT

On a more positive note, if you are new to a particular role but need to get exposure quickly, networking is again the best way to go.

Eileen Brown, who heads the Professional Evangelist Team at Microsoft, has a seemingly simple remit: getting customers excited about Microsoft products they have already purchased. This meant her first challenge was to meet people in as many of the interrelated but separate departments across Microsoft as quickly as possible. It was a steep challenge for anyone, something she did not recognise at first. After she arrived at Microsoft, her 'dream job', she was lulled into a false sense of security.

She remembered: 'I thought, *I'm here, I never need to move again!* But that's not the Microsoft culture. So, even if you stay with the company, you will be expected to change roles every few years. So I quickly realised the best way to do that was to go from having an internal job to one where it was required for my name to be at the top of search engine rankings.'

When she described how she achieved the increase in profile she simply laughed: 'I never said no to a cup of coffee! I knew I had to make connections, as my role in the Evangelist team was to get other people excited. I didn't have a desk here for the first six years and I routinely drank six cups of coffee a day — not because I needed them, but that was how I set up my conversations, going from one coffee break to another. My manager joked that my office was in the café.'

Using an IT analogy of being a *hub* connecting to many *endpoints*, she explained the impact this approach eventually had. She explained: 'It was almost logarithmic, in that once I connected a few hubs, many more hubs knew about me, and soon I was overwhelmed with networking connections, which obviously made my job much easier.'

Fiona Edington, a barrister, also recognised the importance of building a strong reputation amongst her network through quality work and keeping the lines of communication open and honest. 'You need to treat all briefs that come across your desk very sensitively because it's your reputation at stake. That means handling it well — or, if you realise you cannot take it on, quickly passing it on to someone else you would personally recommend,' she concluded.

A good recommendation from one barrister to another serves both barristers and the solicitor well. A solicitor then knows he or she can trust the original barrister who made the recommendation — and hence will be likely to continue to send him or her work in the future.

SPREAD YOUR NETWORK WEALTH

As you move roles, change companies or even industries, your network will have a value in securing clients for your new employers or yourself.

Being recognised as having a large network of solid contacts gives you greater currency in the marketplace. Employers buy not just *you* but also *your contacts*. This expectation only increases as you rise in seniority. It's not just your delivery but your relationships that have a potential commercial value. This is because they recognise that a large group of contacts can be good in securing potential business. It also helps you do your own job *faster*, more easily and more efficiently than trying to do it all yourself.

Lis Astall of Accenture confirmed this when talking about what she looked for in potential applicants at senior levels. She expected them to be well-networked and the more senior the position, the wider the network. She recognised that successful applicants needed additional time to build the ever-vital internal network, on which much business is based.

She confirmed: 'I would be looking for someone who at their core was a strong professional — but more than that, I would be looking for someone who has worked with the right clients, had the right memberships, been recognised as an industry expert and even written books on topic. That being said, if they spend 80 hours a week on the job and can only talk about work, that's a worry, as you need someone who can have a rounded conversation.'

This realisation about just how vital networks are, particularly as a woman progresses her career, came to her much later in her own career. Lis remembered: 'It wasn't until I reached more senior levels that my external network began to be of *real value*, not just to me, but to my prospective employers. There are people now who were junior customers of mine when we were all starting out. They are now major buyers in the Civil Service. As you progress, employers want to get an idea of what you can bring with you — not just skills, but also your potential network,' she explained.

Lis continued: 'I started out concentrating on me and my career — but as I became more successful, my network has reached out to various trade and government bodies, such as the Social Mobility Foundation and the National Employment Panel, where I can progress the work of the firm. Once you have developed your network, you can do things three or four times *faster* than if you attempted it earlier in your career.'

Caroline, a logistics company IT Director, had a similar experience. She said she had not given a great deal of thought to networking until she became the first-ever woman appointed to the Senior Executive Board in the late 1990s.

She remembered: 'I realised I needed insight into where the next generation of technology, process and people management were heading. I didn't have that type of knowledge in-house, I was expected to provide it, and so had to work quickly to make those external connections.' To do this, she began attending and running networking events that were both mixed-gender and for women only, and invited industry contacts external to the organisation.

Most of the women mentioned that, as they progressed their careers, the technical skills that had originally brought them to their fields were in the background of their careers now, *if even used at all*. Instead, they developed managerial skills. This was seen as a natural progression, but one that was at times uncomfortable for some who enjoyed the hands-on approach. Some of the women found it difficult to let others become the technical experts on whom *they* now had to rely, rather than driving and mastering new technologies themselves as they had in the past.

There is something difficult about letting go of the day-to-day technical responsibilities as you grow into more managerial roles — but there was also recognition that without this change in duties, there would be little career progression.

Caroline said that as she reached Director level her job became focused on what she could accomplish through her relationships, rather than the technical prowess she had originally brought to the job. In fact, when discussing her goals, Caroline explained: 'Though I came from an IT background originally, in five years' time I would like to be able to walk into a company and be considered for any board position because of the value I put on leadership and developing the right relationships.'

Mary Hensher, also a partner at a major professional services firm, saw networking as vital in mitigating the risk of working in a fast-paced and high stress environment. She saw the collaboration required as a key factor in her making Partner. This approach to networking was certainly a long-term benefit to her Partnership.

Mary remarked: 'In the highly regulated world of financial services, we owe each other a duty of care to make sure that we are all protecting each other with knowledge. There are strict rules about keeping client confidentiality of course, but it is our *duty* to equip our colleagues with the best knowledge we have collectively to serve a client. This needs careful networking to share any relevant knowledge.'

- A large network will help you reach senior levels and is invaluable in a new role.

- When you move onward and upward, your network brings you clients.

- As you move into managerial roles, you will rely less on technical expertise.

NETWORK TO FIND CLIENTS

As Fiona Edington alluded to, developing successful relationships is of particular importance to barristers as they are given work in one of two ways. Barristers are *prohibited* by the Bar Council from directly soliciting for work, so their next case is always first in the hands of a professional colleague such as a clerk or solicitor. Again, like most fields, while there should be complete transparency in the process, it pays to be well-respected by the peers who make such decisions. A solicitor who thinks a certain barrister would handle a case well sends them the brief directly.

Alternatively, a brief may arrive at a Chambers without a specification for a particular barrister. Instead, it is sent to a clerk who then passes it on to whichever barrister in his Chambers he or she thinks is most qualified. This means the network of relationships between barristers, clerks and solicitors is *especially* vital to maintain.

For Fiona, networking came so naturally she didn't recognise she was doing it. She reasoned: 'I am only as good as my last piece of work for a solicitor. So, I do a good job and don't analyse it too much. What I do notice is that certain solicitors pigeonhole me for certain types of cases: some send me military crimes, others Family Law or child abuse. It's what they perceive I do best, though they all have a different perception.'

Similarly, Ana Pacheco at PwC is aware that while many people make networking a strategic part of their career development process, she never felt she was networking with any agenda in mind. Being friendly to colleagues at all levels is of benefit to both her and her larger team. 'I'm equally helpful to all people because you need them when things are stressful.'

She recalled an example when this had served her well. 'I managed one of the largest pitches we had ever done. Those types of pitches are fraught with stress where the slightest detail feels important. We knew they were interviewing many firms, and at some point I decided to make it feel more informal and intimate,' she remarked.

She continued: 'I always made the effort to be polite to the office removals men, asked how they were and thanked them, so they gave me their mobile numbers to call if I ever needed any help. Before the pitch started, I called and they came and changed the whole layout to incorporate round tables and comfier chairs, to give a more collaborative and interactive feel. In the end, we won that work, and I like to think that it's the small things like that, that helped make the right impression. There's no way I could have made those changes at such short notice without knowing the infrastructure team.'

This focus on the web of contact it takes to be successful may sound obvious to some of us — but all too often, when we think of those who can influence our career, we concentrate solely on those who are more senior.

Angela Mohtashemi, also at PwC, was going through the process of aiming for promotion to Partner when we met. When I asked her how important networking was in securing clients, her answers were as certain as other women intent on career advancement.

She explained: 'With every promotion you feel you are raising the bar on your networking skills and expanding your network further. What's more important is getting access to the right clients, and the only way to reach them is through the lead partners who manage the client relationships. You have to *prove* you can be trusted, as they are understandably protective about their clients. They'll only make an introduction if they think you are up to it — and won't embarrass them!'

NETWORK TO COLLABORATE

Often we narrowly classify people as either competitors or clients, without much grey area in between.

When you get comfortable with the 'grey areas', you will find that the relationships you make through networking can be can much more creative than you ever anticipated. Professor Athene Donald was an advocate of stretching yourself out of a narrow field of expertise to find potential collaborators.

Over the years, she found her work on committees particularly useful to this end. She reflected: 'I am not a conventional physicist in that my work is very inter-disciplinary. I do a great deal with biologists, which is great for me; it keeps things interesting. Also, most papers in my field are rarely single-author papers, so you need to reach out. I once met a chap I had sat on a committee with for several years but didn't know particularly well, on a train to London. We sat together, and while I'm a physicist and he is from the veterinary school, we realised how much we had in common and we ended up putting a cross-disciplinary grant proposal in together.'

Working with committees which include members from different but complementary fields allows for much greater scope of collaboration for specialists. For example, physicists won't necessarily meet biologists or vets in the usual round of professional conferences. There is too much disparity between their fields.

Additionally, for Athene, this type of loose connection with people she met through committees also made her feel more able to contact them when she had questions or even suggestions. She remembered: 'I knew a biologist from Birmingham, from a committee I served on. I noticed he had been published by a research council magazine, but in looking through the article I realised his photographs were really poor. I called to offer him the use of our cutting-edge equipment. We ended up collaborating briefly and then even got a joint publication.'

Professor Nicky Clayton, also at the University of Cambridge, was another scientist who used networking to find academics with whom to collaborate. She said: 'When someone talks about their career, it can seem there are clear stepping stones and it was all a strategic and linear process. That's *not* how I have approached it. I've just had a series of research questions that I wanted to answer, born out of fascinating discussions and even challenges from other scientists in my field. That's how my career has progressed.

'But really, you have an idea and it evolves. You make the story of your career *afterwards*, connecting the dots even though they didn't feel connected at the time.' This is an insightful observation. We are much more able to make sense of our career progression in retrospect, than we are when we are fumbling through it at the time.

In fact, her area of research — episodic memory in jaybirds — was born out of challenging discussions with sceptics who doubted that birds had or even needed memory or had the capacity for forward planning. Yet Nicky recognised that birds she had worked with were able not only to remember where they had stored food, but also to retrieve that food according to how perishable it was. This demonstrated just how memory-reliant the birds actually are.

Over the years, she met several sceptics at conferences and at other universities, who doubted that this process occurred, but who went on to collaborate with her and eventually became some of her biggest advocates.

Nicky's experience illustrates how networking with a wide variety of people, including those who may seem initially sceptical of your ideas, can positively affect your career. We tend to want to work primarily with people who agree with us and even are similar to ourselves on some level. This is natural and frankly is one of the main motivations behind why so many men hire younger men in their own likeness to bring up the ranks behind them.

But as Nicky's experiences demonstrate, this is not the only way forward; a different approach can indeed lead to unforeseen benefits.

She reflected: 'Meeting them offered me a complementary perspective, which challenged me to make my own research much more theoretically robust, multi-dimensional, and the process of getting there that *much more fun.*'

Perhaps this should be the rallying cry for greater diversity in these male-dominated fields.

- Networking helps prepare you for getting and handling board level responsibilities.

- Don't just look upwards. Be friendly to office juniors; you will need their support.

- Committees and collaborations can add a new dimension to your network.

INTERNAL NETWORKS

Nancy Woodhull, the late editor of *USA Today*, was at one time one of the most powerful women in publishing. She was noted for the way in which she facilitated the success of other women.

When she was at the helm of one of the country's largest newspapers, she remarked that it was her duty to 'do something to help another woman every day'. That phrase resonated with me at a deep level. I was struck by how much I also believed it — but also by its sheer simplicity.

Many of the successful women I interviewed found that some form of conscious effort to help other women often makes them feel better. Essentially, when giving, they are also receiving. The process of actively reaching out to other women gives them a new perspective and a feeling of being part of a community much larger than the worlds of their office and home. This is the ethos on which the emergence of women's networks — both internal and external to organisations — is built.

Women's networks within companies are useful to join as they are often high-profile and visible. Involvement can not only raise your confidence and credibility, but allows cross-networking with other departments within a business to widen your personal network. To this end, increasingly, many organisations are setting up their own internal networks for women in an effort to support and retain talented females.

Eileen Brown was one such woman, who has started women's networks — both inside Microsoft where she is the most senior technical woman, and for women in the industry as a whole. She found it challenging at first to get some women excited about the offering when she set up the internal network. She remembered: 'Some would question why they needed a network, as they were already doing the job. So I structured it to have more of a *lunch and learn* feeling, often on a technical topic.'

Eileen smiled: 'Once, after Microsoft installed new voice mail systems where you could manipulate your in-box through a voice-activated system, I decided to hold a networking meeting on using this technology. Some of the women who had been dubious of the network came because they were curious about the technology but didn't want to ask a male colleague to help them set it up. So they came along to our meeting and learned something — as well as entering the dialogue and meeting others.'

Eileen eventually went on to start another pan-industry network for women in IT, called Connecting Women in Technology. She explained: 'We organise a twice-yearly conference for our female employees, as well as for those female employees who work for Microsoft's competitors — but in between each conference we also share best practice with senior women from various companies that are *technically* our competition. We have a conference call and ask each other everything, from what we do to retrain our women returners, to how to keep homeworkers engaged.'

She elaborated on the value this type of information sharing has: 'We realise that we all face the same challenges and want to keep the few women we already have. The truth is, if we don't support the good women we have, they may leave but probably will end up in a company that can get these things right — so it's in our interest.'

When asked why this was of particular importance, Eileen mentioned that in the IT industry it is still far from being considered normal to have women in the field. She declared: 'Until the proportion of women in any industry reaches 30 per cent, it will never be considered normal. We have a long way to go, especially as we often lose women over 40 who don't feel valued or respected and have the confidence to say, *I don't need this anymore*. But that is a huge loss of intellectual property and a real waste.'

Rebecca George has also been heavily involved in promoting and leading women's networks for over a decade, running internal networks for both IBM and Deloitte, as well as spearheading a *Women in IT* forum on behalf of the former Department of Trade and Industry.

As we talked, Rebecca realised that the networks she had been most heavily involved with were primarily for female audiences. She had not been conscious of the fact until our interview — but realised she did want to be a source of encouragement to other women. This is what made her a natural advocate for other women in the industry.

Such is the appetite for support that, sometimes, women's networks are started *within* divisions of much larger companies. For example, Jane Lewis helped organise an internal networking group for her division within Microsoft. She had devised an informal programme for her network, Women in Premier Field Engineering. The network works with managers to make them aware of unconscious bias and how to encourage women to apply for roles within the team.

Jane, like Eileen Brown, is also a member of the project team that is involved in organising an industry-led network called Connecting Women in Technology. It brings women from IT firms such as Google, Dell, Cisco, Intel, Nortel, IBM and Microsoft together for networking several times a year, with a focus on career aspirations and managing work and family demands plus other relevant themes and topics.

She said: 'I am passionate about women finding out how great it can be to work in IT — that you can be creative, energetic, feminine and have fulfilling work.' She continued: 'And this is how I express it and get to do interesting work above and beyond my job description, which is something Microsoft is keen to promote for all their employees.'

Jane explained: 'I worry sometimes, because you can hear absolute horror stories about what it's like to work in the City in some organisations. I hate the thought of a woman thinking that is what IT is like. It would be terrible to let a bad experience in one company ruin your image of an *entire* industry. I like to point out that it can be different. Leaving IT would be a terrible waste.'

THE SET-UP

While there is increasing enthusiasm for internal women's networks, there is also a growing recognition that they need to be set up well, from the start, to ensure their success.

To this end, the question of leadership is one with which companies must first grapple in order to give the women's network the clout it needs to succeed. For example, it is vital that the champion be a high-ranking star within the organisation as a whole, whether that person is a woman or a *man*.

It is imperative to make the chair of any gender committee a senior-ranking executive who understands the issues, has the clout and credibility with other members of senior management, and is someone who normally works with other issues of strategic importance. In some organisations, this means enlisting the help of more than one partner or senior director.

By assigning the most senior and respected employees of either gender, it sends a message to both men and women that the organisation takes women's career development *seriously*.

It demonstrates that gender equality is a business imperative and not just an exercise in political window dressing. It also provides women with access to communicating with the most senior channels, rather than being relegated to the too-often overstretched HR or diversity team.

Furthermore, the network must be funded with a commitment of more than just pilot funding and featuring leaders whose paid role is to help manage the network. Some firms are beginning to credit such volunteers with more than mere kudos. However, unless they are given time within their working day to concentrate on facilitating the women's network, it can turn into a very stressful additional responsibility at the end of their day job.

Leaving the committee to the hands of well-meaning but time-pressed volunteers can set up the network for failure and the inevitable question of the value of such groups when they flounder.

Asking an internal women's network to fundraise for themselves after an initial pilot period, or indeed giving them no budget, creates programmes which are too minimal to be effective which gives unhelpful fodder to critics. I myself experience this when I am asked to reduce my fee because I am working with a 'poorly-funded women's network' — both inside and outside companies. If a network is to have real impact, it must be given real resources.

As explained in Wittenburg-Cox's and Maitland's *Why Women Mean Business*: '...Women's networks ... remain voluntary rather than business initiatives, dependent on personal dedication of already busy women to sustain them and struggle to gain continued corporate funding after start–up. If it is not worth investing in, don't bother'[1].

Joining an internal women's network is potentially one of the quickest ways you can begin to network *now*. It will give you a sense of camaraderie and connection with other women in your organisation as well as inspiration that others can thrive in the environment. It demonstrates to your boss that you are taking your profile seriously and want to become well-connected to others — which is a benefit for them as much as it is for you.

Internal women's networks will help you gain confidence as you move into the mixed-gender networking and external networks that are vital to the success of women in these fields.

---

[1] Wittenburg-Cox, A. & Maitland, A. (2008) "Why Women Mean Business", Jossey Bass, p. 170

- An internal women's network can widen your personal network enormously.

- A successful women's network needs a high-ranking leader.

- Joining such a network says that you take your profile — and career — seriously.

TEN

EXPLORING EXTERNAL NETWORKS

The reason there are so few female politicians

is that it is too much trouble to put make-up on two faces.

— Maureen Murphy

As an addition or alternative to an *internal* women's network, many people enjoy events that are *external* to their employers, and that feature a mix of people from related industries.

Most women in male-dominated fields will have to do their fair share of networking with men. Indeed, being one of the few women attending is a sure way to stand out. While such events can feel intimidating at first, successful women know there is much to be gained by joining mixed-gender networks. Men can become great contacts and mentors to women, and aligning yourself with the most reputable professional bodies in your industry is a key way to stay current and develop your knowledge.

As we have seen, women want to be included in networking but can't and don't always want to engage with it in the same way as men have historically done — on the proverbial golf course and at the pub. Many of my interviewees indicated that, while they liked interacting with colleagues and others in the industry socially, they didn't enjoy sports or impromptu drinking sessions, both of which have been the backbone to many a male career in these industries.

Furthermore, they don't see why they should engage in pub culture just to get ahead. I agree that you shouldn't have to — but I do think there *is* a place for socialisation, done in a style that is more suited to the way *you* want to interact.

Many women who already spend most of their day surrounded by men find they gain confidence and reassurance through attending industry-wide networks specifically for women.

Women who work in male-dominated fields often find women's external networks particularly useful for making connections with other organisations and to compare *how equality is done* in other companies. Many such networks aim to draw women together, precisely because they are in the minority in their field, for both their professional development and a sense of camaraderie.

It is in this space that many external networks for women who want to network in the UK are created. For example, Positive Energy is a network that holds approximately six events per year. The network also hosts a full day conference, attracting women from around the world who work in the energy industry. Another network, Fresh Ideas, holds evening events as well as an annual mentoring competition for female entrepreneurs and those interested in starting their own business. Women in Banking and Finance is an external network that serves women in financial services, and even hosts its own Toastmasters events for women looking to improve their speaking skills. Women in the City organises a yearly awards luncheon to promote women in business and honour individual high-fliers. We are the City is a network for women at all professional levels, but who work within Canary Wharf or the Square Mile in London.

These are only a few of the external networks operating all across the UK to serve women in progressing their careers, and you can check the Resources at the end of this book to find one that may be of interest to you.

Another network I belong to is the Cambridge Association for Women in Science and Engineering, which draws women from both the 'Silicon Fen' and academia. It addresses time pressures by offering both working lunches *and* evening sessions, for a greater chance that an interested woman can attend as well as meet her own scheduling demands.

As discussed previously, while the emergence of internal networks is undoubtedly a positive move, Maggie Berry would argue there is still a place for *external* networks.

She explained: 'Independent networks allow you to take a look outside of your organisation and get a better understanding of the market. You may feel that a difficult situation is unique to your company, then meet others from other organisations who are going through the *same* situation. You either realise you're not alone or indeed find there are actually better opportunities outside. You can often go away with a better understanding of issues within your company and what some of the larger issues are for the sector as a whole.'

Maggie continued: 'Plus, people and companies change — so, knowing people on the outside means that you are in a better position if you want to move, or indeed when *you* need to recruit.'

Womenintechnology.co.uk helps women to network with technology employers and each other to advance their careers. The network started as an online job board, where job advertisements from a wide variety of companies are posted for online jobseekers. However, the demand for in-person events for women themselves grew so much that they now organise over a dozen events per year, as well as offering professional development training courses.

The events are held in the evening and are focused around a keynote speech from an industry expert, or shorter presentations from women in the field and a panel session where the speakers can field questions from the audience. There is ample time both before and after for networking.

When asked exactly what a woman-focused network offers, Maggie said that attendees are often pleasantly surprised. She laughed: 'I always remember a woman who seemed dubious but came up to me after the event and said: "This is brilliant; it's a technology event, but not like any I've been to — it's full of *women*. The atmosphere is great and everybody is talking to one another!" We do invite men, which for many is the first time they get a feeling of what it is like to be a woman at one of the *normal* IT events,' she grinned.

- Look for a network that doesn't tie you into a male style of interacting.

- An external network helps you understand the market your organisation works in.

- Knowing outside people makes you better placed to recruit people or move jobs.

THE UTILITY OF WOMEN'S NETWORKS

One challenge that Zoë Ingle, who runs Positive Energy, described was the scepticism of a minority of women she met who couldn't see any need for a women-focused industry network. She explained: 'When talking to individuals about the value of the network, some women have been reticent, indirectly saying they don't want to be associated with a women-only network. While we do invite men, it's a forum primarily for women and of those sceptics who do come along, they are convinced of its utility after their *first* visit.'

The Positive Energy network takes a slightly different tack, allowing women to present both about their career story, which attendees find inspiring, and on their specialist topic within energy — which helps raise their profile as an expert.

She remarked: 'Our network focuses on industry issues — like global warming — attracting new talent and so on. It also addresses the challenges faced by women in the field that they may not be as comfortable discussing in their normal male-dominated environments. It gives them the opportunity to speak on their subject matter, because we want the world to see them as industry experts first and women almost second.'

I myself have seen some women shy away from women-focused events, as if their attendance or support would draw further attention to their 'otherness' in not being a man. But the fact that they are women already draws attention to their 'otherness' whether or not they attend a female-friendly event. It is almost as if they have internalised the belief that, since they are one of the token women, any other women would be competition for *exactly the same token spot*. Rather, we should question why many senior management teams seem to allow for only one or two 'token women' at a time.

Sometimes, external women's networks find resistance from the same companies they would like to serve. Zoë occasionally has this experience, whereby a company initially asks why it should support their external network when it has its own internal women's network. They argue that their women are already well supported in-house. When an organisation wants to hold on to the few women it has, the idea of supporting them going to an outside network arouses insecurities and worries that those women may decide to leave for a job elsewhere.

Zoë explained how she gets such sceptics on board: 'If the company is truly doing all it can to support women and it's such a fantastic employer to work for, shouldn't they be sharing best practice and making others aware of their successes? And think how many other new women entering the field you could potentially attract!'

Another concern for some of her attendees is the low value some women put on their own internal networks. Zoë said: 'I have talked to women who were dubious about *our* programme, but that's because *their* company pays only lip service to the idea of an internal women's network. Their experience of a women's network is their employer holding a meeting once a year in the evening, with wine and a style show — but not giving the network the resources it actually needs to thrive and be taken seriously by women internally. And then companies wonder why they aren't getting better results!'

- Attend a women-only network *before* you decide it's not for you. You may be surprised.
- Join both mixed-gender and women-only networks.
- Networks provide great opportunities for speaking and committee leadership roles.

THE WIDE WORLD OF ONLINE NETWORKING

Even if you haven't already embraced it, you can no longer ignore the power of online networking. Sites such as Facebook, MySpace, Flixster, LinkedIn and Twitter appear to be here to stay. For the purposes of brevity, I am going to concentrate on Facebook and LinkedIn. According to its website in March 2009, Facebook has over 175 million active users with 70 per cent living outside the US. While Facebook has long been considered a haven for the under-30 crowd, its fastest growing demographic is people *over* the age of 30.

Similarly, LinkedIn's website claims over 36 million members, more than half of which are outside the US. LinkedIn has more of a reputation as an online networking site for professionals, with the average income of a LinkedIn user being double the national average. LinkedIn works slightly differently from Facebook and has greater potential, in my opinion, for the average professional woman. It is not about finding contacts you already know, but finding those you *need* to know.

Online networking is increasingly attractive to women, as a way of managing many contacts in a time-efficient way. According to their own websites, just over half of all Facebook users are women and nearly 40 per cent of LinkedIn users are women. In fact, on LinkedIn, there are over 3,000 groups dedicated to women networking, and just as many in-person networks also have online groups within their forums. These numbers are vital, as they are both above the tipping point to make it easier for a woman to stay in touch with the women — and men — she wants to.

I admit I am fairly new to social media as a means of enhancing one's professional profile. However, I also realise that these networks have the potential to be much larger, and are much trickier to get right, than traditional relationship-building. Through using them effectively, you can be considered the expert to whom people go for answers on a particular specialist topic, as well as someone who is helpful to know because of the strength of your network.

Like face-to-face exchanges, it is vital to choose the right online networks to use. There are too many to count and more being born every day. Like face-to-face networks, the best way to develop strong ties is by being faithful to one or two in particular. Andy Lopata, one of the UK's leading business networking strategists, was able to explain their utility and the options they provide for the professional woman wanting to raise her profile.

He explained: 'Within large organisations, you can find out if someone is working on a similar project to you and compare notes. Outside your organisation, you can connect with experts from around the world who can help you find the answer you've been looking for. Sites such as LinkedIn offer the opportunity to ask your network for the answers to your key challenges. Used wisely, these can offer a tremendous source of ideas, market research and solutions.'

For example, I am sometimes asked by an event organiser or journalist for the name of someone who could act as a speaker or be interviewed. Rather than trawling through my email address book, I have posted such requests to my LinkedIn contacts. I am just beginning to understand the power of online networking and was dubious about its potential at first.

Sensing my initial scepticism, as a busy woman who is over 30 years old and not adept at all in the latest communication technologies, Andy did admit to me that you could have a long and happy career *without* accessing these new online tools. However, he felt that avoiding them could: '…Leave people at a disadvantage. Traditional routes to raising your profile have been rapidly overtaken by blogging and social networks. You can reach so many more people in seconds. There is no other route I'm aware of that offers such exposure so efficiently.'

This is particularly important for women in male-dominated fields, as they need to be remembered by their contacts for something other than their gender.

He explained: 'In the past it was very difficult to maintain contact with previous colleagues when we, or they, moved on. With social networks you can stay in constant touch. It becomes much easier to retain the ability to go back to people when you need their help, advice or input.'

As much of a proponent as he is of online networking, Andy agreed they should never completely *replace* your traditional networking methods. He said: 'You can initiate and manage a relationship online but you can't develop it — certainly not to the same extent that you can when you can see the whites of the other person's eyes.'

Similarly, he does not advocate linking to people you don't know; the goal of online networking for professionals is not quantity, but quality. It reduces the impact of your efforts if you can't honestly make a recommendation for them.

THE PERILS OF ONLINE PROMISCUITY

Think carefully which online networks you should consider, if you are looking to raise your professional profile. Andy suggested: 'Currently, the most recognised site for career development is LinkedIn, which is heavily populated by recruitment consultants and head-hunters. Use a long-term strategy when picking any social network. Only commit to as many networks as you can manage, because you are better off focusing on a few and working on them.'

This echoes the way you should approach traditional networks: don't over-commit. If you spread yourself thin over too many, you may not be able to deliver on regular updates or help other members. This approach reminds me of how Philippa Snare at Microsoft said, *The best technology merely mimics and enhances what humans already do*; commit to a few groups and grow those relationships rather than expecting a scatter gun approach to deliver any real returns.

When deciding which networks to use, it is easy to lean towards specialist networks. While these have their place for gaining specialist knowledge, it would be wise to stay active in the largest and most established, as these are more likely to thrive in the long run. As Andy Lopata suggested: 'People will gravitate towards niche networks. With the growth of social networking, there are now too many networks for even the most committed online networker to cope with. The big networks, like LinkedIn or Facebook, will continue to thrive because I don't see how all of the smaller ones can sustain themselves without a huge pot of money, a truly unique and well-communicated story, or a niche.'

A word of warning in this brave new world: if you have never met the person face-to-face, it is harder to judge other's people reactions to your messages and, in some cases, even be sure with whom we are really communicating. For my own LinkedIn profile, for example, I only make links to people I have met in person a few times and whom I actually connected with ... and I hope the feeling was mutual!

One way to test the water and protect yourself is to avoid being too free with your opinions. They can be easily misinterpreted online and you can't read facial or vocal cues the way you can in a face-to-face interaction. When asked how a woman could protect herself from making contact with the wrong people, Andy suggested: 'Find out what people you know and trust say about new connections. If they have met them and can vouch for them, that may set your mind at rest. If you are meeting someone you have only ever met online, do so in a public place, such as a coffee shop, at a busy time, or at a networking event where there are plenty of other people around.'

Just because a meeting is under the auspices of a business interaction does not mean that you should ignore the same rules you would apply to meeting a blind date, for example. Additionally, having one profile for friends on say Facebook and another for colleagues on LinkedIn is a good way forward — if, like me, you want to keep the two separate and don't want colleagues or potential employers to see photos of what you got up to on holiday with your girlfriends 15 years ago, let alone last summer.

Alternatively, you could have a single account, such as with Facebook, but have various privacy settings so you can better control how much information any individual sees.

If you are concerned about privacy, and how to avoid colleagues seeing your latest holiday snaps or photos from your younger, and let's say *less-polished* days, I have heard of more than one woman who keeps two separate profiles on Facebook. Each profile has separate security access controls. The first is for friends and family; the second is for those she might know through work, and hence with whom she wants to maintain a professional image whilst tapping into the larger audience of professional women who are increasingly using the site.

Do you think it would be better to just opt out to protect your privacy? Think again. Simply not having an account is not the protection you might think it is, as friends who are members will often post photos that may include your name and hence are tagged for others to view. In fact, as I initially did, you may find that there are probably already photos of you on Facebook, posted by friends or family. As with so much else in playing with *the boys' club*, it is worth playing the game but on your own terms.

- Keep social and professional online networks separate.

- Ignore online networks at your peril.

- Most in-person networks have online groups you can also join.

CONNECTING OTHERS

One of the most important pieces of advice I hope you would take from this book is how important it is to be a connector of people if you want to raise your own profile.

Being the connector has worked well for all of the successful women I interviewed, and is a sure way to make sure you are well-regarded by others. Maggie Berry knows the value of staying in touch — *and* the lateral thinking that it requires.

She explained: 'I connect people all the time. Don't underestimate what you know, because the knowledge you take for granted may be what someone else is looking for. I often hear people say, *I've been trying to find that out for ages; do you know anything about it?* In fact, I don't always need to know the answer; it is enough just to know someone who does. Listen out as people are talking and you can offer, *I've read something about that recently, or even, One of my colleagues back at the office is an expert in that; shall I ask her to send you the information?*'

Similarly, as part of her job, Rebecca George of Deloitte makes connections for other people. She stays in touch with colleagues and past clients in all aspects of the Civil Service, and thinks laterally about their needs.

She explained: 'I keep in touch with everyone, and ask them how their priorities or challenges are shifting. I am genuinely interested in what's going on for them — but it also makes *me* useful to others, as I can talk about patterns or trends I am noticing.' She quipped: 'Some people tell me they could ask half a dozen people … or just ask me, since they will know I have probably already spoken to those half a dozen people.'

Eileen Brown operated on this same principle. She explained with a descriptive IT analogy how she saw networking as the intermingling of *hubs* and *endpoints* and how this affected how she became a connector for others. She explained: '*Endpoints* want information; they don't think laterally to pass it on. They come looking for advice and help or to make a sale. *Hubs*, on the other hand, give information out because they are well connected to *endpoints* who recognise their utility. And occasionally, you will have hubs talking to each other, which is where the *most* information and energy is exchanged.'

You don't have to be a technical wizard or industry expert to become a hub; rather, it's more about how you process requests and how well you think laterally that makes you a hub or an endpoint. If an endpoint doesn't know the answer to your question, they will leave it at that. A hub understands that they don't have to know everything; rather they will find someone who does.

The key is in recognising early on who is a hub and who is an endpoint. You may simply have to make time to have 'random conversations', as Eileen put it, to find a *golden hub*. And as she explained, you can change from being an endpoint to being a hub: 'I may have a mentee who asks me something I don't know the answer to — but I can point her in the right direction. She then becomes an endpoint with a few connections. As her career and connections develop, she can become a hub and useful to other endpoints.'

Eileen continued: 'For example, most of my Facebook connections do not respond to my updates because they are endpoints. However, a few people will get in touch and say they are interested in what I have posted too, and ask how they can be involved; they're the hubs.' The key for any woman wanting to raise her profile is to connect others and be recognised as a hub.

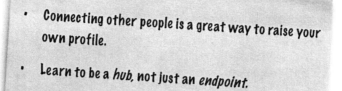

- Connecting other people is a great way to raise your own profile.
- Learn to be a *hub*, not just an *endpoint*.
- Offer help to people you have just met, to keep the dialogue going.

BEING THE WOMAN WHO SEEMS TO KNOW EVERYONE

If your ship doesn't come in, swim out to it.

— Jonathan Winters

What you will find if you are doing it right is that networking is more about giving than receiving. Not recognising this is one of the surest ways to feel let down when you leave your first event with no dream job offer coming from it.

It is about developing relationships and following through by offering any help you can. Don't offer your *business* services initially, unless that is what someone asks for; find other ways to help and stay in touch. It might be that you can make a new contact for them. I offer articles I think a person may be interested in, or the name of someone else I know would make a great speaker for them, based on what we have been talking about.

Another good tip for those new to networking is to give yourself a *get-out clause*. Go along but reassure yourself you *only have to stay* until 7.30 or 8pm, for example. Maggie Berry plays this game with herself and reasoned: 'Give yourself a limit of staying just until 8pm. Invariably, once you get in and start to have a few conversations, you enjoy it and stay at least until your self-imposed deadline and usually past that time, even. Don't tell yourself you have to stay all night. Just give yourself a target and each time challenge yourself to stay a bit longer — if you like.'

Another trick if you are new to networking is to bring a friend. In addition to attending her own events, Maggie receives frequent invitations to other events most nights, so is used to going to things on her own — yet she still advises those who feel intimidated to bring a friend.

She said: 'You won't need one once you arrive, since people are so happy to talk, but if it helps you get over the threshold of even attending, then by all means bring someone. Additionally, if I am going to an event for the first time, I will spot the organiser and ask them to introduce me to people. That usually kick-starts me into the flow of meeting people. Even better, if I know who is going to be there, I will say to the organiser, *Oh, I would really love to meet the speaker. Can you introduce me when you get a chance?*'

When networking, sometimes you can find yourself 'stuck' in a group or with a person with whom there's just no connection. Everyone is there to network, so don't feel bad about saying, *It was really nice to meet you. I'm going to say hello to a few other people before the speeches start.* If that feels difficult, just say that you are going to meet someone you already know, or that you are going to get a drink or visit the ladies before the speeches start. At the end of the day, no one will be truly offended. You're all adults and you know *why* you are there — to meet new people.

Maggie also suggested joining a pre-existing group. This can feel intimidating at first, as it seems as if you are 'breaking into' a group that appears to be best friends already, but most often this is not the case. She said: 'Sometimes you arrive and it looks like everyone has already paired up or people are laughing like they have known each other for years — but they don't. Often when I ask if I can join them, they say, *Oh, we've just met each other tonight.* That is hugely reassuring and often people are just looking for other people to join their group to add a new dimension.'

This is also a clever way to excuse yourself from a one-to-one conversation that you want to disengage from, or to liven up the dynamic. Simply say to the other person, *Let's join this group!*

Ana Pacheco found building her network has been invaluable to her success, even if she doesn't consider herself to be the most strategic networker. She explained: 'Sometimes it's the little things. You remember some of the context from what you were last discussing and ask them how their holiday to Morocco was, or how their child is doing at school if it came up. Even if you can't recall the details, people are often impressed when you can just remember they were going on holiday the last time you spoke. It's the details that help build the relationship.'

In the words of PwC's Janet Davies: 'Networking is everything.' I don't know a single successful woman who does not have a high quality network of friends and colleagues on which she can rely. Attending cross-company networks can provide a wealth of information for savvy women who are researching their next employer. It can give women in these fields the confidence and camaraderie necessary to thrive when moving *beyond the boys' club*. Just as importantly, knowing the right people for any given job allows women to do more within less time — a vital skill for any professional with their sights on climbing the career ladder.

- Boost your nerve by attending events with a friend or giving yourself an *escape time*.

- Join a pre-existing group if you get stuck with one person.

- As for introductions, don't be shy; you may never get another chance.

ELEVEN

MENTORING

> *If you can't be a good example, then you'll just have to be a*
>
> *horrible warning.*
>
> — Catherine Aird

Successful women often cite the influence of a *mentor* on their career. They have benefited enormously from sharing ideas and raising questions with their mentor: someone more senior than them professionally, who can help guide the way and give career advice. And most women recognise they are much stronger as a result of these interactions.

For those who seek these types of relationship, the benefits are hard to overstate. An overview of more than 100 mentoring surveys conducted by the East Mentors Forum[1] found that nearly half of all respondents in such studies reported that mentoring increased their opportunities for career advancement. Seventy-five per cent said the experience was positive, citing higher salaries and increased job satisfaction among the most tangible benefits.

In fact, I don't know a successful woman who has *not* had some type of mentoring relationship in her past, whether or not she recognised it as such at the time. While many of the best mentoring relationships seem to occur spontaneously, rather than leave their development to chance, proactive successful women seek out mentors for themselves.

---

[1] "Mentors Develop the New Leaders", Times Online, Steve Farrar, March 30, 2008

MY OWN FIRST MENTOR

In my experience, actively seeking a mentor has worked very well for my clients as well as for myself. I've had many mentors from whom I have learned, perhaps in small doses with just a handful of interactions, whereas others have given more time on an ongoing basis.

What they all have in common is that I was able to learn from their experiences and make better and more informed decisions for myself.

A good mentor may have travelled much of the same path you are interested in following. They will share their experiences and lessons with you as a means of making your own voyage easier and more fulfilling.

One of my first mentors was a professor, Dr Dana Brotman, who lectured in Psychology at my undergraduate university, St Mary's College of Maryland. She'd had life experiences I admired and loved to hear about. She had travelled to Ireland and fallen in love with a British man (how similar that would be to my own path was yet to be discovered!). She had lived in New York City and developed a successful career as a psychologist; all of this was wildly glamorous and inspirational to me. Plus, she was deeply passionate about her field, psychopathology, which was a fascination we shared.

She was an amazing professor and we would share ideas during her office open hours — never calling it *mentoring* but undoubtedly knowing the value it gave me.

In my final year, I shyly shared with her my dream of moving to Europe after graduation. Unlike many adults who encouraged me to be more 'realistic' about my career plans, considering I had not a single contact in Europe, Dana was enthusiastic and encouraging. She shared with me one of the key lessons I now live with: never to regret the risks you took, only those you did not.

Her encouragement was the seal of approval I needed. My confidence boosted, I began planning for the journey that would change my life forever. I also began to understand the power of a good mentor.

THE INFLUENCE OF EARLY MENTORS

Now, when I speak with women who work in male-dominated fields, I hear echoes of what I found in my own PhD research. Young women were much more likely to enter these fields if they had a mentor, usually someone in the family who worked in the same field. Mentors like these could explain the utility and applications of science, for example, as well as the benefits and drawbacks of working in these sectors.

The role of fathers, in particular, was important as girls were more likely to have fathers in such fields than mothers. In fact, American researchers who surveyed 40,000 women born between the years 1909 and 1977 found that women born in the 1970s were three times as likely to follow in their father's professional footsteps. This could be due to a variety of factors: fathers taking a greater interest in their daughter's education, a wider variety of fields opening up to working women and the overall increase in levels of educational attainment for the average woman during that period[2].

That being said, the role of a parent working in an aligned industry was not essential. It also extended to the role of *influential others* — family friends, uncles or neighbours — for girls interested in these fields. In short, women who entered male-dominated fields often had early experience of mentoring.

Likewise, mentoring was vital to the women I interviewed. They all learned to watch what worked for other people. Regardless of whether they identified a past colleague or employer as a 'mentor', their interviews illustrated how they all had been mentored by watching others. They learned by modelling behaviours, either following the same path — or in some cases, as we will see, doing the opposite.

I have always believed there are three types of people in the world: those that learn from their own mistakes, those that don't learn from their own mistakes and are doomed to keep making them until they do learn, and those that learn from the mistakes of other people. The savviest women learn from the mistakes of others, so they don't necessarily have to make the *same* mistakes themselves in order to learn from them.

[2] "Like Father, Like Daughter" podcast, Scientific American, www.sciam.com, March 4, 2009

Believe me: any professional woman who takes risks will make mistakes — but learning from the mistakes of those who have gone before will speed up the learning process. If your mentor will share with you what went well for her *and what didn't*, you are 'quids in' regarding advice.

Some of the women I interviewed could not identify a single mentor who stood out, nor even qualify any guidance they received as mentoring. However, other women could remember their first mentors in particular, with almost perfect accuracy. In some cases this was because they had initially found themselves floundering at work, and quickly realised they needed to seek out extra guidance.

Janet Davies, at PwC, experienced this situation early on in her career. 'On the first day of my first job, I was told I would be managing a team of people. This came as a complete surprise and certainly hadn't been mentioned in the interview. I was all of 23 and faced with the prospect of managing people both older and younger than me, with completely different mindsets. So I quickly sought out a wonderful mentor in the Human Resources department at Sainsbury's, where my husband had been a graduate trainee. My own employer didn't place a high value on training for managers, and I didn't want them to know how ill-equipped I felt. So I went outside the company for the help I needed, so that they didn't know how much I had to learn!'

- First mentors often have the largest impact.
- Having no mentor will have a big negative impact on your career.
- You can learn the most from the mistakes other people make.

A SENSE OF PERSPECTIVE

Jackie Gittins spoke highly of the mentor who had worked with her for the past ten years. She explained: 'She originally recruited me to PwC. She's moved on now but still provides the perfect amount of emotional and intellectual challenge. We can talk about anything from marriage to a difficult client assignment. She always reminds me to look at what my part is in any challenge, which is very humbling and changes my perspective.'

Seeing things through a new lens was one of the key benefits successful women mentioned when talking about building their support network.

Whilst tradition in many male-dominated fields suggests that people develop mentoring relationships at the pub or on the golf course, Jackie and her mentor meet for the ballet and talk tactics over a meal. This is a great example of women making mentoring work for *them*, based on what they enjoy, rather than the traditional male model with which they have been surrounded.

Matilda Venter was another woman who maintained a close relationship with a mentor from her past. She said: 'He worked at PwC, so continues to help me consider how to build the best internal relationships, approach clients and how to not take things at face value. He taught me to understand the underlying reasons for people's behaviour and not take things so personally.'

The gift of receiving a larger perspective was a benefit named by many women who had mentors. When you are in the thick of an issue, it can seem overwhelming and all-important. As the saying goes: *There is nothing new under the sun*. The chances are that your mentor has often been there before and can help you realise the entire future of your career is not reliant upon one deal, piece of research or job decision alone. They can help you to see the larger picture, which can be like a breath of fresh air and a welcome relief.

Matilda, for example, recalled a time her mentor had helped her take on a new perspective. She said: 'I worked for a European client and had difficulty overcoming cultural differences. I had a hard time establishing a good relationship with a key client contact. It was terribly frustrating. My mentor helped me stop getting caught in the detail and take more of a strategic view — and try to connect with the individual on a different level. It actually led to a very good relationship in time.'

Jane Lewis was another woman who had found very useful the sense of perspective that mentoring can offer. She participated in the formal mentoring scheme at Microsoft as both mentor and mentee — but still found it reassuring when her mentor simply reminded her: 'Jane, take a reality check!' when she was making an issue bigger than it needed to be.

STRUGGLING WITHOUT A MENTOR

Just as successful women find having a mentor useful to their own development, there were also women who struggled without them. This was a good reminder of the usefulness of *proactively* building a support network.

When Harriet Crawford returned to academic life, after a career break as a research fellow at Lucy Cavendish College at the University of Cambridge, she found there was no mentoring system in place. She said: 'This was a great loss, to be honest. It would have been extremely useful to have someone to advise on publication, understanding college politics and giving lectures. But getting that kind of guidance was just something you did by the seat of your pants.'

Academia is fiercely competitive. It has a relatively rigid hierarchical system that takes years to negotiate. This left Harriet to make her own way with a minimum of formal guidance. Looking back at her career, she is sanguine about the impact it had on her experiences.

She reflected: 'If I had a mentor when I got my first academic post at UCL who said, *You've got a very respectable record of publications and your teaching reports are very good, why don't you go for promotion?* I probably would have gone for promotions earlier. There was always a feeling of *Oh, I'm lucky to be here, I mustn't rock the boat*. It helps to have someone telling you to go for it. And of course, I'll never know what opportunities I missed by not having a mentor.'

Similarly, Laura Hinton recalls that it was only when she decided to tender her resignation to her previous employer that she was given direct help and mentoring to advance her career. She explained: 'I told them I didn't know where my career was going and that I wanted to resign. They immediately turned around and told me how well they thought I was doing and that they wanted to keep me. This feedback came as a relief but was a total surprise! To sweeten the deal, they gave me a big project to work on, and a team of mentors who I could now more easily access to talk about my career prospects in and out of the company. I was also given a politically astute line manager for the new project. I shadowed him for nearly five years, learning a great deal about how to get high-profile projects done, and how to handle politics, in the process. But the irony was that this type of mentoring support was not forthcoming until I said I was going to leave, which is disappointing.'

It is a sad irony that it is often only when we feel overwhelmed and ready to give up on a challenge that help is then offered.

At the same time Laura began to receive mentoring, she was also given intensive presentational skills training. She rightly took this as further evidence that her employers wanted to invest in her, that they saw her as someone with a great deal of potential. She laughed: 'It helped me see they were willing to put their money where their mouths were! It sent me a clear message I was valued and they took my potential contributions seriously, which further boosted my confidence.'

THE PARTNERSHIP TRACK

Laura's example does highlight a problem prevalent in some firms that operate as partnerships. Accountancy and law practices, for example, are criticised for not giving enough feedback to mid-level employees about their progress, and hence their chances for partnership. Partnership is considered by most to be the holy grail of a law or consultancy career; you are given a percentage in the equity of the business, and hence the stakes and demands on your time are high.

The challenge is that these types of partnership are based on many years of work beforehand, for example seven years in the case of law firms. There are many casualties along the way — notably women, who face having to make decisions about how committed they are to sustaining a gruelling workload during their key childbearing years.

As Laura Hinton discovered with her previous employer, this is a great deal of time to be unsure as to what your actual chances are for partnership. Some line managers keep employees in the dark on purpose, as a means to avoid de-motivating those whom they do not think are cut out for it but who are still very useful in the interim. Likewise, they may fear too much positive feedback could create complacency in those they identify as the most promising candidates.

Securing your *own* mentor is simply one of the best ways to avoid feeling in the dark.

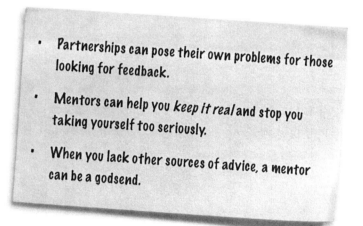

- Partnerships can pose their own problems for those looking for feedback.
- Mentors can help you *keep it real* and stop you taking yourself too seriously.
- When you lack other sources of advice, a mentor can be a godsend.

FIND MALE AND FEMALE MENTORS

Although my specialism is in coaching women for career progression, I do not think the gender of the mentor matters as long as they are genuinely interested in your career growth and are willing to make time for you. In fact, if you work in a male-dominated field, it is vital that you seek male as well as female mentors.

You must be comfortable with men, and get an insight into their standpoint, as they are often the key decision makers and those with real clout. They will help you broaden your perspective and enable you to engage with more senior players than you would be able to access on your own.

I suggest that many of my clients seek both men and women as mentors. The women mentors are often sought for emotional support and strategic guidance, whereas male mentors are better for allowing access to the hallowed halls of the 'inner circle' — a place normally exclusively populated by men.

Janet Davies was one woman who experienced mentoring mostly from men — simply because in her own field, like many, there are not many senior women around. She said: 'It was the men who taught me how to survive in a male environment.'

When asked to explain, she elaborated: 'They lived by the bottom line. They didn't care what colour or gender you were; it was purely about how much business you brought in and the results you achieved. I got on by being keen, likeable and dependable and by not running into a corner every time they did or said something that could have been interpreted as sexist. We have equal opportunities legislation in the UK but I think you make your *own* equality in many ways.'

When I asked her how she managed to achieve 'equality', Janet replied: 'By always believing you are equal. I was raised by my father to know I was equal to any of my brothers, and this has carried on through my working life. Sometimes, if you walk into a room and people don't know you, they may think they can take advantage of the fact that you are a woman. They don't listen or will try and impose something on you. It's like transactional analysis; if they see you as a child and themselves as the adult, it's not a good start, so you have to go in and assert yourself as an adult right from the start.'

The term *mentoring* is a fairly new word, which has only been introduced into everyday language in the last few decades. Obviously, that is not to say that this type of caring and learning relationship did not exist before then — it did, and always has done. For women entering male-dominated fields in those years, it was hard to find female role models at all, let alone a more senior woman who might act as mentor. Men became the default mentoring option for ambitious young women.

TILL YOU FIND A MENTOR, LOOK TO ROLE MODELS

Dame Veronica Sutherland was entering retirement at the time I interviewed her about her long and varied career. She had joined the Foreign Office in 1965 as it offered her a way to travel. While there was no legal requirement for equal pay, she also knew that the Diplomatic Service did indeed pay men and women equally, which was attractive to her.

Regarding mentoring, she explained: 'I go back a long way and *mentoring* was just not a word you used. When I first entered the Foreign Office, I was in my mid-twenties and two men each in their thirties were responsible for licking me into shape. They told me when I needed to contact someone in the Foreign Secretary's office, and rewrote my drafts. I found the whole organisation very supportive and friendly. I didn't call it *mentoring* but it probably was.'

When asked if she had any role models, Dame Veronica answered: 'There were no female ambassadors at the time I started — but there was a woman, Barbara Salt, who had been appointed to the role in Israel but was unable to take it up following an operation which went wrong. So, I knew it could be done. In the 70s, two more women became ambassadors and by the mid 1980s I was made an ambassador myself in West Africa. I was the first British married woman to hold such a post. It's remarkable it took so long but women had to resign on marriage up until 1972.'

In a similar vein, sometimes a client will say to me that she finds it much easier to work with or be mentored by men than women. As I mentioned, I would not advise clients to pick mentors by their gender, but rather to choose based on the sense of camaraderie and chemistry that exists between them. Indeed, I meet lots of ambitious women who would appreciate a guiding hand from a woman who has 'been there, done that', to help them climb another rung on the corporate ladder. Certainly it can be inspirational to work with a senior woman if you can see how she has managed to thrive in your sector — but it is not vital.

What *is* vital is getting a mentor you trust and respect, and vice versa. I am often asked about the motives of senior women who seem to enjoy making life difficult for the women below them, or who are pulling the ladder up after themselves. I often wonder, are those already at the top afraid that there is only room enough for a token woman in the boardroom? It's almost as if we accept that there might be only one or two spots at the top. I am reminded of Madeleine Albright's expression: 'There is a special place in hell for women who don't help other women.'

There might be a feeling that if a woman has had to struggle and claw her way up 'the hard way', and doing so has made her who she is, then such a struggle would benefit other women too. I would believe more in the validity of this 'school of hard knocks' approach if it were also espoused by senior men for more junior men, and that they weren't so willing to promote and help guide those in their own image by default. However, men *have* historically pulled each other up 'the ladder' without worrying about how it might make the younger person 'soft' or hinder the development of their character. And that is one lesson we should definitely take from the men, when observing and learning from *the boys' club*.

- It is not safe to assume that women make better mentors than men. Have both.

- Historically, most of the early mentors would have had to be men.

- Trust and respect are what define a great mentor, not gender.

THE REWARDS OF WO-MENTORING

When I speak at conferences on mentoring, people sometimes ask why they should volunteer to be a mentor to others. We normally concentrate on the benefits of mentoring for the *mentee* — but the results are certainly not one-sided.

The aforementioned meta-analysis of mentoring research by the East Mentoring Forum[3] found that 62 per cent of mentors said mentoring had 'improved their own job performance by enhancing their own knowledge and understanding.'

In my experience, mentoring often gives people a renewed sense of job satisfaction as they pass on knowledge. It is also an outlet to realise just how far they have come in their own development — not something we tend to focus on when the next challenge is always just around the corner. It can also help the mentor keep aware of morale 'within the ranks' as well as offering the *opportunity* to spot the upcoming stars.

Many women I work with initially assume they are not 'experienced enough' to mentor. The truth is, if you wait until you feel you know everything worth passing on, you will never feel quite ready to mentor. It's like seizing opportunities when you are 80 per cent ready, as we have already discussed. People often erroneously think mentoring should solely come from senior management — but even if you are just a few years into a job, you still have knowledge to pass on. Entry-level employees can mentor new hires. New hires can mentor university students!

I routinely challenge my coaching clients to mentor someone, no matter how long they have been in their job or how little knowledge they believe they have. It is always more than someone else has, and you will get more than you imagine out of the experience.

As mentioned previously, mentoring doesn't have to be a long-term partnership. For example, I often find myself in a mentoring relationship with

3 "Mentors Develop the New Leaders", Times Online, Steve Farrar, March 30, 2008

a woman who is just setting up a new business and seeking advice and a bit of supportive feedback. I have also acted as a sounding board to fledgling event organisers — simply because I work with so many as a speaker and know some of the basics that need to be covered, such as the likelihood of getting sponsors or how to give added value to attendees.

There is little in life as *rewarding* as having someone thank you for taking an interest in their career, and seeing them get further ahead than if they had struggled through it on their own.

RECIPROCAL BENEFITS

Matilda Venter is a successful consultant who finds mentoring very rewarding. Many of the other successful women I interviewed also share this experience. She was approached by a more junior client for a mentoring relationship after they stopped working together, which in itself is a great accolade. She explained: 'It's incredibly motivational to help somebody through the process of discovering themselves, and to help open their eyes to what is potentially holding them back.'

Jackie Gittins, also at PwC, works with up to eight mentees at any given time. They are a mix of colleagues and a few who approach her directly because of her reputation for mentoring. Jackie enjoys the interaction and said: 'It's primarily informal — but I notice we tend to work together for two years. I love it because it has allowed me to experiment with my communication style, and connect with a younger generation. It helps keep me up to date, and we talk about everything from what they like to eat to what they want out of work. It's fascinating and keeps me on my toes, whilst staying in touch with the wider world.'

Similarly, Ana Pacheco says that mentoring has played a large part in her success. In addition to receiving mentoring, she volunteers to mentor colleagues from other departments. Her explicit offer to mentor others makes her well-respected throughout the firm.

One of her favourite things to do with a mentee is to help them be a bit easier on themselves. This is something I do frequently in my coaching capacity, as high-achieving women are most often their own toughest critics. Ana remarked: 'Women have a tendency to put themselves down. They point out what they haven't done yet, when perhaps no one has noticed or even expected it. It's funny because I do the same thing myself. That's one of the things I like about mentoring: it helps puts things in perspective for me. I remind them they don't have to do it all in order to get where they want to go.'

She elaborated: 'They often set unrealistic targets for themselves, so I have to help them manage their own expectations which are often higher than those of other people. I point out that while I know what their self-imposed goals were, they actually achieved more than I thought was realistic in the first place!'

Much is made about what a mentee can learn from a mentor — but if we look at it strictly as an unequal relationship, we risk losing much that we could potentially gain: the learning and validation that a mentor can receive. To this end, Philippa Snare at Microsoft said: 'I won't agree to mentor someone if I don't believe I have as much to learn from them as I do to pass on. That's a real challenge as there are lots of talented young people here who are very sharp and ambitious. They help keep me on my toes. It reminds me I'm just here to help facilitate their growth. A good leader knows when a mentee is even *overtaking* them in a certain area and is okay with that. It's humbling but reassuring.'

When asked what mentoring had given her, Philippa responded: 'It just makes you feel a bit better grounded and more realistic about what you can and cannot achieve all on your own. It reminds you that you need others to succeed.'

PRAISE FOR THE MENTOR

Similarly, Laura Hinton recalled the first time she told her mentor about a major win her team had earned at the accountancy firm. As previously discussed, in his note of congratulations he copied in considerably more senior members of the firm, who in turn gave their congratulations to her. However, the flipside is that letting them know that a woman he mentored had achieved so much, was a great plaudit for *him* as well.

Mentors like to be associated with thriving mentees. If they can show a relationship between your success and their advice, even if indirect, they are noted for being a mentor and leader. That in turns serves them well in the long term.

Remember that any good mentoring relationship should have reciprocal benefits for both parties. If you are a savvy mentee, look for ways to show your mentor in the best light possible to their own colleagues and stakeholders.

Other mentors felt they got a great deal out of a mentoring style of leadership even if it was not publicly recognised. For example, Professor of Comparative Cognition Nicky Clayton uses a very hands-off approach to her mentoring and team management. She lets those working in her laboratory dictate their own working hours and holds them responsible for their results rather than their schedule. This approach allowed her to see each member as an individual, with the whole being greater than the sum of the parts.

She said: 'I could question why they don't come in until 9am or leave for the gym at 5pm, but that would just force them to sit here a certain number of hours. I wouldn't make them more creative scientists.'

Uniquely, she saw this approach as almost selfishly beneficial for her. She reflected: 'If I can create an environment people actually want to work in, then I am going to get more out of it anyway. It's something I have learned as I went along. If I can treat each person as special, with their own individual motivations, and give them the freedom to do things their own way, I will get the best out of them.'

While it was generally agreed that mentors benefited from working with mentees, the savvy women I interviewed pointed out that mentoring as leaders within their own teams had a positive knock-on effect for them. They realised that if they raised the bar for themselves, they could then raise it for everyone else.

In this vein, Janet Davies remarked: 'I learned the value of mentoring early on because if you are working with a junior and rather inexperienced team, *your* results will reflect that if you don't lead and nurture their talent. It pays to spend time with them. If I didn't use my mentoring capabilities to help other people within the organisation as individuals, we simply wouldn't progress.'

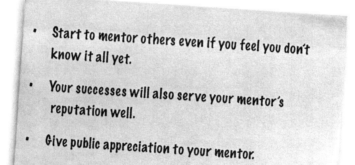

- Start to mentor others even if you feel you don't know it all yet.

- Your successes will also serve your mentor's reputation well.

- Give public appreciation to your mentor.

ALL HAIL THE ANTI-MENTOR

> *Our prime purpose in this life is to help others.*
>
> *And if you can't help them, at least don't hurt them.*
>
> — Dalai Lama

Sometimes one of the best reasons to mentor others is simply because you wish you had benefited from a great mentor yourself. The process of working for a poor line manager, who doesn't give recognition or keep lines of communication open, can motivate people to be a different type of leader and mentor.

A vice-president of marketing for a telecommunications firm, whom I will call Diana, once came to me for coaching on how to develop her leadership and mentoring style. Diana initially felt at a real disadvantage because her relationship with her own line manager had historically been difficult. We developed her skills by taking the opposite approach: we defined what Diana would do with her own growing team, simply by looking at what hadn't been done for her and what kind of guidance she would have appreciated herself. It felt like a huge challenge for her at first, since Diana hadn't been in a position to model good mentoring behaviour, but she went on to develop a very loyal team.

Mary Hensher would agree with this method. When asked what role mentoring had played in her success, she answered: 'If I am perfectly honest, I have learned as much from watching people do things wrong. It sounds terrible, and there are definitely role models out there, but I honestly think you learn more from watching what people do wrong and the projects that initially fail. You want to avoid repeating their mistakes to build up a track record of success.'

Similarly, Barrister Fiona Edington recalled an 'anti-mentor' from whom she learned a good deal: the first woman she shadowed during her pupillage after finishing her law degree. Fiona remembered: 'She warned me that after six months with her I may find some things I will want to do just like her, but that I would probably find just as many I want to do differently. That was true, and I learned a lot about the approach I wanted to take.'

When recalling what she did learn, she remembered that she respected the way this 'anti-mentor' was a rainmaker, meaning she brought lots of work into the Chambers. That was great for her own reputation as well as for the other barristers who picked up the work she wasn't able to handle personally.

Fiona said: 'I learned it's far better to bring in your own work, through good relationships with solicitors and hard work, than it is to be reliant on others to hand me the briefs they don't want or have time to manage.'

She explained the system by which barristers are sometimes given work. At the end of the day, when a barrister realises they won't have time for the brief the following day, they quickly pass the case on through the clerks in the late afternoon. She pointed out: 'Briefs that are taken on by barristers, who think they are going to get to them and then cannot, can do a disservice to their clients as well as to their peers. At the last minute, around 4:30pm, they have to be quickly disbursed and if you are a woman who needs to leave to get home to children or has other caring responsibilities, it is very hard to pick up this type of work.'

Fiona continued: 'That's another reason I like to bring in as much of my own work from solicitors as I can, so I am not reliant on others handing out extra work, literally at the last minute. It is extremely important for me to be out of the office as soon as I can or to work from home if possible so I can be with the children for homework or bedtime.' She recognised this pattern of handing out briefs after 4pm could have a very discriminating effect on women with family responsibilities or any other type of personal commitments; they just couldn't start cases so late in the day, which meant they could lose out on these types of opportunities.

Her way round it, as demonstrated by her anti-mentor, was to ensure her relationships with outside solicitors were strong enough so she was not reliant on the potential work of other barristers, doled out at the eleventh hour.

- When you thrive under a good mentor, the mentor gains kudos as well.

- Being a good mentor causes you to raise your own standards.

- You can become a great leader even if you have never worked with a great leader.

FORMAL OR INFORMAL MENTORING

There is a debate as to the value of mentoring schemes as organised by companies, versus naturally-occurring relationships.

Company-sponsored programmes certainly have their heart in the right place, and are increasingly popular — but without the right guidelines and resources they can often fail. At best they are popular because they are perceived as being a cost-effective way to engage senior staff with juniors. At worst they are a tick-box exercise that falsely reassures an organisation into thinking it's doing enough to develop its people without putting in the right amount of support and additional development.

Another danger is that it can also remove the onus of responsibility from the individual of finding a match that is a perfect fit for herself. This can make her complacent in using the process or understandably disheartened if the assigned match does not work out.

I often lead workshops for employees at the University of Cambridge. At the end of one such session, a woman confided to me that, as a result of our previous session on how to develop effective mentoring relationships, she had taken the initiative to find her own mentor. Previously, she had been assigned a mentor who offered to meet her in three months' time when she emailed him regarding an issue she was having. Realising that her career was in her *own* hands, she plucked up the courage to approach another academic she respected, who offered to have a coffee with her just a few days later.

Her initial mistake? Assuming her employer would make the best choice for her in a mentor, and then feeling let down when the process didn't work as smoothly as she would have liked.

Some of the successful women I interviewed had their own opinions as to what works best when seeking a mentor. Janet Davies, for example, experienced both formal and informal mentoring schemes during her career. She reasoned: 'I personally feel that informal mentoring works best as it is voluntary and based on mutual respect. It's not an exercise in being paired up with somebody according to someone else's agenda. The chemistry and trust must be there for it to work.'

Similarly, Jackie Gittins has developed all of her mentoring relationships organically. They are not part of an overall project where relationships are randomly assigned. She emphatically believes that the would-be mentee should seek out the right mentor for herself. Jackie said: 'I would hate to be assigned a mentor. While it's something you have to have, at its core it's the trust, connection and rapport that make it work. It would be difficult if not impossible to achieve that in a formal mentoring programme where matches are made for the participants. You have to have that human connection first.'

IF IT LOOKS LIKE A MENTOR, FEELS LIKE A MENTOR...

Most women admitted they had learned something from almost every person who was willing to engage with them, no matter how long the interaction or even the topic of conversation.

They made opportunities to speak and *listen to people who might not have even realised they were 'mentoring' at the time*. While the term itself is fairly new, that does not mean these women have not been engaging in mentoring throughout their lives. For example, Eileen Brown said she never had a formal mentor. She then said she'd had many 'information mentors': people who had passed on key pieces of advice or learning at the right time for her to hear it. She joked: 'Any woman I have a glass of wine with becomes an information mentor — we share tips and what has worked or not worked for us.'

Whilst Eileen is undoubtedly now a mentor to many, she still found the fact that people approached her for guidance slightly surprising. She explained: 'I don't have a degree or an IT qualification to my name! I look around and see I am surrounded by people who seem to have a proper career path. I sort of fell into each job I've had. I don't feel I can give structured career advice, when my own career path has been so informal!'

Instead, what she has done is make the most of every 'random conversation' and opportunity that's come her way. She has taken opportunities she wasn't looking for, learned from them, and then looked for ways to do things even better. This is undoubtedly why dozens of people at Microsoft and further afield look to her for advice.

The academics I met also engaged in mentoring, often with their students or previous students, but didn't initially conceive of it as mentoring as such. For example, Professor Athene Donald described the way laboratories work together as *familial* in style. In this realm, mentoring permeated through several generations of scientists. She explained: 'It's like genealogy; I think of my former students as my children and the post-docs they are supervising as grandchildren. I may not know a particular individual, but I probably know their supervisor, which allows me to always be able to speak to someone I know about potential collaborations. It keeps it in the family.'

Having worked at Cornell University in the US as well as in the UK, it was apparent that Athene's 'family' was well extended. She said: 'I never set out to network but there is a sense of a large family spread throughout US, Canada and Europe. I can also meet people who have worked with my mentor, which makes us feel like we are part of a larger family.' She smiled playfully: 'And like all families, there is always someone you end up loathing — but you are still connected in some way.'

Professor Nicky Clayton, also at the University of Cambridge, studies memory in birds — jays in particular. She too came from an academic background and also discussed mentoring as 'familial' in style. This was remarkable as I had not mentioned to her that Athene had used this very word to describe the relationships. She described how her PhD supervisor introduced her to the idea of running her laboratory almost as a family; drawing on each person's strengths whilst downplaying their weaknesses and letting each member get on with their own work.

She remarked: 'There is a term in German, which is *Doktor Vater*, meaning *Doctor Father*, and that sums up how my mentor's laboratory was run. He and his wife would host lots of parties at their house and be very hospitable. It's a tradition I have tried to keep going. My husband, who is a senior lecturer at Queen Mary's, and I routinely have colleagues and students to our house for meals and regularly have drinks with them at least once a week to encourage collaboration rather than competition.'

- Seek out your own mentor; don't wait for your company to do it.
- Treat every conversation as the potential for 'mini-mentoring'.
- Mentoring can substantially extend your own network.

SETTING MENTORING UP

Sometimes we make the mistake of assuming a mentor must be from within the same company or industry background. While there are benefits to working with someone in your company whom you respect, this approach may miss some of the main gains to be had from mentoring.

A good mentor need not have your industry expertise. This allows them to ask you questions that haven't been asked before, rather than working with peers who all agree 'we just don't do it that way here', a type of collusion that mentors from different backgrounds will not share.

Additionally, there is also less likelihood of them feeling threatened by your successes, which is a concern I hear from clients who don't want to appear as if they are vying for their boss's job. Search widely from other companies in your sector, or indeed from other sectors, for mentors who seem approachable and who have successes that you respect.

One former client, in the oil and gas industry, worked with a manager who was known to be disagreeable and difficult. She told me she had received some of her best mentoring over coffees from a senior woman at a competing company, whom she had met at an industry conference.

MAKING THE APPROACH

A good mentoring relationship is built on mutual respect, candour and trust, with a clear communication of what is expected on each side. Early conversations should explore why you have approached this particular person as a mentor. Besides being flattering, it gives them an idea of what you are looking for in the relationship. Another good way to sound them out is to mention some of your goals, which can help you determine whether it will be a successful partnership.

This is not the time to ask for them to open up their book of contacts for you. While many mentors eventually do offer this type of support, it should never be a first request. It gives the impression that you as a mentee are more concerned about whom your mentor knows rather than about learning from the mentor themselves!

And remember, their list of contacts took them years to build; why would they share that information before they knew you well and have complete trust in you? When you first approach a potential mentor, you *can* say that you are looking for someone to bounce ideas off while you are working on a certain project, or as you integrate into a new role, or while you prepare yourself for a possible promotion. This gives both of you an exit strategy with a loose time limit, so that neither party feels they are locked in for life. It means your request for mentoring is likely to be met with agreement; with an end date, you keep focused on getting the most out of the relationship while you both can.

GIVE YOUR MENTOR FEEDBACK

Mentors are like the *rest* of us: they like feedback, to know whether you are following their advice and how you are getting on. To this end, you should always show a willingness to listen to the advice a mentor gives and follow their suggestions. Mentoring is not a forum for your complaints — you will be given guidance that you will be expected to follow. That's its gift.

Mentees make a great impression on a mentor when they act on the advice given to them. This is a critical point. Often people who are looking for guidance don't take the advice they are given. If you keep ignoring advice and yet continually solicit feedback, you run the risk of *pestering* the mentor whilst demonstrating that you have no follow-through — not a good professional reputation for anyone. Tell them when you have followed their advice, what you learned and how you changed the direction slightly for your own path. Give the quality of feedback you would like to receive! Most professional women I meet would love more feedback; mentors are no different.

Additionally, share with your mentor what you are getting from the relationship, and share information you find that might be relevant to them.

The *most* successful mentoring relationships are those where both people feel they are benefiting. Send them articles you see, or things that you might hear on the political grapevine, opportunities for speaking or interesting projects, even nominate them for industry awards — anything that might be of interest to them.

Of course, you may want to continue to be mentored by this person for the foreseeable future. That's fine — but allow the relationship time to develop into that pattern, rather than explicitly saying you want their help on a continual basis. Additionally, even when in a good mentoring relationship, always keep your eyes open for anyone else you may want to approach as a mentor. This can be simultaneously, or after your current mentoring relationship has ended. This is not being disloyal. Mentoring is not like marriage, where the ideal is a one per person basis! Indeed, the most successful professionals have several mentors in various industries, at different companies and with different perspectives. Whilst finding one can seem like a real triumph, finding several, most of whom you outgrow as you develop, is actually the best way forward.

Just remember, mentoring can feel challenging which is good. It provides the advice you say you would like to have — but it may not always be easy to hear. Be ready for your assumptions about how things are done to be challenged. We learn more from those who stretch us than from those who agree with everything we say. I am not advocating taking your mentor's advice at all times. Rather, figure out what works best for you. Advice is usually given because it worked for the person giving the advice. Additionally, the advice usually will stretch you out of your comfort zone, which is the whole point. Work with your mentor and learn all you can, then whilst staying in touch, move on to greener pastures once you have identified a new skill set you need to develop. Continue the cycle of development by then challenging yourself further, by becoming a mentor to someone else.

Mentoring clearly has many benefits and is one of the best activities you engage in with a variety of people, throughout your career. You can learn from the mistakes and lessons learned by those who have gone before as well as gain reassurance when you are on the right path. Proactively seeking out mentors will set you apart as a woman who is intent on winning the game when she engages with the boys' club.

- Look *outside* your company or sector for mentors.

- Say what you want from mentoring and how long you wish it to last.

- Follow up on any guidance — or be prepared to lose your mentor's interest.

TWELVE

COACHING

> *A 'No' uttered from deepest conviction is better and greater*
> *than a 'Yes' merely uttered to please, or what is worse, to avoid trouble.*
>
> — Mahatma Gandhi

In previous chapters, I have mentioned many of the career strategies employed by successful women who work in a man's world, to help them get ahead in their careers.

Some are as tried and tested as time itself, such as mentoring and informal networking. Others, such as media and presentational skills training, are fairly new interventions — but are increasingly being used as cutting-edge methods of career development.

Executive coaching, while using some of the skills employed by gifted leaders for generations, is a relatively new method of support. It is fast gaining recognition for its dramatic utility both by employers as well as by individual women themselves.

As an executive coach myself, you might think it would be natural for me to say this. However, many of the women I interviewed had experienced executive coaching in some form or another. They found that developing a coaching relationship, one that provides a sounding board whilst developing your confidence, was one of the surest ways forward.

In my coaching practice, I have yet to work with a client who did not make some type of major career progression during and after our time together — even if it does not always lead down the path they originally anticipated. For example, some women initially think they want to leave unfulfilling jobs that they are actually able to turn around. Similarly, some women realise only through the coaching that a career change or a new direction is exactly what they want.

A good coach will challenge and stretch you, whilst helping you overcome unhelpful patterns of thinking and behaviour. The women I interviewed, most of whom had worked with coaches, viewed it not as a luxury but as an investment in getting an advantage in their career and personal life.

For example, Lis Astall, one of the most senior women at Accenture, believed strongly in the power of coaching. She in fact worked with three different coaches according to the area on which she wanted to focus. She explained: 'I have a coach that I use to help me unravel problems, simply through asking questions. He helps me work through my own ideas. Another coach helps me on my presentational style and can give guidance to political manoeuvring. My third coach is more of a visionary and helps me place my actions and career in the larger picture, regarding what I want for my life. He challenges me to act in a way that creatively questions my self-imposed constraints.'

When had the coaching made the greatest impact for Lis? She remembered an incident six years before, when she lost a government bid her team had worked on for over two years. She smiled: 'My normal pattern would have made me very demoralised and focusing on aspects I had no control over, asking *what if?* My coach helped me unlock some of those patterns, making me realise that *cynicism did not define me*. It was just an approach I had used for a long time. He reminded me I could choose to change, through using language and different thought patterns, which I did.'

One remarkable aspect of this story, and indeed of the power of coaching, is that Lis admitted this breakthrough session with her coach had occurred more than *six years* beforehand, with just a few top-up sessions in between — but that the positive patterns she had developed were still with her after all that time. The *aha!* moment was still as fresh and relevant for her today as it was when she made it all those years ago.

COACHING VERSUS MENTORING

Like most of the successful women I interviewed, Lis benefited from mentoring relationships as well. She clearly saw a place for both coaching and mentoring in her professional and personal life. What was the difference for her?

She reflected: 'Mentors for most people come from within your organisation and often have a personal stake in your development. My mentors mention jobs and opportunities they've heard about, which is great. They write references and are more likely to know the detail of your work. A coach, on the other hand, helps you see the bigger picture.'

Also, as Lis explained, there was a difference in the amount of support she could expect from someone she was paying — and mentoring, which was given freely, but generally less frequently. She said: 'I pay for coaching, so the time is mine and mine alone, so it remains clean. It also means I can ask for as much or as little interaction as I want. There's a danger of overloading a mentor with requests for time, which can make me feel guilty. Mentors are doing it out of the goodness of their hearts and in the little spare time they have. Plus, with a coach I can swap them if I don't feel it is working out well.'

Another difference is that the client doesn't have to worry about internal politics with a coach, as opposed to an internal mentor, or give back in terms of reciprocal development. Another key difference is that good coaches have received coaching-specific training, as we will discuss, whereas most mentors have not.

The fact that coaches are objective outsiders is a real draw for many of my own clients, who are used to taking other people's opinions, even subconsciously, into account within their normal decision-making. For a time-starved professional woman, having the time to focus on what she wants and which direction is best for her is one of the most frequently-cited benefits.

I remember once talking with a couple about my work. When the wife asked about the value of coaching, the husband quickly said: 'It's for people who don't have wives they can talk to.' Not only was this patronising to a beneficial process enjoyed by both married and single clients, it completely missed the gift of objectivity that the process offers. Clients know their loved ones give good advice and want the best for them — but they recognise they all have their *own version* of what is 'best'.

Indeed, I would agree that many of my professional female clients *need a wife* in that old-fashioned sense of the term — not only for use as a sounding board, but as the much needed logistical support in the day-to-day running of a household that many of the men with whom they compete in the workplace expect and receive as a matter of course from their other halves.

THE GIFT OF INDEPENDENCE

The above interaction reminded me of a client I had, whom I will call Serena. She was a well-paid marketing executive and her husband was a graphic artist. Serena was the main breadwinner, and in our sessions she admitted she would like to reduce her hours to spend more time with their small daughter. Her husband could understand her wishes — but concern for their financial situation meant that he could not be completely objective with her. What's more, she didn't want to discuss it with him until she had made up her mind more firmly, as she didn't want to feel she was 'letting him down', or risk him talking her out of her feelings.

One last point that Lis made, about the difference between mentoring and coaching, was how a mentor, especially one you work with, may not always be able to see whether you need a change in the direction of your career. I added to the discussion that sometimes it is not in a mentor's best interest to see that you need a career change, especially if it's away from a role that serves them in some capacity.

Lis agreed: 'I have had funny conversations where I have asked a junior colleague if they want me to wear my *mentor hat* or my *friend hat* before I give advice. I've had to say, *Well, as your mentor and boss, of course I do not want you to leave the company — but as your friend, I can see that this may be a great time for you to try something new.* It can be a very difficult conversation to have because you have a stake in it. At the end of the day, I firmly believe you should have both mentors and coaches, as they each have a different but vital role to play in helping you move forward.'

Similarly, Caroline the IT Director of a global logistics company was one of the many women I interviewed who had worked with coaches and mentors during her career. When asked the difference between the two, she was clear: 'A mentor will tell you exactly what to do, whereas a coach will help you find your own right answers.' She worked with her most recent coach for 18 months before making the large step up to IT Director.

When asked what the relationship gave her, she replied: 'The coaching was all about me, a one-to-one focus on my career and me as a person. It helped me take time out of my schedule, even just once a month, to focus on where I am going. My coach helped me remove the obstacles I was putting in my own way without even realising it. I didn't initially believe I was ready for such a large promotion.

'My coach helped me question why I didn't think I was ready, when all the behaviours showed me that I clearly was. It previously felt like a step too far — but she helped me make more of my strengths and see what else I needed to do in order to get ready for the role.'

I asked Caroline for her main piece of advice for anyone thinking of working with a coach. She said: 'Choose one yourself. In the past it has only gone sour if I was assigned someone without any choice. You need to like and trust the coach if you are going to honestly open up to them. For me, that's only worked when I could choose the coach myself. Whereas I started out doubting how well the process could work, I would now recommend coaching to any senior professional.'

TAKING CONFIDENCE TO THE NEXT LEVEL

As you put together your career development plan to succeed as a woman in a man's world, you will begin to give thought to what you want from a mentor, with whom you want to network, what type of additional training you want to receive.

To take your confidence and career to the next level, you must start to think about what you want in a coach. The relationship will only succeed once you are clear what your goal is for the relationship, as well as why this is the right *time* for you to start a coaching relationship.

The many women with whom I work all have different presenting issues. It may be management of a new team, help in growing into a new role, aiming for a promotion — but in most cases, almost everyone wants to develop their *confidence*. This is a very achievable goal, and one that most women will need to address at multiple points in their career.

It's not surprising that confidence is an issue when faced with *new* challenges, simply because confidence is most often based on what you have *already* achieved — which women routinely minimise, rather than on goals you have not yet reached.

Maggie Berry invested in working with a coach, as recommended by a friend, early in her role with womenintechnology.co.uk. 'I needed time for me, to see how I was going to maximise the opportunities for myself. So, for example, I made a decision to change the title on my card from *UK Communications Director* to *Director*. There was only me running the organisation and I wanted to convey that I was in charge. The first title potentially narrowed my focus and didn't give me the authority I realised I deserved,' she said.

'Deciding to invest in the coaching came from a very positive intention. I didn't want to leave my job; I just knew there were opportunities out there that I was not making the most of. I needed to give myself time and space to think about the direction in which I wanted to head,' she explained.

Maggie chose to pay for the coaching herself, and saw it as an investment: 'I didn't want to be beholden to the parent organisation, and paying for it myself helped keep the boundaries clean for me.' Whilst I always advocate asking your employer to provide or pay for any type of executive coaching you may need, some women value the demarcation. This is especially true if you are certain you want to leave your employer.

To this end, ask whether your employer provides coaching or hire one privately. For example, I personally work with a mix of companies who want to develop their female staff, and with individual women who contact me to help them take their career to the next level.

Philippa Snare first realised the power of coaching when she met a well-respected young woman at a Financial Services event. She remembered: 'I knew she worked in one of the most traditional of sectors, and yet she was very well known for her contributions. I was impressed and asked her how she made her voice heard amongst all the men — and she replied she had a great coach!'

She continued: 'I began to work with the same coach on making the 360-degree feedback we got at Microsoft more robust and actionable — two things it wasn't at the time. After she helped my team, I continued to work with her, one-to-one, to build my confidence, particularly in dealing with senior executives from the US whom I found myself intimidated by.' Philippa's coach recommended exercises that were highly creative but initially surprising and very challenging.

She recalled: 'As part of the coaching, I went to a recording studio on Abbey Road with a group of other executives who were completely suited and booted. We arrived to participate in music therapy, with a hippy woman smiling at us over a pair of bongos. We started with trepidation, but I just felt I should give it my all as I wouldn't be in this situation ever again! In truth, it was one of the most powerful days I have ever had — though I certainly didn't expect it to be. Each individual had to come up with a *power phrase* we then had to announce with clarity and conviction to the group. The others then repeated it back to us as they had heard it. I chose a statement about being respected and valued. It was emotional because the group would repeat it weakly and in an uncertain voice if that's what they had heard, which gave you an indication of how you came across to others. It was hard, but we got there in the end.'

The experience was surprisingly powerful for Philippa, in ways she didn't even realise until she returned from her next trip to the US. She remembered: 'On the plane back, I realised I hadn't been second-guessing myself or replaying every conversation I'd had with colleagues who used to intimidate me. I used to give myself a hard time for the things I *should* have said. The sessions freed me from making assumptions about other people's judgements, in a way I hadn't been anticipating.'

The coaching can also help you put into perspective personal issues that can affect work, and even turn them into learning tools that better your confidence and the way you interact with colleagues overall.

Private banker Joanna Hewitt was one such woman who found that she had also grown, since working with a coach, through what was initially a trying time in her life. She was coping with the onset of dementia in her mother, whilst maintaining her career. When describing the coaching, she said: 'I gained a sense of maturity in myself, a certain belief in my own ability and skills and an awareness of other people's behaviours. I was taking my colleagues' bad behaviour personally, and I realised they have their own issues. If a colleague comes to work and is difficult, I now realise, perhaps he's experienced family problems before work. It doesn't make his behaviour right, but it's a new way to look at it, which makes it easier.'

POLITICAL SAVVY

Others used coaching as a means of negotiating the ubiquitous world of *office politics*. This is a game women who work in male-dominated fields must play, despite the fact that they never helped create the rules. There is sometimes confusion as to how to negotiate the boardroom, the politics of presentations, unspoken agreements — negotiating everything from job titles to pay rises, and how to put forth a sense of gravitas and professional poise, even while you feel you are still learning the ropes.

It is with these challenges that some of the women found coaching to be most helpful in redefining politics to incorporate influencing skills, creating awareness and good old-fashioned diplomacy — all of with which most women more easily identify.

Angela Mohtashemi reflected: 'I just get a feeling that a lot of what goes on in meetings is discussed beforehand at the pub, the dinners, or the football club — and that these discussions play a larger part than I would *like* to recognise. But now I have a coach who is helping me influence that process as best as I can. The challenge for me is that I used to network to bring in clients, and now I have to network for the sake of my own career, which is a big difference.'

Jackie Gittins also had used coaching to help her better understand office politics. She explained: 'I needed to understand myself and my natural preferences better. For example, being an extrovert, I found it difficult working with introspective men. I'd become impatient, because it's not my style. Through the coaching, I realised I needed to be the one to adapt in order to be more influential with data-driven people. So, I learned how to mix my natural tendency to descriptively story-tell with the type of empirical data that's more widely respected by many colleagues in a corporate setting. Making this small change has been huge for me and has enabled me to engage more credibly and powerfully with the board, for example.' Jackie recommended coaching for any woman who wanted to 'learn how to play to her strengths, take a new approach or who is just feeling stuck'.

Some savvy women decide to work with a coach after a promotion, to help them grow into the role more quickly. Vickie, a previous client, came to me after a promotion to a Director level position within the pharmaceutical industry. Vickie remembered: 'I realised I'd put everything I had into reaching that level — but that if I wanted to continue to grow, I would have to identify new behaviours and look at the blind spots that I wasn't even *aware* of.'

Which blind spots? She elaborated: 'I didn't think of my colleagues and clients in the same way. With senior people in the company, I subconsciously engaged in parent-child type relationships where I assumed they knew best; they were the authority and I wouldn't necessarily voice my own opinions. I treated my clients as equals however, and expressed my views readily. I figured clients were paying for my opinions and guidance, but forgot that my employers were too! I needed to step up my approach and be more consistent, no matter who I was talking with.'

She gave an example of how she was employing this strategy as a result of the coaching: 'I got involved with a new internal project, sponsored by a board member. In the past, I know I would have been intimidated by him as he can be quite challenging; it's his way of testing people out. I would have previously shrunk back from him and felt overwhelmed. This time, I treated him like a client and gave my opinions and didn't back down, which established my credibility. That simple change gave me far greater impact than I could have had just a year ago.'

Additionally, Vickie also credits coaching with helping her see how her competitive nature was also potentially getting in the way of progressing her career. She explained: 'I've always been incredibly competitive, which means I would usually work with people who were junior to me rather than peers. The coaching provided the *aha!* moment for me; I had to challenge the assumption that people at my level are pure competitors. This eventually enabled me to engage in collaborations with peers I would have never even seen before. My eyes weren't open to those opportunities before.'

Her advice to other professional women? Vickie recommended: 'You should work with a coach when you reach a level of *discomfort* with where you are. You feel you can do more, but don't know how to take that next step or even what the next step actually is. If I didn't use the coaching to become aware of my blind spots, it would have limited my career in the long term.'

YOUR FIRST NINETY DAYS

Rebecca George worked with a coach at several points in her career. Whilst at IBM she was chosen for a senior leadership programme developed by the Whitehall & Industry Group (WIG), a non-profit organisation that seeks to promote understanding between the private and public sectors. Whilst there, she met with a group of cross-sector leaders for 18 months; their meetings were facilitated by a coach whose style impressed her. When Rebecca then prepared to leave IBM after nearly 20 years, to take a role at Deloitte, she contacted the coach to work with her privately to help her make the transition during the first few months on the job.

Rebecca described the relationship as: 'One of the best investments I ever made in myself.' What difference did it make? She replied: 'For example, it sounds simple, but she asked me how I would introduce myself to new clients and colleagues. I gave a half-hearted response which didn't impress either of us! We created a much stronger introduction which both gave me credibility *and* demanded that others take me seriously in my new role. I learned to say, *I've just joined Deloitte to look after key influencing departments of government. I've come from IBM and most recently was running their central government business for the last seven years.*'

She makes a great point about the power of introductions. They are deceptively simple, in that we have to make them every day but rarely give them much thought. She was wise to work on introductions, as well as on other areas affecting how *she* would set the tone in this new role.

Rebecca said: 'My coach reminded me that, as I was in a newly-created role, it was vital for me to set my objectives early and agree how they would be measured. She also encouraged me to build my new network quickly, as I previously had a strong network at IBM but was now an outsider at Deloitte. Getting her help was invaluable in helping me make a successful transition over my first few months.'

Whether making a career transition, growing into a new role or aiming for advancement, working with an executive coach clearly makes the difference for many successful women who need to understand *the boys' club* in order to begin to move *beyond* it.

LEARNING TO TAKE YOUR OWN ADVICE

> *He who asks is a fool for five minutes,*
>
> *but he who does not ask remains a fool forever.*
>
> — Chinese Proverb

When I first speak to a potential client, one of the first things I tell them is that *I don't give advice.*

To those new to coaching, this sometimes comes as a surprise; they often expect me to give them a prescription for the perfect career. Instead, I tell them I will help them find and act on their *own* advice. My goal is eventually to render my services to them redundant. My aim is always to create a more confident woman who is able to guide herself long term. While I do work with many clients on an ongoing basis, the set-up is more like Lis Astall's, who meets with her coach for sessions, only when she has a new challenge that arises.

I do not want my client to become dependent on *me*, but solely on *herself.* That work starts in our very first session, at which I hold her accountable for the actions she wants to take, based on the discoveries she makes about herself during this initial session and every other subsequent session. Some potential clients joke that it is a questionable business model — before telling me they are reassured by this approach. The truth is, I'd rather have the word of mouth referrals that occur from stronger and satisfied clients, and these do now make up the bulk of my business.

Similarly, some of the successful women I interviewed also mentioned problems that arise from becoming too dependent on others for guidance.

Relying on other people to make your career what you want it to be gives your power away, and doesn't allow you the joy of proactively finding your own path.

Learning to be proactive in career development was an essential step taken by many successful women. For example, Athene Donald noted that for most academics the best way to build a profile is through your record of publications. Some of the most successful academics she knew were those who had looked to move away from the area that was their supervisor's research specialism, and to seize these opportunities early on.

She explained: 'I knew a researcher who had spent just a summer in the US. In a short time he showed great initiative by managing to link with someone there and produce a joint publication, so that he could have more research under his own name rather than the auspices of his supervisor. Similarly, some of the post-docs here supervise undergraduates and will even publish with them. Both of which demonstrate great initiative as it shows you don't have to wait for a grant or fellowship. You are creating your own path rather than waiting for one to be bestowed upon you.'

Athene further explained the benefit of this approach: 'There's a joke about people who never move out of their specific academic area to work with others or become more cross-disciplinarian, though they can become quite successful. People say they are still really *working on their PhD*, because they've never really moved on.'

Philippa Snare of Microsoft had also experienced a light bulb moment of her own, which developed her confidence in sticking to her principles and finding her own way. She had worked for a woman she respected and emulated. After several years, her boss made an unethical decision which put pressure on Philippa to take a stand either against or with her mentor. In the end, Philippa realised she had spent years making her boss look good — no doubt, this is a smart foundation on which to build — but that she had been repaid with a moral dilemma. She took the high moral ground and told her boss she disagreed with her actions, a move that could have cost her job. She had to find her own path, and that started with her sense of integrity.

She remembered: 'I reached a point where I felt very disillusioned with her; but I realised I'd rather lose my job and *stick to my values* than sweep the incident under the carpet and lose respect for myself. I was disappointed with her but realised that while she was making the wrong decisions for her career, I couldn't allow her to make those same decisions for me.'

In the end, Philippa was moved to a different department and her boss moved on but the experience gave her the wake-up call she needed. In a quiet moment, she recalled: 'I used to give my whole life to a job, but now I realise there are some things I'm prepared to sacrifice and my integrity is *not* one of them.'

This incident was a real watershed for Philippa. When I asked what other impact it had had on her, she said that her approach to work had changed. Her role up till then had been wholly internal-facing; she learned through this experience that, whilst making her boss look good as she had always done, she also needed to take a more *external* focus herself and become an ambassador for her own efforts.

Philippa explained: 'I'm not particularly motivated by moving up the corporate food chain, but now I want to collect as many *experiences* as I can. And that means me asking myself what I am going to get out of a role in a way I never used to. What am I going to learn? Who am I going to get to meet? Who do I want to be reporting to? How am I going to grow? These questions now must have better answers than they did before!' Her answers demonstrate her passionate intention to find her own path.

TOO MANY COOKS

There is another benefit to finding the strength to take your own path. Women who habitually need the approval of everyone else before they take a risk are seen at first as collaborative and just in need of a bit of guidance — but this is not a way to advance a career in the long term.

Women often use this technique of over-participation as an extreme way to avoid confrontation or blame if a risk doesn't pay off in the long run. As you build your career, however, you will need to be seen to be able to make decisions on your own and with a minimum of input from other colleagues. This is one of the benefits of working with a coach. It happens behind closed doors and in a safe environment where you can expect confidentiality.

If taking decisions without input feels frightening, then take a series of smaller risks — use your own best judgement. Start with lower-profile decisions to build up your confidence. If it goes awry, be ready to explain the reasons you made the decision and what you would do differently next time. Then take appropriate steps to rectify the situation. Rarely is a problem beyond any hope of salvation; most problems are much larger in our *heads* than they are in reality.

Starting to minimise the damage is often one of the best ways to calm yourself, as a reminder that there are still plenty of things over which you *do* have control; your response to any supposed disaster-decision being one of them. In the end, employers are looking for a high level of pro-activity and will soon tire of holding your hand. You owe yourself a proactive life.

Getting the best support you can, through working with a coach, is one way that successful women make it through what at times can feel like a minefield. Having the space to focus on yourself, and the direction of your life and career, is not a luxury for a professional woman. It is a vital piece for women who want to lead the happiest, most fulfilling lives they can. It will make decisions easier, the path more rewarding and the experiences more enjoyable. Getting the *right* support at the right times is not just an investment for yourself, but in the women who will follow and look to your path for guidance.

- Agree with your coach specific goals right at the start.

- Free from internal politics and self-interest, a coach can help you see the big picture.

- The benefits of coaching will spill over into other aspects of your life.

FINDING THE RIGHT COACH

Once you understand that working with a coach could help you reach the next level in your career, there are steps to take to ensure you find the best person for your needs. There are as many coaches out there as there are issues that could be addressed in a session, and not all of them will be a good fit for you.

For example, I specialise in coaching professional women working in male-dominated fields who want to develop greater confidence and a sharper sense of career direction. I am *not* the coach to go to if you want to find a boyfriend, stop smoking or lose weight. There are coaches out there who do great work in these areas, but if these goals are your primary focus, we would not be a good match. As I often joke, I am not the coach to go to for a free colonic irrigation with your fifth paid session! All joking aside, there are a great number of people offering coaching services – some much better qualified than others. Just like searching out the best network or mentor, it's up to you to find a great match for yourself.

Finding the right coach could take time, but it's an investment worth making. I find it disappointing that there is no one single accreditation body or level of education or type of training that an executive coach should have undertaken in order to practise. Since the industry is so young, it is still finding its way regarding how best to train people and what a good coaching session even looks like. I find it positively scary that a person could read a book or attend a weekend workshop and then claim to be coach.

When I was initially searching for a training programme for myself, I looked for training rigour in the absence of any strict industry-set guidelines. I would suggest the same to you. Otherwise, you may find that your hairdresser has undertaken more hours of training than your prospective coach.

Now believe me, I am personally well acquainted with the transformative power of a great blow-dry, but until there is a type of training and level of experience set by the industry it will be up to you, the *consumer*, to find a well-qualified coach. Coaching is a large investment in terms of mental energy, time and money – make sure the person you work with is well-qualified to handle those responsibilities.

To add to the confusion, there is no single body representing all certified coaches. Instead there are several, each with its own varying membership requirements. These major players are the International Coach Federation, the Association for Coaching, the European Mentoring and Coaching Council and the Association for Professional Executive Coaching and Supervision.

I am personally aligned to the International Coach Federation, and am increasingly asked about my accreditation in a market that is full of well-intentioned but untrained and unaccredited coaches. The ICF is an organisation that provides credentials for both coach training programmes and individual coaches through a peer-review process. The ICF also enforces a code of ethics and a set of core competencies that each of its accredited coaches must adhere to. While any coach can be a *member* of the ICF, ask for an *accredited member* coach as that is a more rigorous process to undertake and is one way organisations are increasingly separating the wheat from the chaff.

That is not to say that the only good coaches are accredited or indeed that all accredited coaches are the best. However, it does mean they should adhere to both a system of ethics and peer-reviewed core competencies that many 'professional' coaches do not.

Please don't be misled into believing that a degree in your field or charging fat fees is a guarantee of quality. I had a PhD that addressed the issues faced by women who entered male-dominated fields before I set up my practice, but I still knew that I wanted additional coach training in order to best serve my clients ethically. To this end, ask any prospective coach where they did their training and what credentials they have that are specific to coaching. If they dismissively respond that while they don't have a great deal of formal training they do have a 'PhD in Results!' – as I once heard someone claim – be very wary.

Additionally, while it is not yet an industry requirement, a good coach will also be receiving external supervision. This enables them to take any potential ethical issues or problems they are having with a client to a safe place to discuss with a more senior mentor and coach – it can give you the impact of having two coaches in one and is reassuring to know that your coach is also getting the support they need.

KNOW WHAT YOU WANT TO GET WHAT YOU WANT

When you have identified a few prospective coaches, get a good idea of what would be a great result from the coaching, before you have that initial conversation with any of them:

- Do you want to be promoted within the next year?
- Do you need to build a stronger relationship with your team or line manager?
- Are you looking to make a career change?
- Do you want to get a better sense of balance between your home and work lives?

Get specific in your own mind what your ideal result would be, and listen for your coach to ask you about these goals. Also, think about how you want the relationship to work. Do you want to work face-to-face or is the telephone more convenient? Telephone coaching doesn't always sound very attractive to clients initially, but often when they see how convenient it can be or how much a good coach *can actually hear*, they are often surprised.

I personally work with some clients face-to-face and others by telephone, and many with a mix of the two, depending on what is convenient. There are other coaches who will work by Skype or email.

WHERE TO START YOUR SEARCH

When searching for anything, remember, there is nothing as powerful as a *personal recommendation*. Most of my work now comes from referrals or people who have seen me speak – as we discussed elsewhere in the book, it is much easier to market yourself when other people are willing to 'toot your horn' for you. I have had clients in New York and continental Europe with whom I have worked on the telephone recommend me to friends in London, with whom I have worked face-to-face.

Ask women you know and respect who they would recommend. I love when past clients give my details to potential clients –it's a real compliment and it means that my previous client has done some of the pre-work in recognising we would be a good match.

If you don't know where to start looking, associations such as the ICF have an online coach referral service where you can search according to geography, topics of choice, level of credential and even fees.

There are a few questions you should ask any prospective coach, as well as asking for examples of successful coaching from their experience:

- What is your coaching experience?
- What type of people do you normally coach?
- What is your coach-specific training?
- What is your coaching specialism?
- What is your specific *process* for coaching?
- How are sessions conducted and how frequently?

Once you have had an initial discussion, if you don't find the coach from a personal recommendation, you can ask for references from other satisfied customers. Additionally, speak to a few different coaches about their approach, and this is a vital stage to be listening to your gut. Coaching is one of the most important relationships you will have. There should be a connection between you and the coach that just 'feels' right to you.

Finding and working with the right coach will be both fun and challenging. It will stretch the bits of you that need to be developed whilst celebrating and strengthening the skills you already have. You owe getting the best support you can to yourself, your team and the women who will follow you into your traditionally-male field, and view *you* as a role model of a woman who clearly knows how to move *beyond the boys' club.*

- Know your objectives before you start looking for a coach.

- Consider how, and how often, you want to talk with your coach.

- Accreditation and personal recommendations are a great guide.

THIRTEEN

MOVING BEYOND THE BOYS' CLUB

If you take one thing away from this book, I hope that it is that no matter who you are, *you and you alone* are responsible for your career. No one will do it for you.

You don't need to do anything unnatural or false in order to get on … but you may need to adjust how you think about career progression. Because, as you have read through the experiences of savvy and successful women, in order to *move beyond* the boys' club you have to *understand* the boys' club.

Too many intelligent and hard-working women put their faith in the people above them to be totally objective and without personal bias when deciding who deserves a new opportunity, a job promotion or public recognition. The trouble is that these decision makers, these people who have a great deal of say over the progression of your career … are in fact just *human*.

The people who hand out kudos are not telepathic, nor should they be. Because workplace cultures in male-dominated fields were built to serve men, they are also not likely to be particularly observant of the woman who keeps her head down and waits to be noticed. They don't *see* good work without it being pointed out to them, for the simple reason that they have grown up knowing that being assertive, making the right connections and building their profile is how *men* get ahead. That is how *they themselves* got into that position of authority.

This is what makes it *your* job to point out your worth to them. Point out the relationships you have built, the business you have brought in, the leadership you have demonstrated, the projects you have completed, the money you have saved or earned for your employer. As I said in the introduction, *no one* will ever care about your career as much as you do.

Luckily, thanks to the successful women who have broken through before you, a woman who learns to *play the big boys* at their own game is no longer automatically branded an interloper, or a ball-breaker, or 'trying to be one of the guys'. There are ways to even up the odds without losing your dignity or femininity, and without compromising an atom of your professionalism.

The single biggest key to your success will be through making connections for both yourself and others and *seizing the opportunities* that arise. As a woman, you already do this all the time, in every other aspect of your life: you introduce friends to each other; you share insider tips about reliable plumbers, miracle–working hairdressers, books you've loved and the best schools for your children.

The single biggest favour you can do for yourself is to apply the same attitude of helpfulness and facilitation to your career. Talk to everyone, regardless of your respective levels in the food chain. Learn about them as people, and become a properly-rounded person in their eyes — not just a cipher at a desk or on the end of a phone.

Make introductions. Offer suggestions. Celebrate your wins — and notice how, when more people know who you are, people celebrate along with you. Give favours freely; they make you feel great about yourself, as well as remind you how much you *already* know and can offer the world.

Remember, you are *not* aiming for perfection. Perfectionism is a very common trait among high-achieving women who work predominantly with men. However, as your male colleagues already know, perfectionism is also the enemy of progress. Waiting until you are perfect, and not just 80 per cent ready, will hinder you from saying yes to all kinds of opportunities. Nobody, including the most high-flying and inspirational of women, knows everything they need to know, but the women who succeed choose to say *yes* to opportunities and know they can get the support and knowledge they need *along the way*.

It will take courage to begin to take your career to the next level— but like your first days in any job, it's surprising how quickly it all becomes natural, empowering and even *enjoyable*. Work is more satisfying when you perceive it through the prism of *relationships* and greasing the wheels for people. You will begin to realise the responsibility for your career is firmly within your control — as it should be because it is *you* who is moving *beyond the boys' club*.

The direction that path takes is yours to choose.

FOURTEEN

ADDITIONAL RESOURCES

CAREER NETWORKS OR INFORMATION

Anita Borg Institute for Women and Technology
ABI's mission is to increase the impact of women in technology. It provides resources and programmes to help industry retain/develop women in technical careers. (US based)

www.anitaborg.org

Association for Women in Mathematics
Global network for women at all levels working in maths-related fields.

www.awm-math.org

Association of Women Solicitors
Mentoring scheme, networking, returners' courses, lectures and seminars.

www.womensolicitors.org.uk

Aurora
Job board and The Times 'Where Women Want to Work Most Top 50'.

www.auroravoice.com

British Federation of Women Graduates
Network for women graduates across the UK.

www.bfwg.org.uk

British Computer Society
Career development, networking, forums with women's special interest group.

www.bcs.org

British Women Pilots' Association

Promotes aviation to women. It offers an annual awards ceremony, careers guide, scholarships.

www.bwpa.co.uk

Cambridge Association for Women in Science and Engineering (CamAWISE)

Networking events, career development and mentoring based in East Anglia.

www.camawise.org.uk

Capability Jane

Job resource and board for women looking for high quality flexible working arrangements.

www.capabilityjane.com

Central European Centre for Women and Youth in Science

Promotes, mobilises and networks women in science in Central Europe. Offers workshops and women scientists database.

www.cec-wys.org

Chicks with Bricks

Created with the support of women in architecture and construction. Organises events with speakers.

www.chickswithbricks.com

City Women's Network

London-based network for women from a range of industries.

www.citywomen.org

City Women's Club

Selective network for senior female professionals in the financial services.

www.citywomensclub.com

Dress for Success

Charity that donates work wear for disadvantaged women entering the workforce.

www.dressforsuccess.org

Engender
Scottish network and research organisation.

www.engender.org.uk

Enterprising Women
Networking, awards and resources.

www.enterprising-women.org

European Federation of Black Women Business Owners
Pan-European organisation to promote women entrepreneurs.

www.blackwomeninbusiness.com

European Platform of Women Scientists
Gives women scientists a voice in research policy debate. Currently building a convention of networks.

www.epws.org

European Professional Women's Network
Pan-European network of more than 17 women's networks.

www.europeanpwn.net

European Women in Mathematics
Pan-European organisation for women working in maths-related fields.

www.math.helsinki.fi/ewm

Everywoman
Networking organisation, annual conference and awards.

www.everywoman.co.uk

Fresh Ideas Events
Networking events, competitions for professional women from all backgrounds.

www.freshideasevents.com

Girl Geeks Dinners
For women in technology. Chapters and regular events in the UK and abroad.

www.girlgeekdinners.com

Global Women Inventors and Innovators Network
Event and support for women inventors and those working in innovation.

www.gwiin.com

High Tech Women
Meetings and mentoring.

www.hightech-women.com

Institute of Chartered Accountants (England and Wales)
CPD, with women's special interest group, networks.

www.icaew.com

International Coach Federation
Accrediting body for coaches and coach training programmes.

www.coachfederation.org.uk

iRelaunch
Group to support career re-entry for those in all stages of a career break.

www.irelaunch.com

Medical Women's Federation
Grants and bursaries, networking, support.

www.medicalwomensfederation.org.uk

MentorNet
E-mentoring network for diversity in engineering and science, particularly for women and others underrepresented in these fields.

www.mentornet.net

MentorSET
WES/Awise mentoring.

www.mentorset.org.uk

Mums in Science
Online network and forum for advice for mothers combining a science career and family.

www.mumsinscience.net

National Association of Women Pharmacists
E-mentoring and telephone networking scheme; return to practice support;
CPD guidance.

www.nawp.org.uk

National Association of Women in Construction
Network, events, advice and contacts.

www.nawic.co.uk

National Center for Women and Information Technology
Advocacy and support for women working in IT.

www.ncwit.org

National Women's Network
Network for women in management roles.

www.national-womens-network.co.uk

New Life Network
Website dedicated to advice on finding work, legal rights, starting your own
business and retraining after redundancy.

www.newlifenetwork.co.uk

Oxford Association of Women in Science and Engineering
Support network for women working in science and technology.
Runs lectures.

http://wwwusers.brookes.ac.uk/p0071266/oxawise.htm

Positive Energy
Network, events, annual conference for women in the energy industries.

www.positive-energynetwork.com

Portia
A gateway web portal to support women in SET. Offers a range of services
to individuals and companies.

www.portiaweb.org

Professional Speakers Association
For subject experts who speak for a living.

www.professionalspeakersassociation.co.uk

Prowess
Advocacy and support for organisations promoting women's business ownership.

www.prowess.org.uk

SET Women
Voice for women in SET. Activities include a national conference and regional/local networking groups.

www.setwomen.co.uk

Society of Petroleum Engineers
Network and advocacy for petroleum engineers with women's special interest group.

www.spe.org

Society of Women Engineers
Events and network for women in all fields of engineering.

http://societyofwomenengineers.swe.org

Thinking Women
Discussion and networking group promoting the achievements and progression of women in society, politics and the workplace.

www.thinkingwomen.org

Toastmasters
Speaking skills clubs across the world.

www.toastmasters.org

UK Resource Centre for Women
Government-led organisation that provides advice, services and policy construction for underrepresented women in SET.

www.ukrc4setwomen.org

We are the City
Network group mixing social and professional events for professional women.

www.wearethecity.com

WEConnect
Leading UK supplier diversity initiative spearheading the connection of women-owned business and multinational corporations.

www.weconnect.org.uk

Wise
Women in science, engineering & construction.

www.wisecampaign.org.uk

WiTEC
European Association for women in SET. Access to international network and events.

www.witec-eu.net

Women in Architecture
Network and support for women architects.

www.diversecity-architects.com/WIA/wia.htm

Women in Banking and Finance
Mentoring, networking events, awards, magazine.

www.wibf.org.uk

Women in the City
Annual awards luncheon for successful businesswomen.

www.citywomen.co.uk

Women's Environmental Network
Campaigning organisation for issues linking women, health and the environment.

www.wen.org.uk

Women in Games
Network and events for women working in the video gaming industry.

www.womeningames.com

WOMEN-Omics
Website dedicated to the issue of women's promotion as an economic opportunity.

www.women-omics.com

Women in Technology and Science
Ireland-based network and information resource.

www.witsireland.com

Women in Telecoms and Technology
Network and events for women working in the telecommunications industry.

www.wittgroup.org

Women in Film and TV
Events and awards.

www.wftv.org.uk

Women in Physics
Network, events and an annual conference.

www.iop.org

Women in Property
Online database, mentoring, networking events.

www.wip.propertymall.com

Women in Technology
Offers IT career advice to women, training sessions and advertises latest jobs.

www.womenintechnology.co.uk

Women's Engineering Society
Membership organisation for women engineers. Regional activity organised through networks. Annual dinners, jobs/careers section.

www.wes.org.uk

Women and Manual Trades (WAMT)
Provides a range of services to women wanting to enter the construction industry. Offers training courses and a careers page.

www.wamt.org

Working Families
Charity that offers advice to individuals and employers on legal rights regarding flexible working.

www.workingfamilies.org.uk

FURTHER READING

- Babcock, L. & Laschver, S. "Women Don't Ask: Negotiation and the Gender Divide", Princeton University Press, 2003

- Bayley, S. & Mavity, R. "Life's a Pitch: How to Sell Yourself and Your Brilliant Ideas", Corgi Books, 2007

- Canfield, J. "The Success Principles: How to Get From Where You Are to Where You Want to Be", Collins, 2005

- Christian, K. "Your Own Worst Enemy: Breaking the Cycle of Adult Underachievement", Regan Books, 2002

- Ferriss, T. "The 4 Hour Workweek: Escape 9-5, Live Anywhere and Join the New Rich", Crown, 2007

- Frankel, L.P. "Nice Girls Don't Get the Corner Office", Warner Business Books, 2004

- Gilberd, P.B. "The Eleven Commandments of Wildly Successful Women", MacMillan Spectrum, 1996

- Harrington, M. "Women Lawyers: Rewriting the Rules", Knopf, 1993

- Hewlett, S.A. "Off-Ramps and On-Ramps: Keeping Talented Women on the Road to Success", Harvard Business School Press, 2007

- Holden, R. "Success Intelligence: Timeless Wisdom for a Manic Society", Hodder Mobius, 2005

- LoPata, A. & Roper, P. "...and Death Came Third: The Definitive Guide to Networking and Speaking in Public", Lean Marketing Press, 2006

- Moore, D.P. & Buttner, E.H. "Women Entrepreneurs: Moving Beyond the Glass Ceiling", Sage, 1997

- Nicolson, P. "Having It All? Choices for Today's Superwoman", Wiley, 2002

- Reardon, K.K. "The Secret Handshake: Mastering the Politics of the Business Inner Circle", Doubleday Publishing, 2000

- Stanny, B. "Secrets of Six-Figure Women: Surprising Strategies to Up Your Earnings and Change Your Life", Harper Business, 2004

- Tannen, D. "You Just Don't Understand: Women and Men in Conversation", Ballantine, 1990

- Tannen, D. "Talking from 9 to 5: How Women's and Men's Conversational Styles Affect Who Gets Heard, Who Gets Credit and What Gets Done at Work", Virago, 1995

- Thomson, P. & Graham, J. "A Woman's Place is in the Boardroom", Palgrave, 2005

- Wittenburg-Cox, A. & Maitland, A. "Why Women Mean Business", Jossey Bass, 2008

SUPPORT RESOURCES

Krissy Jackson
The IT Girls Coach

www.itgirlscoach.com

Carole Collins
Image Coach and Master of the Federation of Image Consultants

www.carolcollinsimage.com

Andy Lopata
Leading Business Networking Strategist and co-author of ...And Death
Came Third

www.Lopata.co.uk

Michelle Brailsford
Executive coach with a passion for working with women

www.jupiterconsultinggroup.com

Judy Reith
Coaching for parents

www.parentingpeople.co.uk

Talking Talent
Specialists in maternity coaching

www.talking-talent.com

International Coach Federation
Accrediting body for coaches and coach training programmes

www.coachfederation.org.uk

Association for Coaching
Accrediting body for coaches

www.associationforcoaching.com

European Mentoring and Coaching Council
Membership body promoting good practice for both mentors and coaches

www.emccouncil.org

Association for Professional Executive Coaching and Supervision
Membership body for promoting good practice for coaching
and supervision

www.apecs.org

BEYOND THE BOOK

Suzanne Doyle-Morris, PhD, is available to speak at conferences and deliver workshops training specifically on the career development strategies discussed in the book. She wants all women who work in male-dominated fields to succeed and understand what it takes to move beyond the boys' club.

Get greater benefits of *Beyond the Boys' Club* through:

- *Beyond the Boys' Club Career Development Programme for Women*

- Keynote speeches for events and conferences

- One-to-one executive coaching with International Coach Federation accredited coaches

- The Doyle Morris Coaching and Development monthly newsletter

- The www.doylemorris.com blog on topical career issues for women who work in male-dominated fields

The Beyond the Boys' Club Career Development Programme for Women is a series of workshops which can be delivered in-house. These include tailor-made interactive group discussions as well as one-to-one ongoing coaching support — the perfect ongoing development tool to complement the invaluable lessons in the book. The programme has also been extended as an external development programme for individual women.

To find out how the *Doyle Morris Coaching and Development* team can help your business, visit www.doylemorris.com.

To find out more about the book, the *Beyond the Boys' Club Career Development Programme for Women*, or to download Dr Doyle-Morris' Speaker Sheet visit www.beyondtheboysclub.com.

To book Suzanne as a *keynote or conference speaker*, e-mail suzanne@doylemorris.com

NOTES

NOTES

NOTES

ABOUT THE AUTHOR

Suzanne Doyle-Morris, PhD, is an executive coach, international speaker and author. She specialises in professional development for women as leaders in the workplace. She gives an international perspective, as a native of Washington DC who has lived and worked in four countries. She is currently based in the UK and has worked with clients from Microsoft, Cisco, UBS, Barclays Wealth, University of Cambridge, Clifford Chance, O2, and Coca Cola Hellenic.

She has always been fascinated by the stories of successful career women and has a BA in Women's Studies & Psychology. She received her MPhil and subsequent PhD in Educational Research from Cambridge University in the UK. Her doctoral dissertation focused on the experiences of successful women in male-dominated fields. She founded Doyle Morris Coaching & Development in 2005.